WILLIAM & CATHERINE

THE LIFE AND LEGACY OF THE BOOTHS

FOUNDERS OF

The Salvation Army

WILLIAM & CATHERINE

THE LIFE AND LEGACY OF THE BOOTHS
FOUNDERS OF
The Salvation Army

·A NEW BIOGRAPHY·

TREVOR YAXLEY
WITH CAROLYN VANDERWAL

BETHANYHOUSE
PUBLISHERS
MINNEAPOLIS, MINNESOTA

William & Catherine: A New Biography
The Life and Legacy of the Booths, Founders of The Salvation Army
by Trevor Yaxley with Carolyn Vanderwal

Copyright © 2003
T. F. & J. B. Yaxley

Cover design by Dan Thornberg
Cover photo of Catherine Booth: The Salvation Army International Heritage Centre. Color added by designer.

Manuscript prepared with the help of Rick Killian, Boulder, Colorado. *www.killiancreative.com.*

Crest on chapter pages used by kind permission of United Kingdom Territorial Headquarters.

Published by Bethany House Publishers
11400 Hampshire Avenue South
Bloomington, Minnesota 55438
www.bethanyhouse.com

Bethany House Publishers is a Division of
Baker Book House Company, Grand Rapids, Michigan.

Printed in Canada

Library of Congress Cataloging-in-Publication Data

Yaxley, Trevor.
    William & Catherine : the life and legacy of the Booths, founders of the Salvation Army / by Trevor Yaxley with Carolyn Vanderwal ; foreword by John Dawson ; preface by Winkie Pratney.
        p.   cm.
Includes bibliographical references and index.
    ISBN 0-7642-2760-2 (alk. paper)
    1. Booth, William, 1829–1912. 2. Booth, Catherine Mumford, 1829–1890.
3. Salvationists—England—Biography. 4. Salvation Army—History. I. Title: William and Catherine. II. Vanderwal, Carolyn. III. Title.
BX9743.B7 Y39   2003
287.9'6'0922—dc21   2002152602

Dedication

This book is first dedicated to the entire team at Lifeway Ministries Trust Inc. You have laid down your lives for the sake of the gospel in our nation. Your courage and faith inspires me daily.

and

To all those who have served or are faithfully serving in The Salvation Army. We owe you an enormous debt of gratitude for your inspirational example of sacrificial living and perseverance. Thank you.

and

To the joys of my life, my family: Jan, my soulmate for the past four decades, our son David (now with the Lord), Mark, Rebecca, son-in-law David, and Renee, Shania, and Safia, who would have to be the most beautiful grandchildren anyone could ask for.
You delight my heart.

Acknowledgments

Our sincerest love and thanks to Carolyn Vanderwal for her hard work, inspiring faith, and incredible diligence in pulling this project together. Her research, writing, and editing have made this book an accurate depiction and powerful teaching tool. She and her husband, Peter, are an outstanding example of faith outworked and an immense source of support, encouragement, and love to Jan and me.

I am also particularly grateful to Rick Killian for his labor of love in doing the final edit of the manuscript, which went far above and beyond the call of duty!

I would like to thank Karen Thompson, Susan Mitchum, Jim Bryden, and others of The Salvation Army's archival services for their prompt help and direction in researching this project. Without their counsel and guidance, this book would not have been possible.

My special thanks also goes to the British Library, whose careful preservation of the letters of William and Catherine was invaluable to this project. These letters added the personal touch to the story of the Booths that showed both their humanity and their passions. Such careful work to preserve primary documents for the following generations is an effort rarely noticed. In many ways they are the true historians who record history without interpretation and give us genuine access to the lessons of the past.

And lastly, my special thanks to Pat Judd, Steve Laube, and the staff of Bethany House Publishers for catching the vision of this book and seeing its value. I have rarely worked with a group so competent and full of the love and wisdom of God. Their input and guidance in the development of this manuscript turned an otherwise arduous research project into a real and vibrant word for the body of Christ today. May God bless them richly for their continuing efforts, excellence, and integrity in publishing books that encourage and instruct ministers in their callings, strengthen laypeople in their walks with God, and reach out to new generations with the liberty of the gospel of Jesus Christ.

Table of Contents

Foreword 11

Preface 15

The Vision: Who Cares? 21

Chapter 1: *A Mind Hungry for Truth and a Heart for
the Oppressed*. 27
CATHERINE'S EARLY YEARS (1829–1852)

Chapter 2: *Hell No!* 47
WILLIAM'S EARLY YEARS (1829–1852)

Chapter 3: *And the Two Shall Become One* 65
WILLIAM AND CATHERINE'S COURTSHIP (1852–1855)

Chapter 4: *One in Marriage, One in Ministry*. 88
A YOUNG MINISTER AND HIS WIFE (1855–1861)

Chapter 5: *Obedience at Any Price*. 109
YEARS AS AN INDEPENDENT EVANGELIST (1861–1865)

Chapter 6: *Prayer, Faith, and the Power of the Holy Spirit* 124
THE MISSION BECOMES AN ARMY (1865–1878)

Chapter 7: *To Gain, Train* 150
PREPARING A SOLID FOUNDATION IN THEIR CHILDREN AND
RECRUITS (1878–1886)

Chapter 8: *High Cost* 173
ENDURING PERSECUTION AND THE STRUGGLES OF A
GROWING WORLD MOVEMENT (1878–1885)

Chapter 9: *On Trial for Righteousness* 197
THE ARMSTRONG CASE (1885)

Chapter 10: *A Broken Heart* 211
CATHERINE'S FINAL YEARS (1886–1890)

Chapter 11: *Finishing the Race* 231
WILLIAM'S FINAL YEARS (1890–1912)

Epilogue: The Challenge. 259
Appendix A: English System of Currency in the Time
of the Booths 266
Appendix B: A Timeline of William and Catherine Booth and
The Salvation Army 267
The Booth Family Tree 280
Endnotes 281
Bibliography 291
Index 293
About the Authors 300
The First Wave Army. 302

Foreword

Blood and Fire" indeed! "The power of the blood of Christ and the fire of the Holy Spirit!" This famous phrase came to hold another meaning for those heroic workers who shed their own blood when attacked by vicious mobs, refusing to compromise their calling. This is a story we need to know.

The story of The Salvation Army is truly amazing. It has moved me to repent of having a small expectation of God. The Booths were innovators who understood the needs of their generation. When most churches looked the other way while their wealthiest members used the advances of the Industrial Revolution to exploit others, the Booths used the latest technologies to help break the straitjacket of religious presuppositions about ministry. In a time before women's suffrage, they employed dynamic women as apostolic leaders. While others walked past the poor in the streets without a second glance, they turned uneducated street people into preachers who could not be ignored. Most remarkably, in an era of empires, they used the military motif as a framework for service and humility. They took the discipline, commitment, and long-term planning venerated by the military culture and infused it with new meaning: instead of conquering others, it would set them free!

The Booths' leadership of The Salvation Army reveals a legitimate polarity within the styles of biblical leadership. More directive than democratic, it represented the resurrection of apostolic leadership in a day when the prevalent rule was pastors subject to committees. To this day The Salvation Army is the only major movement within the body of Christ that embodies the militant personality expressed in the epistles. Because of generations of service to the poor and needy, the Salvationists have been able to represent the Lord of Hosts without being mistaken for advocates of violence. Imagine if any other Christian movement put on military uniforms—it would probably be roundly condemned in spite of our labeling it "an army of love."

A few years ago, after preaching on the boardwalk in Atlantic City, I was presented with a gift by local Salvationists—a beautifully preserved antique Salvation Army Officer's uniform. It is one of my treasures. It speaks to me. The stiff high collar and radical insignia came to symbolize commitment unto death for those who wore this garment. Just to look at it fills me with reverence for the Booths and the other pioneers of the Army.

I also have personal reasons for recommending this book to you. It was while serving as the Urban Missions director for Youth With a Mission, one of the world's largest mission societies, that I first glimpsed the awesome power of united, dedicated believers in impacting a world-class city. I was reading *The General Next to God* by Richard Collier on a flight from Chiang Mai to Bangkok at the time, and the story of the first generation of The Salvation Army became my inspiration. To me it represents the high-water mark of urban missions. It demonstrates city-transforming power that has challenged subsequent generations to match its impact.

But I have an even deeper debt to The Salvation Army. Many years ago a young woman knelt at the penitent bench in a storefront mission on Cuba Street, Wellington, New Zealand. She was giving her heart to Jesus. She was my great-aunt, and through her, the grace of God began to pour into my troubled family.

"Make your will, pack your box, kiss your girl, and be ready in a week,"[1] Booth once said to a volunteer; I feel similarly commanded by the life and example of "General" Trevor Yaxley every time I have worked on a project with this remarkable man of vision.

Trevor has served us well by using the story of the Booths as a way to prophesy to this generation. Well researched and well written, this gripping tale of two of the greatest heroes of modern faith should be read by Christian leaders and new believers alike. I needed this book. God used it to rekindle my own devotion to evangelism and discipleship.

William Booth once remonstrated:

> The chief danger of the 20th century will be religion without the Holy Ghost, Christianity without Christ, forgiveness without repentance, salvation without regeneration, politics without God, and Heaven without Hell.[2]

Between the bookends of time, from the Booths' day to this, it would seem that this statement is in many respects true. It is easy to see why the story of a man with such foresight is still relevant to us today.

However, I believe we have turned a corner and are now moving into a day the likes of which we have never seen before. The heartbeat of God is "intimacy with believers" and a "longing for souls." There is a distinct parallel between the Booths' time and our own. The landscape of the nations displays vividly our inability to handle human affairs with any level of success. We have once again hit an all-time low. These are abnormal days, and they require abnormal men and women with an inordinate appetite for self-sacrifice. Our world is now extremely vulnerable to the impact of passion-filled prayer and applied Christianity. God is once again raising an army as in William and Catherine's day. An army that will not have to whistle to keep up its courage, but one that is saturated with the presence, power, and glory of God. If we are willing, God can teach us lessons from the lives of the Booths and make us world-changers for Jesus as we enter the twenty-first century, just as William and Catherine were world-changers at the start of the twentieth.

Thank you, William and Catherine Booth. Thank you, Trevor. Thank you, Jesus.

—JOHN DAWSON, LOS ANGELES, 2002

Preface

Since its humble beginnings, The Salvation Army has pioneered its work in over one hundred countries, and its shelters, rescue homes, farm colonies, and emigration bureaus have done more to reclaim the fallen than any other organization in the world. Even now, nearly a century and a half after its inception, it still ranks as the number one charity organization in the U.S. and other nations. We might perhaps truthfully say that The Salvation Army is doing more to rescue the fallen than are all other agencies combined. Now, here in this book, the vision, ideals, and methods of the Booths, who are long since gone, still speak.

It is surprising how relevant their story remains today, especially to those seeking to deeply impact this world spiritually and socially, seeing real, lasting change brought to the lives of individuals and nations. The Booths' influences into the political, social, and spiritual arenas of their day leave us with an incredible example and blueprint of how we might also successfully impact those areas in our own societies.

Some might argue that the Booths were just called for their time, but if we look at why God used William and Catherine, we will get a glimpse of the heart attitudes I believe God is still looking for in those who will change nations today.

Why *did* God use William and Catherine Booth?

William and Catherine Cared for Nothing More in the World Than Saving Souls

The Booths' passion for souls is clearly portrayed in the following excerpt from a sermon by William entitled "The Seven Spirits of God":

What is your duty here? Oh that you realized your true business in this region of death! Having eyes, oh that you could see!

15

Having ears, oh that you could hear! Having hearts, oh that you could feel! What are you going to do with this graveyard? Walk about it in heartless unconcern, or with no higher feeling than gratitude for having been made alive yourselves? Or will you content yourselves with strolling through it, taxing its poor occupants for your living while leaving them quietly in their tombs as hopeless as you found them? Heaven forbid!

God has sent you into this dark valley for nothing less than to raise these doom-struck creatures from the dead. That is your mission. . . . Go and do it again. Go and look at them. Go and compassionate them. Go and represent Jesus Christ to them. Go and prophesy to them. Go and believe for them. And then shall bone come to bone, and there shall be a great noise, and a great army shall stand up to live and fight and die for the living God.[1]

Catherine also echoed this passion for souls in her description of those they were looking to recruit into their Army:

We want men who are set on soul-saving; who are not ashamed to let every one know that this is the one aim and object of their life and that they make everything secondary to this.[2]

Everything the Booths called The Salvation Army, and all those under their military leadership, were geared to one thing: the taking back of the citadel of souls from sin, Satan, and the quicksand of evils in secular street society of their day. A Salvationist had to be truly devoted and willing to sacrifice everything—old friends, family ties, wealth, possessions, comfort, security, acceptance, social accomplishment, and so on—to see the beachhead established, the spiritual breakthrough made, and the citadels won back for God's Kingdom.

William and Catherine Were Willing to Risk Everything to See Souls Saved From Sin

The Booths were intolerably ahead of their time. Famous Christians opposed them for their disrespectful abandonment of traditional, religious, and *sheltered, safe* methods of ministry. Their Army sang to converted bar tunes and used outlandish gimmicks and advertising to get people to listen or come to their meetings. They were loud, disturbing, and doggedly committed to their cities' highest good—the changing of people's hearts. Catherine once expressed the fundamental reasoning behind such practices:

Here is the principle . . . adapt your measures to the necessity of the people to whom you minister. You are to take the Gospel to them in such modes . . . and circumstances as will gain for it [the Gospel] from them a hearing.[3]

Unconventionality was their trademark. They didn't even look like other ministers of the day. Yet while William's clothes were often baggy, his tired face baggy, and his eyes baggy, he always preached with such power, conviction, and compassion that all who heard him felt literally pulled up from their seats, lifted up from the crowd, and deposited at the altar of surrender to the living Christ.

Above all, William Booth loved Jesus and loved people for Him. Nothing mattered as much to him as presenting Jesus in His purest form before others so that they might come to know Him as William did:

The great multitude are like children; they require to see and hear God revealed before their very eyes in visible and practical form before they will believe. And to reach these crowds, God wants men and women to walk about the world so that those around, believers and unbelievers alike, shall see the form and hear the voice of the Living God; people who shall be so like Him in spirit and life and character as to make crowds feel as though the very shadow of God has crossed their path. Will you be a shadow of God?[4]

The Booths let nothing stand between them and being like Jesus, regardless of what it cost them or what it looked like to other people.

William and Catherine Understood and Loved the Poor

When William was only a teenager, his father lost his entire fortune and died wholly destitute. He was left behind watching his devoted and godly Methodist mother trying to take care of their family alone, encouraging them to be good and not give up. He grew up in poverty and understood the struggle and suffering of being poor. What little money he did make to support his family came from pawnbrokering, where profits were often at the expense of family heirlooms being traded in so that those who couldn't find work could have room and board for at least one more week. He knew what poverty could do to someone. The poor were his kind of people, and he knew them and loved them deeply. Catherine's heart echoed this compassion as all her life she deeply felt God's call to be a defender of the oppressed and helpless.

William and Catherine Knew What It Was Like to Be Rejected, Persecuted, and Hated

From the time William first preached on the street in Nottingham, he was jeered at, mocked, and ridiculed. As a woman in Victorian England, Catherine sorely felt the sting of exclusion from not only society's decisions but also participation in the leadership in the church. Throughout the early years of the Army's ministry, its young soldiers had to dodge missiles of rotten fruit, dead animals, rocks, and brickbats from crowds that did not appreciate being called out from the deeply entrenched wrong that filled their nation. Salvation Army missionaries and evangelists saw themselves as real soldiers—doing battle with the enemy to win back that which had been wrongfully taken. Theirs was a war of holy love:

> He loves you. He has told you so again and again. He has proved His love by His deeds. Love compels the one entertaining the affection to seek the good of its beloved. He knows that sin is the enemy of your peace, and must mean misery here and hereafter. For this reason among others He wants to deliver you from it.[5]

Salvationists were roped, punched, kicked, spat on, and pelted with ships' rockets and burning sulfur, while entire gangs of hundreds, even up to thousands, rallied to stop the little holy band. But the Army marched into town anyway, covered in slime but not ashamed. Kneeling in the center of the town they lifted up their battle cry: "Lord Jesus, in Your name we claim this city for God," and then they got up to take it, regardless of the circumstances!

William and Catherine Understood and Loved Holiness of Heart and Life

The Booths did not have just a radical social mission, they also had a radically saving message. The gospel they preached was a return to the old paths of righteousness with a call to complete consecration of heart and life to the Person and purposes of God. It was a God-centered proclamation with the ancient teeth and fire of personal to global transformation built into its platform and preaching. They challenged their people:

> The first thing God asks is that . . . [we] possess the character that He approves. You might say the character that He admires. The very essence of that character is expressed in one word, holiness. . . . No other qualities

or abilities can take its place. No learning or knowledge or talking or singing or scheming or any other gift will make up for the absence of this.[6]

While "less creed and more deed" is a Salvation Army fundamental, their great foundational doctrines were repentance, faith, and the need for a holy life. To the Army, repentance was not just being sorry for sin but a real turning away from sin. Faith was not some brief intellectual act but a real reliance of the soul upon Christ, beginning instantly but continuing through time and eternity.

Holiness meetings were held every week in Salvation Army missions around the world to lead Christians into a sanctifying experience. Such holiness for them was not just imputed but also imparted by the indwelling Spirit. How else could they hold indoor and open-air meetings every night of the week—and two or three times on Sundays—summer and winter, rain or shine, unless they had the power of the Holy Spirit? What else could have kept every Salvation Army soldier at his post seven days a week and taking part, if possible, in every meeting?

A strenuous life must have supernatural strength. The general realized this and made sanctification, or the filling of the Spirit, a fundamental Salvation Army doctrine. The Booths built on an apostolic foundation, preaching neglected aspects of God's Word often feared and avoided by those who sought salvation without a real surrender to the Person and purposes of God. Mere legislation and devout moral intention are never enough to bring redemption to ruined men and women; only a gospel of grace, power, and holy abandonment preached in the Holy Spirit could bring about the real and radical reclamation in the world in which William and Catherine ministered.

The Booths and their holy army visited more countries, spoke more frequently, won more souls for Christ, and rescued more fallen men and women than did any other person in street ministry history, probably more than all of them put together. Things changed for the better wherever they ministered or planted a new outreach—and isn't that what we are looking for in our service to God today?

—WINKIE PRATNEY, 2002

On April 9, 1865, Robert E. Lee met Ulysses S. Grant in the parlor of a private home at Appomattox Court House. He surrendered his army, bringing to an end four long years of death and devastation called the American Civil War.

In the same year, a thirty-six-year-old Englishman by the name of William Booth declared war on the powers of darkness by founding The Salvation Army.

—Paul Smith

THE VISION: WHO CARES?

A vision without a task makes a visionary;
A task without a vision makes for drudgery;
A task wedded to a vision makes a missionary.
—LEONARD RAVENHILL

In June of 1885, *The War Cry* published a series of letters from General William Booth entitled "Theoretical Religion." The articles reveal William's desire for all Christians to live like Christ. The degree of unreality that infested the lives of many who professed to follow Christ saddened him. He was deeply disturbed by the churchgoing crowds whose songs and prayers were so blatantly contradicted by their lives.

As he thought of the multitudes of people in London alone who lived out their lives in complete ignorance of their eternal welfare and destiny, a question began to form in his mind: *Cannot Christians reach a devotion that will truthfully answer what we say we believe about these perishing multitudes?* While thinking on this, William received the following vision from God. Its powerful imagery thrust his heart into the unfathomable realms of human depravity, evoking an immediate response. Such a vision cannot be ignored!

He first wrote of it in the June 15, 1885, edition of *The War Cry*, laying it down as a challenge to Salvationists around the world. Its message is as relevant and challenging to Christians today as it was to those over a century ago.

I saw a dark and stormy ocean. Over it the black clouds hung heavily, through which thunder rolled; and every now and then vivid lightning flashed. The winds moaned, and the waves rose and foamed and fretted and broke, and rose to foam and fret and break again.

In that ocean I saw myriads of poor human beings plunging and floating, shrieking and cursing, and struggling and drowning, and as they cursed and

21

shrieked, they rose and shrieked again, then sank to rise no more.

Out of this dark angry ocean I saw a mighty rock rise up above the black clouds that overhung the stormy sea. Around the base of this rock I saw a vast platform and up on to this platform I saw with delight a number of the poor struggling drowning wretches continually climbing out of the angry ocean.

As I looked more closely, I found a number of those who had been rescued scheming and contriving by ladders and ropes and boats to deliver the poor strugglers out of this sea. Here and there were some who actually jumped in regardless of all consequences in their eagerness to save the poor drowning multitudes. I hardly know which gladdened me most, the sight of the poor creatures who climbed the rocks and reached the place of safety, or the devotion and self-sacrifice of those whose sole purpose was to rescue others from the sea.

As I looked I saw that the occupants of the platform were quite a mixed company. They were divided into different sets or classes and they occupied themselves in quite different ways. It was only a very few, comparatively, who seemed to make it their business to get the people out of the sea.

What puzzled me most was that though all had been rescued at one time or another from the ocean, nearly everyone seemed to have forgotten all about it. The memory of its darkness and danger no longer troubled them; and what was equally strange and perplexing to me was that these people did not seem to have any care—that is, any agonizing care—about the poor perishing ones who were struggling and drowning right in front of them, many of whom were their own husbands and wives and mothers and sisters and children.

This lack of concern could not have been because they were ignorant of what was going on. They lived right in sight of it all. They talked about it sometimes and regularly went to hear lectures, which described the awful state of things.

I have already said that the occupants of this platform were engaged in different pursuits. Some were absorbed night and day in trading in order to make gain, storing up their savings in boxes and by other means. Many passed their time by amusing themselves with growing flowers on the side of the rock; others by painting pieces of cloth, performing music, or by dressing themselves up in different ways and walking about to be admired. Some occupied themselves with eating and drinking. Others were greatly taken up with arguing about the poor drowning creatures in the sea and what would become of them, while many appeased their conscience by participating in round after round of curious religious ceremonies.

As I looked more closely I saw that some had found a passage up the rock leading to a higher platform, far above the black clouds that overhung the ocean. From this elevated platform, they had a good view of the mainland, which was not very far away, and to which they expected to be taken off at some distant day. Here they passed their time in pleasant thoughts, congratulating themselves and each other on being rescued from the stormy deep, and singing songs about the happiness they were to enjoy when they should be taken to the mainland.

All this time the struggling, shrieking multitudes were floating about in the dark sea, quite near by, close enough to be pulled to safety. Instead, however they continued to perish in full view of those on the rock, not only one by one, but sinking down in shoals, sinking down every day in the dark and angry sea.

As I looked, I found that the handful whom I had observed before were still toiling in their rescue work. Oh, how I wished there had been a multitude of them! Indeed they did little else but fret and cry and toil and scheme for the perishing people. They gave themselves no rest, and bothered everyone around them to come and help with the rescue work. In fact, they came to be voted a real nuisance by many quite benevolent and kindhearted people, and many who were very religious too. But still they went on, spending all they had and all they could get, on boats and rafts and drags and ropes, and every other imaginable thing they could invent for saving the poor wretched drowning people.

There were a few others who did much the same thing at times, working hard in their own way, but the people who attracted my attention were those who were totally committed to the task. They went at it with such fierceness and fury that many, including those who were doing the same kind of work in a milder way, called them mad.

And then I saw something more wonderful still. The miseries and agonies and perils and blasphemies of the poor struggling people in this dark sea moved the pity of the great God in Heaven, so much so that He sent a Great Being to deliver them. This Great Being whom Jehovah sent came straight from His palace, right through the black clouds, and leapt into the raging sea among the drowning, sinking people. As I watched I saw Him toiling to rescue them, with tears and cries, until the sweat of His great anguish ran down in blood.

As He toiled and embraced the poor wretches and tried to lift them on to the rock, He cried out continually to those already rescued—to those whom He had helped up with His own bleeding hands—to come and help Him in the painful and laborious task of saving others from the sea.

What seemed to me to be so strange was that those on the platform to whom He called—who heard His voice and felt they ought to obey it, at least they said they did—those who loved Him much, and were in full sympathy with Him in the task He had undertaken—who worshipped Him—or professed to do so, did not respond. They were so taken up with their trades and professions and money saving and pleasures and families and circles and religion and arguments about it and the preparation for going to the mainland, that they did not attend to the cry that came to them from Him out of the ocean. If they heard it they did not heed it. They did not care and so the multitude went on struggling and shrieking and drowning in darkness and anguish.

And then I saw something that seemed to me the strangest of all that I had seen in this strange vision. I saw that some of these people on the platform whom this wonderful Being wanted to come and help Him, heedless of His cries to them, were always praying and crying for Him to come to them. They wanted Him to come and stay with them, to spend His time and strength on them.

Firstly, they wanted Him to make them happier. Secondly, they wanted Him to take away the doubts and misgivings they had respecting the truth of some letters which this great Being had written them. Then, they wanted Him to make them feel more secure on the rock—so secure that they would be quite sure they should never slip off again. Finally, they wanted Him to make them feel quite certain that they would really reach the mainland some day, because it was well-known that some had walked so carelessly as to miss their footing, and had fallen back into the stormy waters.

These people used to meet and get as high up the rock as they could, then, looking towards the mainland where they thought the Great Being was, they would cry out, "Come to us! Come, and help us!" And all this time He was down among the poor struggling drowning creatures in the angry deep, with His arms around them, trying to drag them out, and looking up—oh, so longingly, but all in vain, to those on the rock, crying to them, with His voice all hoarse with calling, "Come to Me! Come and help Me!"

And then I understood it all. It was plain enough. The sea in the vision was the ocean of life—the sea of real human existence. The thunder was the distant echoing of the wrath of God. The lightning was the gleaming of piercing truth coming from Jehovah's Throne. The multitudes of people shrieking, struggling, and agonizing in the stormy sea were the thousands and thousands of poor harlots and harlot-makers, of drunkards and drunkard-makers, of thieves, liars, blasphemers, and ungodly people of every kindred and nation and tongue.

Oh, what a black sea it was! Oh, what multitudes of rich and poor, ignorant and educated, and yet all so alike in one thing—all sinners before God. "All alike in one thing?" No, in two things. Not only the same in their wickedness, but unless rescued alike in their sinking, sinking, sinking, down, down, down to the same hell.

The great sheltering Rock was Calvary. The people on it were those who had been rescued. The way they employed their energy, gifting, and time represented the occupations of those who profess to be rescued from sin and to be living for God. The handful of fierce determined saviors were Salvation Soldiers, together with other believers who shared the same spirit. That mighty Being was the Son of God, "the same yesterday, today, and forever," who is still working to save the dying multitudes about us from this terrible doom of damnation. His voice can be heard above the music and machinery and hue-and-cry of life calling on the rescued to come and help Him to save the world.

"Who Cares" Vision Poster

My comrades, you are rescued from the waters—you are on the rock. He is in the dark sea, calling on you to come to Him and help Him. Will you go?

Look for yourselves. The surging sea of perishing souls rolls up to the very spot on which you stand. This is no vision or imagination I speak of now. It is as real as the Bible; as real as the Christ who hung upon the Cross; as real as the Judgment Day will be; and as real as the Heaven and hell that will follow it.

Look! Don't be deluded by appearances—men and things are not what they seem. My vision was merely a picture, but the reality is far more harrowing than any vision or picture can possibly be. All who are not on the rock are in the sea. Look at them from the standpoint of the Great White Throne and what a sight you have. Jesus Christ, the Son of God, is in the midst of this dying multitude, working to save them. And He is calling on you to jump into the sea, to go right away to His side and help Him.

Will you jump? Will you go to His feet and place yourself absolutely at His disposal? As when a man on a river-bank sees another struggling in the water, lays aside the outer garments that would hinder his efforts and jumps in to the rescue, so will you who still linger on the bank thinking and singing and praying about the poor struggling souls lay aside your shame, your pride, your care about other people's opinions, your love of ease and all other selfish loves that have hindered you for so long, and jump to the rescue of this multitude of dying souls?

Does the surging sea look dark and dangerous? Perhaps so. There is no doubt that the leap, for you as for every one who takes it, means distress, scorn, and suffering. For you it may mean more than this. It may mean death. He who calls to you from the sea, however, knows what it will mean; and knowing it, he still beckons you and bids you come.

You must do it. You cannot hold back. You have enjoyed yourself in religion long enough. You have sung. You have had pleasant feelings, pleasant songs, pleasant meetings, and pleasant prospects. There has been much human happiness, much clapping of hands, very much of Heaven on earth.

Now, then, go to God and tell Him you are prepared to turn your back upon it all, and that you are willing to spend the rest of your days grappling with these perishing multitudes.

You must *do it. You must go down amongst the perishing crowds. Your happiness now consists in sharing their misery, your ease in sharing their pain, your crown in bearing their cross, and your Heaven in going to the very jaws of hell to rescue them.*

Will you answer His call? Will you go?[1]

---

[1] William Booth, "Theoretical Religion," *The War Cry* (June 15, 1885). "The Vision" section (pages 21 to 26) can be photocopied and distributed without further permission for use in classrooms, Bible studies, and discussion groups. Such copies must appear as in this book and contain this permission note: "From *William and Catherine: A New Biography*, © 2002 T. F. & J. B. Yaxley. Published by Bethany House Publishers, 2003."

CHAPTER 1

A Mind Hungry for Truth and a Heart for the Oppressed

CATHERINE'S EARLY YEARS (1829–1852)

We cannot tell what may happen to us in the strange medley of life, but we can decide what happens in us — how we take it, what we do with it — and that is what really counts in the end. How to take the raw stuff of life and make it a thing of worth and beauty — that is the test of living.

—JOSEPH FORT NEWTON

At nine years of age, Catherine Mumford skipped happily alongside her rolling hoop, breaking rhythm momentarily to give the hoop another push with the stick she held in her hand. The cool, northern England sea breeze blew her dark curls across her face as she ran playfully in front of the shops near her Lincolnshire home in the little town of Boston. Rounding a corner, she let the hoop slow down, catching it before it wobbled to a stop.

The peace of the quiet neighborhood was suddenly shattered by shouting and hooting. As she turned onto the side street, two young boys pushed past her and ran to where a crowd was forming, not far from the corner. Continuing cautiously, Catherine looked on with curiosity as the boisterous crowd grew larger and louder and began to come toward her. Taken aback by their jeering and jostling but curious to know what was happening, she held her hoop tightly and backed into the shelter of a shop doorway to watch the procession pass by.

Her eyes scanned the unruly mob and came to rest on the pair that were at the center of attention. In front, a stern-looking constable was half pushing, half dragging a dirty, disheveled young man along the road. Catherine could tell by the way he lurched and stumbled that he was drunk. As she watched from her place of safety, the cheeky young boys taunted the drunkard, shouting abuse and laughing as he staggered at the side of the policeman. Though still a child, Catherine had sat in many temperance meetings, listening intently as her father expounded on the evils of drink. Here before her now was a perfect example of its destructive power. She could stand silent to this scene no longer.

With all thought of personal safety forgotten, she flung her hoop over one arm and ran to the man as he stumbled past the shop doorway. The officer and the man stopped instantaneously, confronted by the bold young girl who stood resolutely in their path. Catherine's dark eyes looked up into the man's face, searching for the soul behind the glazed, drunken eyes. As she locked eyes with him, she reached out, took his hand, and smiled as if to say, "It's okay, you are not alone. I'll walk with you." The shocked policeman turned to growl at her and order her home but was silenced as he witnessed the calming effect the little girl had on the man. Together they continued toward the lock-up. Catherine bravely marched alongside the drunk, steadying his steps and ignoring the jeers and laughter of the crowd, happy to befriend someone so needy.[1]

Though this public display of boldness seemed out of character for timid young Catherine, it was early evidence of the compassionate courage and strength of conviction that eventually characterized her life. By nature she was a shy, nervous, and physically delicate child. Underneath her reserved exterior, however, beat an unusually intense heart that was extremely sensitive to the hurt and needs of those around her. Catherine was stirred with compassion toward those who suffered injustice or pain. She felt this way for all defenseless creatures, be they humans or animals.

Catherine had learned as a young child that every life is precious. She was born in Ashbourne, Derbyshire, England, on January 17, 1829, the only daughter to Sarah and John Mumford. She had four brothers, only one of whom lived beyond childhood. Catherine's childhood memories began on a somber note when, as a two-year-old in her mother's arms, she looked upon the lifeless form of her older brother, who couldn't have been more than three or four at the time of death, laid out for his funeral. So real an impression did death make upon her at this tender age that almost sixty years later she recalled, "I can remember to this day, the feeling of awe and solemnity with which the sight of death impressed my baby-mind."[2] Her conscious life began with an understanding of the reality of death and of the sanctity of life. With sickness a frequent companion while growing up, Catherine meditated much more on death and eternity than most children. She grew up intense and contemplative, questions of morality, justice, and truth ever on her mind.

Catherine's mother was converted as a young adult when the Methodists established their work in her hometown. Her conversion came after sixteen weeks of severe illness following the tragic breaking of her first engagement and resulted in immediate tangible freedom for her soul and healing for her body. She was a woman of strong convictions who would adhere to the principles in which she believed regardless of the cost. She did not begrudge God for the death of her children; with heaven as an ever-present reality, she rejoiced openly that her three eldest children were already there.

The Army flag that fired passion in Catherine's spirit, displayed outside her birth place, 13 Sturton Road, Ashbourne, Derbyshire.

Mrs. Mumford was adamant that her daughter not be influenced by the bad behavior of other children, and so she herself became Catherine's closest friend, her playmate, her spiritual adviser, and her teacher. A strong and clear sense of right and wrong was developed in Catherine under the watchful eye and influence of her mother. By the time she was just four years of age,

Catherine's conscience had been sharpened to the point of being both powerful and effective. Her mother often told how she was summoned back into Catherine's bedroom late one evening by the sound of sobbing. The four-year-old was lying in the dark room, unable to sleep, tears streaming down her face. Hearing her cries and thinking she must be in pain, Mrs. Mumford rushed to her bedside and began questioning the distraught young girl. Catherine sat up and tried to catch her breath. With her eyes fixed on the floor, she confessed to her mother that she had not told her the truth on some matter earlier in the day. As soon as she had finished, she looked into her mother's face and began to weep again. Tears flowed freely as she apologized and promised always to tell the truth. Mrs. Mumford did not excuse the little girl or brush aside her confession. Instead she allowed repentance to take its path and then prayed with Catherine until the girl felt the comfort and forgiveness of both her mother's and God's love. Catherine's gentle, repentant heart was formed as she grew to know the love of her Heavenly Father and consequently desired to do what pleased Him.[3] Looking back later she said, "I had the strivings of God's Spirit all my life."[4] Catherine could not recall a time when she did not pray and when she did not desire to please God.

Catherine was a very observant and intelligent child. She was quick to grasp the alphabet and was able to read at three years of age. By the time the family moved to Boston, England, when she was five, her education was well established under the careful and loving guidance of her mother. The text from which she had learned to read was the Bible. Standing on a little stool alongside her mother's high-backed chair, she would read aloud from the heavy book resting on the arm of the seat between them. The worn pages of the family Bible came alive to Catherine as she read, her active imagination and compassionate, merciful heart creating a way for her to enter into its stories. The great heroes of the faith became the heroes of her childhood, and as her character was formed, an understanding of the love and fatherhood of God was birthed within her. By the time she was just twelve, Catherine had read the Bible aloud from cover to cover a total of eight times.

Catherine's father was a coachbuilder by trade, a keen politician, and a preacher in the local Methodist church. When they moved to Boston he threw himself into the growing temperance movement, giving lectures and using his home as a base for temperance work. Prominent supporters of the movement visited Catherine's home, and she would always listen to the lively discussions, even joining in to the delight of her father and his guests.

Catherine loved her father. One of her greatest joys as a child was to ride by horse and cart through the pretty English countryside beside him as he frequently let her take the reins. She loved to talk with him, and it was from her father that she received a great deal of her education. Mr. Mumford's passion for politics, his zeal for the temperance movement, and his love of a good debate made mealtimes both lively and stimulating. Perhaps because his only remaining son was educated in a boarding school, he related to Catherine more as an adult son than the young girl she was.

The 1830s were politically volatile years in Britain. The highly controversial Catholic Emancipation Act of 1829 paved the way for Catholics to enter politics, and with the first of the Reform Acts passed in 1832, electorates were reorganized and voting rights extended to thousands of middle-class men. These revolutionary new laws heralded changes that forced Britain's elite upper class to share power and influence. Catherine's father followed the political scene closely and explained the ins and outs of the issues of the day to his attentive young daughter. Quick to learn, Catherine soon formed her own ideas on politics and logically argued and debated with her father.

One issue on which father and daughter were in total agreement was that of the evil of alcohol. At just seven years of age, Catherine had "washed her hands of strong drink,"[5] a genuine conviction that was never to be shaken. When she was twelve, Catherine became secretary of the local juvenile temperance society, which organized meetings and collected subscriptions. An avid reader, she devoured all the material she could find on the case against alcohol. Each article she read and every argument she absorbed fueled her longing to do more. Her compassion for those helplessly lost to the destructive power of alcohol had developed into a fervent sense of responsibility, and she earnestly desired to be an influence for good in any way possible. However, what could a young girl do?

Then, one evening when she was still about twelve, it occurred to her: She could write! As she began to compose in her mind the outline of an article, Catherine kissed her parents good-night and climbed the stairs to her bedroom. Taking care to make sure the door was securely locked behind her, she placed the candle on her bedside table, took out her paper, and began. The words flowed with ease and she wrote furiously, desperately trying to keep up with the thoughts that formed her argument. Losing track of time, she continued into the early hours of the morning until at last she felt she had presented her case on temperance with clarity and passion. Collapsing into bed, Catherine tried to sleep but could not escape the fear that grew in her heart as she contemplated her plan to send the article anonymously to the editor of the magazine to which her father subscribed. Negative thoughts plagued her weary mind. *Surely they will know it was written by a child. My handwriting will certainly give it away.* As sleep eluded her she determined to approach a trusted friend and fellow temperance advocate to copy it in his own hand-writing and send it off on her behalf. In the morning she set her plan into action.

Catherine kept secret this latest venture and waited nervously for each new issue of the magazine. When finally she saw in print the words she had penned, she felt as though she would burst with excitement. Even more thrilling was the praise her father gave her unknowingly as the anonymous writer of the article, the first of many that were published. In spite of this remarkable achievement, Catherine seems to have remained the conservative and humble child, never divulging the secret of her penmanship to her father.

Although the temperance movement captured much of her focus as a youth, Catherine was moved by the plight of those trapped in every form of oppression and evil. The influence of the modern missionary movement pioneered by William Carey had by this time spread to most evangelical churches in England. Interdenominational mission societies formed to support the spread of the gospel in Africa and Asia. Their efforts were encouraged by fresh reports from the field. Perhaps the most notable during Catherine's childhood were the stories of Dr. David Livingstone, who began his work in Africa in 1841. Although slavery had been abolished throughout the British Empire in 1833, the evil network of slave trading still thrived on the African continent. From the horrors of slavery to stories of spiritual darkness from the heart of Africa, Livingstone's accounts captured the imagination of Christians with a growing concern for the plight of those who did not know Christ.

Catherine attended many missionary meetings conducted in her area and was stirred by the stories she heard of the unsaved in foreign lands. As always, she looked to see what she could do about their circumstances. Catherine never had to pray for compassion: it was a God-given gift that stirred her tender heart to action on behalf of any who were oppressed. She raised money from her friends, and she denied herself treats and sugar in order to increase the funds. She was struck, even as a young girl, by the strange complacency of Christians who seemed content to do so little when the need was so great. Later in life, as she reflected on this time, she stated,

> I can remember a sort of inward pity for what I thought then the small expectations of the church. . . . I can remember how disappointed I felt at

the comparatively small results which seemed to give satisfaction.[6]

While Catherine's compassion for those in need grew over time, there are few experiences that seem to have formed her young outrage at injustice more than the loss of Waterford, her pet retriever. Her love for animals was never stronger than for him. From the moment her beloved pet became part of their family, he and Catherine were inseparable. Without siblings at home or friends to play with, Waterford became her cherished companion. They went everywhere together, and he brought great joy and happiness to her childhood years. So loving and devoted was this little retriever that if he heard her crying in her bedroom he would whine outside the door until she let him in to comfort her.

Toward the end of her life she recounted the story of his death, recalling vividly the trauma of the day.

> Wherever I went the dog would follow me about as my self-constituted protector, in fact we were inseparable companions. One day Waterford had accompanied me on a message to my father's house of business. I closed the door, leaving the dog outside, when I happened to strike my foot against something and cried out in sudden pain. Waterford heard me, and without a moment's hesitation came crashing through the large glass window to my rescue. My father was so vexed at the damage done that he caused the dog to be immediately shot. For months I suffered intolerably, especially in realizing it was in an effort to alleviate my suffering that the beautiful creature had lost its life. Days passed before I could speak to my father, although he afterwards greatly regretted his hasty action, and strove to console me as best he could. The fact that I had no child companions doubtless made me miss my speechless one the more.[7]

The loss of Waterford deeply affected Catherine's world. Her strong sense of justice and her ability to reason logically and draw her own conclusions in life were now focused on the personal pain she was suffering. She struggled for three months to come to terms with what seemed to her to be so cruel and unnecessary. She wrestled with her feelings of resentment and bitterness toward her father and toward God. From her later writings we know that during her troubled twelfth year Catherine came into sharp conflict with all of the premises of her childhood: chiefly, of God's existence and His work as a loving Father reaching out to all of His children. It is probable that it was at this time, at the instance of Waterford's death, that she was tempted to discard her faith in God entirely as she struggled to reconcile her concept of a loving

Father God with the horror of unjust suffering. *Is there a God?* This was an inevitable question that had to be faced and worked through by someone who felt so keenly the pain of unfairness and affliction.

Writing of this experience at another time, she stated,

> When not more than twelve, I passed through such an ordeal of fiery temptation for about the space of three months as but to reflect on makes my soul recoil within me; at that age I frequently watered my couch with my tears, and the billows of the Almighty seemed to go over me. Many a time my whole frame has trembled under the foul attacks of the adversary, and His attacks were so subtle and of such a nature that I could not then on pain of death have revealed them to anyone, so I endured alone and unaided by any earthly friend these fearful conflicts of soul . . . but the storm passed, and my mind regained in great measure its former vivacity.[8]

We are not told how Catherine overcame the inner struggle that could have led to her falling away from faith. We can only assume that her experience of the love and faithfulness of God to this point in her life enabled her to choose to believe in His goodness regardless of her loss. For any who make such a choice, the grace of God is sufficient to endure all kinds of personal suffering.

This questioning of God's very existence was the first of three crises that became turning points in her walk of faith. Although the battle was intense, Catherine emerged triumphant, successfully negotiating the first of three important steps that would forge the foundation of her faith in Jesus Christ. Having faced her personal loss and pain, she maintained her faith in the existence and love of her Heavenly Father.

During these three months, Catherine's withdrawal and poor spirits troubled Mrs. Mumford. She wondered if it would be helpful to send Catherine to school. The decision was reinforced by the persuasion of a good friend, a sincere Christian lady who was the principal of a local girls' school.

Catherine quickly adapted to this new sphere of life. She loved to learn and happily applied herself in every class. She mixed easily with the other students and soon made friends. Catherine's good character and leadership abilities were quickly recognized, and she was appointed as class monitor. The schoolmasters accurately discerned her unshakable conviction to tell nothing but the truth and were always happy to accept her version of any classroom or schoolyard incident. Her natural teaching ability was also put to good use as she took it upon herself to help those who had trouble completing their work. She fell in love with history and showed natural talent in composition; geography made her long to visit foreign lands, while mathematics for a time plagued her as she thought it taught in a "senseless way." Eventually, however, she worked through this distaste for numbers and it joined her favorite subjects.[9]

Although she loved school, not every day was a happy one. Her compassionate heart got her into trouble many times with angry outbursts over the injustice of other children being teased and even in response to her own being teased as the "principal's pet." She always deeply regretted the outbursts and was quick to apologize for her anger. Despite her repentant nature, these fits troubled Catherine for some time following each incident. She knew her classmates could see only a small portion of the rage she truly felt, and she didn't know what to make of this inconsistency. A deep sense of conviction rested on her life because the wickedness that she saw in her heart stood in stark contrast to how good others seemed to think she was. She realized instinctively that it didn't matter what anyone thought of her if there was sin buried in her heart. This conflict between the true nature of one's heart before God and outward appearance led her to question the surety of her own salvation years later. But for the time being, it merely threw her more passionately into her studies.

Her school days were short-lived, however. In 1843, when she was fourteen years of age, a serious curvature of the spine became apparent, the only remedy for which, it was announced, was months of rest, lying flat in a hammock. For any active teenager, such a verdict would seem like a term of imprisonment. Catherine's love of books was the one redeeming feature of this new phase of life. Although her body was frail and immobile, her mind hungered after knowledge. She began to study and devour books on many subjects, including theology, church history, doctrine, and the works of Finney, Wesley, Newton, Fletcher, and others. She would not just read them but would study their theories, making notes and giving great thought to the conclusions they made. Little by little the intellectual basis of her beliefs was being shaped and formed. Yet, despite the undeniable contribution and logic of each of these godly men, their conclusions did not always agree. Thus it was during this period of her life that Catherine faced her second crisis of faith: *How can I know what is truth?*

As she read, questions sprang up in her mind and conflicts arose between opposing points of view on all sorts of issues concerning God and faith. Just as it seemed she would be overwhelmed by the confusion of contradictory theories, she made a decision on how she would discern the truth of God from the writings and thoughts of men. She learned to trust the voice of the Holy Spirit within her and the evidence of the Bible itself. Speaking of this decision some years later, she shared,

> When I was fourteen years old I rejected all theories about God and religion which contradicted my innate conceptions of right and wrong. I said, "No, I will never believe any theory which represents that a course of procedure is good and benevolent in God, which in man would be despicable and contemptible. I cannot receive it." I could not then put it into this language, but I remember distinctly the feelings of my soul. I said, "No, all that there is in me akin to goodness and truth God has put there, and I will never believe that what God has put in me contradicts what He has put into this book. There must be a mistake somewhere," and thank God, I came to the Scriptures for myself, which I recommend you to do. Don't imagine that the repugnant views of the character of God which have been forced upon you by professed theologians will form any excuse for your rejections of His book or of the Divine authority of it in the great day of account. God will say, "Had you not the light for yourself?"[10]

At just fourteen, Catherine wrestled with the concept of truth. She set as life principles both the infallibility of the Scriptures and the discernment of the truth of God by the inner witness of the Holy Spirit. Theoretical knowledge was discarded as being of no value unless confirmed by personal experience. Catherine continued her study with great fervency, submitting all she read to the plumb line of Scripture and the inner working of the Spirit of God. She discarded all doctrines and theories that did not pass these tests. This second step in the foundation of her faith was a crucial one. By it, she would in later life disregard the theories and doctrines of the popular Christianity of her day to follow after Christ's example. Strangely enough, Christianity as exampled by Jesus himself was getting lost in an age of intellectualism and the scientific "supremacy" that had fathered the Industrial Revolution.

In making her way through this crisis, Catherine succeeded where many nineteenth-century believers failed. She grew up in a time when the question of belief for many was shipwrecked on the shoals of skepticism and doubt. It was an era of revolution, from the political revolutions that broke out in Europe during the 1840s to the revolutionary new thinking that emerged throughout the remainder of the century as theologians and philosophers alike began to question the biblical worldview. Biblical criticism, liberalism, and the theory of evolution presented major challenges to the beliefs of the Christians of the day. Many philosophers picked up Friedrich Nietzsche's battle cry: "God is dead." Man, they alleged, had finally outgrown the need to believe in a Supreme Being and was now ready to create his own morality and justice based on humanistic thinking. So many ideas about the Christian faith floated around during this time that many believers were overwhelmed and either fell away or settled for a faith that was more religious than real. Catherine's belief in the infallibility of Scripture and the witness of the Holy Spirit cut quickly through such philosophy, providing for her a strong and sure foundation for her faith.

Mrs. Mumford nursed Catherine while she was bedridden. Although she was concerned by the intensity with which her daughter threw herself into her reading and study, she had long ago accepted the intense drive and intelligence that was so much a part of Catherine's personality. Finally, after more than twelve months of lying prostrate, Catherine's spine had improved enough to allow her to get up a little each day. She began to attend chapel services with her mother again and was able to receive visitors. Her term of confinement was over.

Among the regular visitors to Catherine's home at this time were cousins from Derby. One in particular began to pay frequent visits to Catherine. He was a good-looking and intelligent young man whom Catherine had known since childhood. He was obviously enamored by his pretty young cousin and found her conversation intriguing. His feelings toward her quickly deepened into love.

As the days and weeks passed, Catherine found herself thinking more and more of her cousin. She liked him. He was kind and intelligent, and she enjoyed his company. Yet, even as her heart softened toward him, she was troubled by the fact that he was not a Christian. Her conscience roared within with the words, "Do not be yoked together with unbelievers." Perhaps it would be for her to lead him to salvation.

Her cousin, although not a Christian by Catherine's definition, was more than happy to accompany her to chapel. This experience seemed to confirm in Catherine's heart the decision she must make. While Catherine's focus during the service was on the minister, her cousin's eyes were clearly on her. She sat engrossed in the preacher's message, while her cousin scratched a little picture in the pew in front of them, trying to capture her attention. She was not impressed! When he returned to visit after some time away, obviously still very much enamored with her, Catherine had made up her mind to put an end to their relationship. Her decision was one she thanked God for to the end of her days. Looking back on this time she later remarked on how grateful she was that she had not "chosen to follow the inclinations and fancies of my own heart, rather than the express command of God which so unmistakably reveals His will to us in this matter."[11]

In 1844, immediately after this first experience of love, Catherine moved with her family to London. The excitement of the city captured the heart of the sixteen-year-old as she visited the great monuments of St. Paul's, Westminster, and the National Gallery. After a time, however, the novelty of life in London wore off. Weightier issues began to press upon her mind.

Her father, once the keen Methodist and local preacher, had become entirely engrossed in his business affairs. His main concern was now for making money. His passion for the things of God had waned, and he was increasingly more concerned with worldly things. Catherine and her mother began to attend the local Wesleyan Methodist chapel, but in the context of her father's backsliding, questions arose in her heart concerning her own salvation.

Looking back on her life she could see the hand of God. She was able to state,

> Before I was fifteen years of age God had in an especial manner taught me what I consider the first and fundamental and all-comprehensive principle of Christ's salvation, of real Christianity—that every act of our lives, every relationship into which we enter, every object at which we aim, every purpose that inspires our souls, should be centered and bounded by God and His glory. I had embraced the idea of Christianity so early, and I can say before God and my own conscience that I sought to carry out that principle.[12]

All her life Catherine had followed after God. She had so much understanding, so much knowledge of God and what it meant to follow Him, and yet she did not have the assurance in her heart that her own sins were forgiven. When she had been faced with injustice in the past, as at school, the violence of her anger had frightened her, and only she had known the extent and intensity of the fury inside. How could a heart bearing such wickedness be regenerated in Christ? While confined for the year to reading in her hammock, she had been impressed again and again by the certainty of the conversion experience of the people she read about and the immediate changes that had come forth after their personal encounters with God. As she reflected on these things, she became less convinced that she had experienced the change of heart that comes with conversion. At the age of seventeen, Catherine faced the third crisis of her faith: *How can I know I am saved?* In her own words, the question that now troubled her mind was, "Do I know God by a personal revelation of Him to my own soul?"[13]

Within her heart there grew an insatiable desire for a personal encounter with God that would bring an assurance of her salvation. She longed for the Holy Spirit's witness in her heart concerning her acceptance before God. This one thing became the ruling desire in her life. For the first time her thoughts and focus became fixed on her own spiritual condition rather than the state of those around her.

She wrestled against the lies of Satan that told her: "You must not expect such a change as you read of in books; you have been half a Christian all your life. You always feared God. You must content yourself with this."[14] She struggled against her own fear of deceiving herself as she rebuked Satan's lies, stating, "No, my heart is as bad as other people's, and if I have not sinned outwardly I have inwardly." As the battle intensified she vowed in her heart, "I will never rest till I am thoroughly and truly changed, and know it as any thief or great outward sinner."[15]

Catherine refused to be saved by logic. She sought God for the gift of faith that would bring about her salvation. The struggle for faith was intense, as she later recalled:

> About this time I passed through a great controversy of soul. Although I was conscious of having given myself up fully to God from my earliest years, and although I was anxious to serve Him and often realized deep enjoyment in prayer, nevertheless, I had not the positive assurance that my sins were forgiven, and that I had experienced the actual change of heart about which I had read and heard so much. I was determined to leave the question no longer in doubt, but to get it definitely settled, cost what it might. For six weeks I prayed and struggled on, but obtained no satisfaction. True, my past life had been outwardly blameless. Both in public and in private I had made use of the means of grace, and up to the very limit of my strength, and often beyond the bounds of discretion, my zeal had carried me. Still, so far as this was concerned, I realised the truth of the words:
>
> > Could my zeal no respite know,
> > Could my tears forever flow—
> > These for sins could not atone;
> > Thou must save, and Thou alone.
>
> I knew, moreover, that "the heart is deceitful above all things, and

desperately wicked" [Jeremiah 17:9]. I was terribly afraid of being self-deceived. I remembered, too, the occasional outbursts of temper when I was at school. Neither could I call to mind any particular place or time when I had definitely stepped out upon the promises, and had claimed the immediate forgiveness of my sins, receiving the witness of the Holy Spirit that I had become a child of God and an heir of heaven.

It seemed to me unreasonable to suppose that I could be saved and yet not know it. At any rate I could not permit myself to remain longer in doubt regarding the matter. If in the past I had acted up to the light I had received, it was evident that I was now getting new light, and unless I obeyed it I realized that my soul would fall into condemnation. Ah, how many hundreds have I since met who have spent years in doubt and perplexity because, after consecrating themselves fully to God, they dare not venture out upon the promises and believe!

I can never forget the agony I passed through. I used to pace my room till two o'clock in the morning, and when, utterly exhausted, I lay down at length to sleep, I would place my Bible and hymnbook under my pillow, praying that I might wake up with the assurance of salvation.[16]

Night after night Catherine sought hard after God, desperate to know the assurance of her salvation. Day after day she would arise again, exhausted but determined to press on until she found her answer.

The evening of June 14, 1846, was an unremarkable summer night. After spending the hours after dinner in her room, pacing the floor and crying out to God in prayer, she fell wearily onto her bed once more. Placing her Bible and hymnbook under the pillow as she had done countless times before, she breathed one last conscious prayer to the Lord: "Father, may it be that I awake tomorrow to an assurance of your forgiveness of my sin." She relaxed into the bed and fell asleep, utterly exhausted.

A few hours later, the sun's rays filtered through the drapes into her room, heralding the start of a new day. Catherine stretched out her aching back and rubbed her bleary eyes. Propping herself up against her pillows, her first thoughts were once more of the Lord. Reaching for her Bible and hymnbook, she laid them on her lap. As she did so, the hymnbook fell open. Picking it up, her eyes rested upon the verse:

My God I am Thine,
What a comfort divine,
What a blessing, to know that my Jesus is mine![17]

In an instant these simple words, words Catherine had read and sung countless times before, penetrated into the depths of her soul with incredible power and light. They became life to her as the Spirit of God brought revelation to her soul in an instant. Her months of struggle were answered in a moment as the truth of her forgiveness, her sonship, and her acceptance before God because of Jesus flooded her soul. Recalling the beauty and joy of the moment, she later said,

> Scores of times I had read and sung these words, but now they came home to my inmost soul with a force and illumination they had never before possessed. It was as impossible for me to doubt as it had before been for me to exercise faith. Previously not all the promises in the Bible could induce me to believe; now not all the devils in hell could persuade me to doubt. I no longer hoped I was saved, I was certain of it. The assurance of my salvation seemed to flood and fill my soul. I jumped out of bed, and without waiting to dress, ran into my mother's room and told her what had happened.[18]

This spontaneous outburst of joy is itself a testimony to the change that had, at that moment, been wrought in Catherine. For a long time she had found it virtually impossible to talk openly about spiritual matters, even with her own mother. Prayers were shared together on occasion, but Catherine could not freely speak of the things God impressed on her heart. The happiness that flooded her as she realized God's favor on her life and experienced the release of the Holy Spirit within gave her such a freedom in expression that she'd never before had.

Catherine had endured and triumphed through her third crisis of faith. She had persevered with God until she experienced the assurance she longed for. This encounter with God was of great importance to her life and also to the work she would undertake in years to come. It helped fashion the principles by which she dealt with sinners seeking salvation in the work that would become The Salvation Army. Her personal experience enabled her to lead others through genuine repentance and surrender to God until they, too, personally experienced the inner peace and assurance of their salvation.

Two years before her death, she spoke on the moment of conversion, saying,

> It does not signify how we are trained or what were the particular circumstances of our antecedent life; there comes a crisis, a moment when every human soul which enters the Kingdom of God has to make its choice of that Kingdom in preference to everything that it holds and owns

as its world; when it has to renounce its world—all that would constitute the worldly and temporal benefits of that soul—it has to give up all that, and embrace and choose God and His righteousness and His Kingdom.[19]

On another occasion she declared,

Saving faith is not intellectual perception of the truth. . . . If a mere intellectual perception of the truth were saving faith, the devil would have been saved long ago! . . . Saving faith is not mere feeling on the subject of religion . . . it is the committal, the giving over of the soul and of the whole being to God. It means such a giving of himself up to God as constitutes him henceforth God's man.[20]

On the issue of the assurance of salvation, Catherine taught,

Don't ever tell anybody he is saved. I never do. I leave that for the Holy Ghost to do. I tell them how to get saved. I try to help them to the way of faith. I will bring them up as close as ever I can to the blessed broken body of their Lord, and I will try to show them how willing He is to receive them, and I know that when really they do receive Him, the Spirit of God will tell them quickly enough that they are saved. He will not want my assistance to tell that.[21]

Catherine could now affirm publicly that she was God's. She became a member of the Brixton Wesleyan Methodist Church, something she had refused to do while she had struggled with her salvation. The next few months were the happiest of her life to that point. She was overwhelmed with the joy and freedom she felt within. She shared her own journey of faith with her friends and was delighted to discover that God would use her to bless and help others in their faith. She experienced for the first time the value and power of personal testimony: her honest account of her struggle to faith and God's answer helped others to find Him. Her times of prayer grew deeper and more intimate as they became times of precious communion with her Savior.

The happiness of this season was overshadowed by Catherine's grief for her father. While she had pressed in to find God, her father had totally abandoned his faith and his views on temperance. The financial stress of his business ventures drove him to drink and brought great sadness and distress to Catherine and her mother.

In September of 1846, just a few months after her conversion experience, Catherine became ill again, this time with a severe respiratory infection. She suffered incredible pain in her chest and back, accompanied by a high fever.

The doctor feared that Catherine might contract tuberculosis, and so she was confined to her room for the winter. By May, she had recovered enough to be able to travel to Brighton to stay with an aunt in the hope that the sea air would hasten her healing.

Catherine's sickness, her physical weakness, and her ongoing back trouble added at this time to her loneliness and the deep sorrow she felt for her father. The pain she experienced in her chest and back was at times excruciating, and the disease left her weakened to the point that she felt as though she might die. In spite of the enormity of the trials she faced, Catherine courageously took every new day as an opportunity to grow closer to God. The peace, love, and joy she experienced through her times of prayer became the strength of her life.

Although her times of personal prayer were precious, her experience in public was quite the opposite. When she was strong enough, she attended chapel services in Brighton and even began to visit others who were sick. She was dismayed as she realized how the boldness she had initially experienced in speaking of the Lord had given way once more to timidity. She struggled even to pray aloud when called on to open a meeting in prayer.

After six weeks of convalescence in Brighton, Catherine returned to her family home in London. Although not fully recovered, she had regained much of her strength and was able to slowly increase her activities. In addition to chapel, Catherine attended Sunday school classes. The first lesson she had to learn was to lead the class in prayer. She objected strongly, pleading her weakness, but to no avail. The class leader, Mrs. Keay, who was the wife of a minister in the circuit, called upon her to open in prayer and the whole class waited, kneeling in silence for up to five minutes as Catherine desperately tried to muster the courage to speak. She implored the leader not to ask her to pray, arguing that the pressure made her feel ill, but her leader was uncompromising. "Never mind," she would say, "you will be of use by-and-by if you overcome this timidity, and employ your gifts. But if you don't you won't."[22] The fear of public speaking was to plague her for years to come.

Catherine's love for the Word of God had deepened greatly after her conversion experience. Where once she read to discover more *about* God, she now read to experience His *reality* in her life and circumstances. Reading the Bible through twice in the next sixteen months, she began to appropriate the promises it contained for her own life. Seeing her heart mirrored in its pages, her understanding of the dealings of God with man grew. As she read, the Spirit of God was able to ignite the richness of truth to bring life to her soul.

With the matter of her salvation now firmly settled in her heart, Catherine began once more to look beyond herself to the needs of those who did not know Jesus.

London was visited by all the renowned preachers of the day, and Catherine would always endeavor to attend the meetings they held in Exeter Hall. The principles she set at the age of fourteen remained the standard by which she judged every message she heard. The Methodist Church of the day was suffering from a decline in the number of conversions, and as Catherine listened and observed meeting after meeting, she began to form her own conclusions on why this was so. In her opinion, the preachers were largely to blame. Although they spoke well, they usually failed to bring their listeners to any point of decision.[23] Furthermore, to Catherine's dismay, the prayer meeting held after the service at the Brixton chapel was virtually discontinued. It was this prayer meeting that had previously given opportunity to those impacted by the message to seek after God. Catherine became convinced that change was needed if they were to see conversions increase.[24]

She was not alone in wanting to see reform come to the Wesleyan Methodist Church. During the 1840s a group had arisen in protest against the established authority within the movement. They objected strongly to the increasing centralization of authority, especially when decisions made by the Conference President effectively overruled and undermined the authority of local preachers in their circuits. Some argued that local preachers were increasingly being consumed with clerical work when what was needed was a revival of the evangelistic passion and zeal of their founder. They began to call for change that would give greater autonomy to local congregations and, in their view, bring the movement up-to-date with the times. Those calling for reform circulated anonymous statements of protest and petitioned their leadership for change.

Although their desire was for leadership reform rather than forming their own splinter group, this wish was soon destroyed. In 1850 the conference singled out those it believed to be at the heart of the dissension and expelled them. These Methodists formed the Methodist Reform Union and took with them thousands of supporters. Strict orders were given by the conference leadership that no Wesleyan Methodists were to attend any meetings held by the expelled reformers.

Catherine had followed the progress of the reformers with great interest. Although she did not directly support their calls for change, she was appalled by the apparent injustice of their treatment by the conference, both before and after their expulsion. Out of sympathy for the outcasts, she attended their meetings of protest and enthusiastically argued their case among her friends. When her class leader cautioned her with the possibility of expulsion for supporting their cause, Catherine refused to back down. Her leader's suggestion that it would be of greater benefit for her to be allied with the more influential section of the church only made her more determined to speak out.

Finally, when it was clear that she would not be silent about something that to her was so unjust, her class leader reluctantly decided to withhold her ticket of membership. [At this time, membership among the Methodists was reviewed on an annual basis as a measure of control by the leadership. If a member was found in conflict with them or their beliefs, it was quite possible not to be readmitted to membership.] Catherine was excommunicated from the body that had nurtured her in faith from the time she was born. As most of her closest friends were Wesleyan Methodists, she lost their companionship as well. History would prove, however, that the greater loss was sustained by the organization she left behind in 1850.

Catherine and her mother joined the Binfield chapel opened by the banned reformers. Unable to hide in the mass of a large congregation, Catherine was asked to lead a Bible class for fifteen girls between the ages of sixteen and nineteen. The twenty-one-year-old Catherine poured her heart into these young girls, devoting hours of preparation to each lesson and spending time in prayer with any who wanted to stay after class. Over the next three years Catherine became their guide and counselor. She grew in wisdom in dealing with the hearts of people, and her skills as a teacher of the Word were strengthened. At all times she strove to ensure the lessons were interesting and practical, challenging her girls to respond to the dealings of God in their lives. She saw some of them converted and was continually delighted in being able to disciple them in their faith.

It is easy to see the hand of God upon Catherine's life from the time of her birth through the turbulent adolescent years to her entrance into adulthood. In spite of the many hardships she endured, both physically and spiritually, she emerged triumphantly, conquering doubt and receiving the gift of faith. The compassion stamped indelibly upon her heart as an infant matured to a powerful sense of responsibility for the state of the afflicted. The trials and testings of her youth gave birth to a courageous spirit that would mature in adulthood, enabling her to face and overcome even greater obstacles.

Looking back on her own childhood years, Catherine once wrote,

I cannot tell you the gratitude I sometimes feel to God for having shielded me in childhood and early youth from the giddy, flirty pleasures of the world. I have to mourn many disadvantages and grievous ones, but oh, I do feel the value of those I possessed. I do see the effects they have had on my heart and character. I see the importance of young minds being engaged with pure and weighty subjects, and the young heart shut up from the fascinations and allurements of unreal and pretended admiration. Oh, if ever I have a daughter how I shall guard the sacred gem of a pure and unsophisticated mind, it is indeed a precious boon to its possessor.[25]

At twenty-three, Catherine's thoughts at times turned to marriage. Her desire for a life partner, someone she could share the journey with, grew. As many young girls before and since, Catherine was quite specific about the type of man she would like for a husband:

As quite a young girl I made up my mind. . . . In the first place I was determined that his religious views must coincide with mine. He must be a sincere Christian—not a nominal one, or a mere church member, but truly converted to God. . . . The second essential, which I resolved upon, was that he should be a man of sense. I knew I could never respect a fool, or one much weaker mentally than myself. . . . The third essential consisted of oneness of views and tastes, any idea of lordship and ownership being lost in love. . . . Of course there must be and will be mutual yielding wherever there is proper love. . . . This is just as true with regard to man as to woman. . . . Another resolution I made was that I would never marry a man who was not a total abstainer, and this from conviction and not merely to gratify me.[26]

These were the absolutes. A less than essential but still desirable trait was that he be a minister, as she felt she could be of most use to God as a minister's wife. Finally, her personal taste compelled her to desire a man who was dark, tall, and, for preference, named "William."[27]

As she formed in her mind the picture of the type of man she would like to marry, Catherine was completely oblivious to the fact that God had already handpicked her perfect life partner. Delighting herself in her Lord and Savior in spite of the hardships she endured, Catherine was soon to receive the desire of her heart.

CHAPTER 2

Hell No!

WILLIAM'S EARLY YEARS (1829–1852)

This is the way I know I am getting closer to God — my heart begins to echo what His heart says: "Souls! Souls! Souls!"

—KARL STRADER

It was late one evening in 1844 as fifteen-year-old William Booth trudged wearily home through the shabby, dimly lit streets of Nottingham, England. The stench of open sewers and the snarl and hiss of marauding cats mingled with the muffled cries of young children echoing behind cold stone walls. William was well accustomed to the dark, oppressive atmosphere of the city streets, yet tonight the sights and sounds compounded upon the strange uneasiness welling up from within. He recalled with clarity the words of Isaac Marsden, a preacher he'd heard some time before at the local Wesleyan chapel: "A soul dies every minute!"[1]

The preacher's words beat in William's ears at pace with his blood. He walked faster, trying to escape the words pounding in his head, but they merely pulsed more quickly through his mind.

"A soul dies every minute!" Marsden had thundered at the somewhat bewildered congregation. The challenging words played over and over in young William's mind, stirring up a torrent of unanswered questions with an urgency he had never before encountered. "I would have given myself to God that very night if my friends Boldie and Will weren't with me," he argued with himself, trying desperately to justify his failure to respond to the challenge. His breath hung heavily in the cold autumn air, lighting up as it drifted by the occasional gas lamp, a light for drunks stumbling along the dark streets.

"A soul dies every minute! A soul dies every minute!"

As he wound his way through narrow alleys, the words echoing more strongly in his ears, his troubled heart was suddenly overwhelmed by an incredible sense of sinfulness. Cold tears trickled down his trembling cheeks and froze on his chin as an urgency to be free from sin's grip rose within him. One by one, memories of past wrongs paraded through his mind. With his heart pounding relentlessly, the Spirit of God fell upon him, bringing both conviction and repentance. He wept as he saw for the first time the true condition of his heart and his need for forgiveness. With the light of the Holy Spirit flooding his soul, he chose to renounce his sinful ways and determined to put right, wherever possible, the wrongs he had done to others. This was the beginning of a new life for William Booth, though his actions from that day forward suggest Marsden's words never stopped echoing in his mind.[2]

By this time he had already earned himself the nickname "Willful Will" among his family and friends. The passionate, fiery, and, at times, impulsive personality that gained him this title did not change with his conversion but rather redirected its interests from serving self to serving God. William seemed well suited to the Methodist movement he joined. Its founder's passion for God, pursuit of holiness, and zeal for the poor and downtrodden struck a chord in young William's heart. After all, he had grown up witnessing the desperate hopelessness that poverty brought to families all around him.

William Booth was born in Nottingham on April 10, 1829, the only son of Samuel and Mary Booth. He and his three sisters grew up in their parents' red-brick terrace home in Sneinton, a small village later engulfed by the expansion of Nottingham. The Booth family professed to be Church of England by religion, although his father rarely set foot inside a chapel. As an enterprising local businessman, he did, however, insist that each of his children attend church for the sake of appearance.

Nottingham was typical of England's cities in the 1800s. With the Industrial Revolution in full swing, the gap between the classes grew wider every year. The impoverished working class filled the city's eight thousand back-to-back homes. Even its women and children toiled long and hard in the struggling stocking-weaving factories, striving to make ends meet. Years of failed harvests, rising taxes, and the corn levies that protected the earnings of wealthy landowners caused more families to plunge into the terrible grip of poverty annually.

William knew what poverty could do to even the most respectable of people. His childhood memories included riotous scenes of mobs of the starving poor looting bakers' shops, filling their arms with precious bread before fleeing. As a young boy he peeked through the front window of his home on Notintone Place as angry multitudes wrenched free the iron railings of his father's fence to use as weapons in their battle against the troops sent to dispel the riots. Prostitution and crime were rampant in the poorer neighborhoods as people struggled for survival.

William's father was a tightfisted entrepreneur and, although not a good businessman, he always managed to earn enough to provide for his family. Unlike many children his age in Nottingham, William was never required to labor for twelve hours or more each day in the factories to help earn enough to buy bread and coal. His childhood was spent attending school and enjoying the fun of boyish games. William's natural leadership qualities came to the fore during childhood, even in the games he played with his friends. Pretending to be soldiers, William was nicknamed Wellington, after the Duke of Wellington who triumphed at the Battle of Waterloo in 1815. No matter what game they played, it was usually William who was captain and leader. He also loved to fish and would set off for the banks of the Trent River as early as five in the morning, hoping optimistically for a catch. His hopefulness was rarely rewarded, and his lack of success at fishing soon became a family joke.

Although his childhood years passed by pleasantly, William's life took a sudden turn soon after his thirteenth birthday. He had known for some time that his father's building business was in trouble. Money was even more scarce than usual, and by the constant frown of worry on his mother's face he suspected their situation was getting worse. William's premonitions were right. His father faced financial ruin. A creditor's sudden call for repayment saw the family plans for young William's future swing from attending a prestigious school for gentlemen to being apprenticed to a pawnbroker.

"Apprentice to a pawnbroker," William murmured under his breath as he strode purposefully through the streets of Nottingham toward Goose Gate for his first day of work. "I'm a pawnbroker's apprentice," he repeated, wondering what his new role in life would entail. He remembered the look of disappointment that had crossed his mother's face when his father announced his decision. *Still,* he thought to himself, *Mr. Eames is the best pawnbroker in Nottingham. I'm sure to learn a lot from him in six years!*

Nearing the corner of Goose Gate, William's destination came into view. His heart beat nervously as he approached the tiny shop and recognized the sign of the three golden balls hanging over the entrance. Pushing the door open, a bell announced his arrival with a sound that soon became forever etched upon his mind.

Frances Eames greeted his newest assistant. Unlike many businesses, his trade was booming. Each new day brought more customers from farther afield, and he had been looking for some time to take on an apprentice to help with the increasing workload. *Young William Booth looks like he will do well*, he thought, sizing up the tall, raven-haired young man. After a short tour of the premises and a stern briefing on what was expected of him, the young apprentice was put to work.

It didn't take William long to realize that he hated pawnbroking. The days were long and the weeks seemed eternal. There were items to sort, paper work to complete, errands to run, and a never-ending assortment of forfeited pledges waiting to be priced and displayed for sale. It was not that he hated the hard work, the long hours, or even the oppressive, musty smell that penetrated his clothes as a constant reminder to him of his workplace. The one thing William grew to loathe passionately was the constant jingle of the front doorbell. It rang out almost constantly throughout the long days, and in William's young mind it soon came to symbolize the terrible plight of the poor. It seemed impossible for him to escape the sound. It rang out around his home, in other shops, and even in his sleep. All served as a reminder of the soul-destroying hopelessness that emanated from the lives of the poor.

Such was a too-common scene as, early one Monday morning a few weeks into his apprenticeship, the bell rang out its familiar sound and William looked up from the pile of clothes he had been sorting. The heavy door creaked shut as a thin woman with a familiar face approached the counter. Mr. Eames greeted the woman while William tried to recall how he knew her. He had seen her somewhere—where? Perhaps she was the mother of one of his old schoolmates?

The woman emptied the contents of her ragged bag onto the counter and stood silently as Mr. Eames examined each item, his trained eye quickly valuing the pledges. William watched on, sighing as a new pile of clothes built up on the counter. In his mind, he guessed at the value of the garments and wondered how close he would be to Mr. Eames's total. As he did so he recognized some of the items—a silk blouse, a deep-blue bonnet, and a young girl's lace dress. He looked up into the woman's expressionless face and remembered immediately where he had seen her last. It was a late Saturday night and they had been preparing to close the shop when she rushed in with a few coins to pay out her loan and redeem her "Sunday best" clothing. William's heart sank as he wondered what sacrifices she had made to look her best for just one day. His eyes rested again on the woman's blank face, pity and compassion mingling with a strange sense of anger that rose within, anger toward poverty. He turned back to his work and tried to shut out the sadness he felt inside.

Day after day his young heart was crushed by the despair etched on the faces of those bringing their most precious possessions to be given only a pittance in return. The haunting sadness in the depth of their eyes added to the picture of hopelessness that gripped and touched him. His senses were bombarded by the destructive grip of poverty as he witnessed the gradual erosion of people's dignity and self-respect. The silk handkerchiefs and Sunday clothes were the first to go; wedding rings were last. For some families, the pawnshop was their only hope to avoid eviction from their shabby dwellings.

Alongside the compassion that grew in his heart for the poor rose a deep hatred for the public houses and bars. Some nights as he dragged his weary body home he would see the husbands of the women he had served during the day stumbling through their doors. To the young teenager, it all seemed so desperately wrong. In the face of such misery, William never dared to complain about his work. Each day was a reminder that he was among the fortunate ones—earning at least a small wage. He was grateful for the opportunity to support his own struggling family.

William's father did not recover from the bankruptcy declared on his business. His mental and physical state deteriorated from the strain, and it was no surprise to the family when he died in September of 1842, less than a year after they had faced ruin. What was a surprise, especially to William, was the eleventh-hour repentance that came on his father's deathbed. As the family gathered round, "Cousin Gregory" led them in singing "Rock of Ages" and took it upon himself to see to Samuel's eternal affairs.[3] To the headstrong young man, his father's words seemed little more than a hypocritical plea to get to heaven.

With his father's death came greater responsibility for his family's welfare. These were desperate times for the thirteen-year-old to assume the leadership and care of his household. William's mother eventually found work in a small haberdashery store in Goose Gate, but as the only male in the family he carried the constant burden of their needs. The daily picture of poverty he faced at the pawnbroker's now threatened his own life. This environment birthed in his heart the compelling desire to help people escape poverty, which would later characterize his ministry years.

When Feargus O'Connor, the radical Irish speaker for the Chartist movement, visited Nottingham, William attended his meetings. The working-class-driven Chartist movement advocated political reform aimed at addressing the huge inequalities that existed between the social classes in England. They had published *The People's Charter* in May of 1838, which called for, among other things, the equality of electoral districts and equal voting rights for all men in England, regardless of their social class. O'Connor spoke with great passion and fervor as he rallied the working class to support their efforts at improving conditions for England's poor. As he listened, William's resolve to help the needy deepened.

His compassion for those less fortunate than himself grew with each new day of his apprenticeship with Mr. Eames. Even more impacting on his tender young heart, however, was the pitiful sight of young children crying and begging in the streets for bread. As he reminisced on his childhood at the close of his life, it was not the fiery words of the Chartists' orators, or the sermons he may have listened to in chapel, the games he played with his friends, or anything he had experienced while attending school that dominated his memories. The vision of children in rags weeping in the street for food remained his most vivid impression from childhood.[4] As he worked each day in the pawnshop, he began to dream of leaving his work behind to make a difference in the world. He dreamed of joining the Chartists and changing England's laws so that no one would live in poverty.

No amount of dreaming, however, would provide for his family; William knew, for now at least, he must continue in his work. Although he didn't know it, as he entered his fifteenth year, a remarkable change was just around the corner. The nature of that change was even more unexpected.

William was ambling home after closing the shop late one evening when he heard the familiar voice of his childhood friend Boldie Newbold. They talked for a while, exchanging news and inquiring about mutual acquaintances. William hadn't seen much of his friends since starting work, and there was a lot to catch up on.

"How's Will Sansom?" he asked, thinking of the fun they used to have together, playing in the Nottingham streets.

"He's doing fine," replied Boldie. "He was at the meeting tonight."

"What meeting is that?" William asked curiously, noticing for the first time that Boldie was all dressed up.

"We've been at a class meeting at the Wesley Chapel on Broad Street," Boldie said. Seeing the look of curiosity on William's face, he continued. "It's a meeting for young people to study the Bible and talk about how they're getting on."

"What do you mean, 'How they're getting on'?" asked William. "How they're getting on at what?"

"Well," Boldie responded, "it's about how they're doing with God." He was surprised by the interest William was showing. He knew the Booths were Church of England and had even seen William at the Broad Street Chapel with an elderly couple on a few occasions, but he didn't expect him to show much interest in spiritual things. They continued to talk, and before they parted Boldie had invited William to next week's class meeting, an invitation that was surprisingly accepted.

William began to attend the meetings, and although he felt distinctly uncomfortable at times, something drew him back week after week. Class leader Henry Carey's penetrating eyes and his question—"How are you getting on with your soul?"—disturbed William. Although not sure what was wrong, he could not ignore the growing feeling that told him things were certainly not right.

The Spirit of God continued to work in William's heart. Little by little he began to realize his need for God. The stirrings of the Spirit grew stronger until finally, influenced by the fiery preaching of Isaac Marsden, he took his first step of faith. When the light of God flooded his heart and mind on his way home as previously described that evening in 1844, William Booth made a decision to renounce his sin and to live God's way, putting right, where possible, the wrongs he had done.

Over the days that followed, he continued to allow God to deal with his heart. At first he hesitated to make a public declaration of his faith—something held him back. "The inward Light revealed to me," he said, "that I must not only renounce everything I knew to be sinful, but to make restitution, so far as I had the ability, for any wrong I had done to others before I could find my peace with God."[5] In his heart he knew there were things he had to do, things that must be put right. The most pressing issue concerned the silver pencil case he carried to and from work each day, a treasure gained deceitfully from his friends. Under the conviction of God, the prized pencil case began to burn like fire against his flesh. Years later he recalled the process of repentance that began in his heart and was worked out into action.

It was in the open street that this great change passed over me, and if I could only have possessed the flagstone on which I stood at that happy moment, the sight of it occasionally might have been as useful to me as the stones carried up long ago from the bed of the Jordan were to the Israelites who had passed over them dry-shod.

The entrance to the Heavenly Kingdom was closed against me by an evil act of the past which required restitution. In a boyish trading affair I had managed to make a profit out of my companions, whilst giving them to suppose that what I did was all in the way of a generous fellowship. As a testimonial of their gratitude they had given me a silver pencil-case. Merely to return their gift would have been comparatively easy, but to confess the deception I had practiced upon them was a humiliation to which for some days I could not bring myself.

I remember it as if it were yesterday, the spot in the corner of the room under the chapel, the hour, the resolution to end the matter, the rising up and rushing forth, the finding of the young fellow I had chiefly wronged, the acknowledgement of my sin, the return of the pencil-case—the instant rolling away from my heart of the guilty burden, the peace that came in its place, and the going forth to serve my God and my generation from that hour.[6]

As the Holy Spirit brought conviction concerning wrongs he had done, William responded with confession, repentance, and restitution before God and, where necessary, before his friends. The uneasy feelings he had felt during chapel meetings were now replaced with the joy of experiencing the forgiveness and love of God. As he responded in obedience, the Holy Spirit brought peace to his heart, and he knew that he was saved.

Salvation became a reality for William, a reality that remained with him for life. Some years later he wrote,

My brethren, if you have salvation you are sure of it. Not because . . . you have heard it preached. Not because you have read with your eyes, or heard read by others in that wonderful book, the wonderful story of the love of God to you. Not because you have seen with your eyes transformations of character wrought by the power of the Holy Ghost; changes as marvelous, as miraculous, as divine, as any that ever took place in apostolic or any other days. These things may have led up to it. But these things, wonderful as they may be, have not power to make you sure of your part and lot in the matter of salvation. Flesh and blood has not revealed this to you, but God Himself, by His Spirit has made this known.[7]

The Spirit of God bore witness within fifteen-year-old William Booth that he had been made new. For William, the joy of a new start in life brought with it a sober understanding of the responsibility of obedience.

This newfound desire to follow God spilled over into every area of his life. Soon after his conversion, William began to feel uneasy about working on Sundays. Although the pawnshop officially closed at midnight on Saturday, the staff were often kept working without a break long into the early hours of Sunday morning. Business was booming. Compelled by his conviction that to work on Sunday was against his Christian principles, William informed his employer that he would no longer be able to continue work beyond midnight on Saturday.

Mr. Eames was not impressed. His position was clear. "You can work with the rest of us until we shut up shop, or you can leave."

Standing strong in his decision despite the threat of losing his job, William quickly discovered his employer was serious. He was fired! For choosing to live by his convictions, his only source of income and his support for his family were cut off. Joining the hordes of unemployed in Nottingham, he was faced with scant opportunity of finding work. The streets were packed with slow-moving crowds, each person desperately searching for employment, prepared to stand in line for hours at the slightest glimmer of hope that work might come along.

However, William's street-walking was short-lived, for in a remarkable turn of events God intervened. After just a few days, his employer realized he had lost his most valuable worker. William was reinstated and became the only employee who was allowed to finish work on the stroke of midnight each Saturday. His stouthearted desire to obey God no matter what the cost, evident from the moment of his conversion, thus became a hallmark of his life and teachings.

William's interest and focus in life now turned to the things of God. He attended every chapel meeting possible, eagerly learning from the revivalist preachers who traveled the country in the 1840s. Hungrily he devoured every word they uttered, learning not only the truth they declared but also the techniques they employed to capture people's attention. From one he learned the value of simple stories that brought home a point, from another the use of parables, relating spiritual truths to ordinary, everyday activities.

Two years after his conversion, he sat spellbound by revivalist preacher James Caughey. The Irish-American's flamboyant style captivated the entire congregation, but none more so than William. As he preached he painted vivid pictures with his words, challenging his hearers to a response. The Word of God was surely as a sword in his hand, piercing to the depths of William's soul. During these meetings William's life was revolutionized, and without hesitation he dedicated himself to the service of God. "I want to be right with God, I want to be right with myself, and I want to spend my life helping others to be right,"[8] he stated emphatically as he reflected on his decision at that time to live his life in the service of God. Kneeling that day before the Lord he determined, "God shall have all there was of William Booth."[9]

James Caughey, born 1810, greatly inspired the ministry of William and Catherine Booth.

From that moment on he was branded with a consuming passion to save souls. The same sense of desperate urgency that almost a century before had consumed John Wesley now also gripped William Booth. In many ways he began to tread in the footsteps of Wesley, his heart beating with compassion for the multitudes of poor and weary who would never darken the doorways of the lavish churches and cathedrals of the day.

Their reluctance to come to church troubled William. He noticed how the revivalist preachers, having concluded their sermons with a challenge, followed the Methodist tradition of urging people to the communion rail to publicly accept Christ. The poor, who were so much on his heart, never came forward. In fact, the poorest of the poor he dealt with day in and day out at work rarely entered the chapels at all. When they did, they were shown little welcome. In an age of pew rents, where the best seats in the house were reserved for those willing to pay the most for them, sections for the poor were not only sparse but often out of sight. The church catered readily for those that could support it but often showed little concern for the rest. The poor simply did not fit into church culture. They were ashamed because they did not have suitable clothes to wear and chose to stay away rather than face the scorn and pity of others. None knew this more than William, who worked late every Saturday evening sorting, folding, stacking, and hanging "Sunday-best" clothing on racks in Eames's pawnshop.

Whatever the reason, William was not one to let the grass grow under his feet. If the poor did not come to the gospel, then he would take the gospel to the poor! When his friend Will Sansom, also inspired by Caughey's meetings, proposed they start holding open-air meetings to preach the message of salvation, he leaped at the chance. With the compassion for the poor that ruled their tender young hearts it was no surprise that these became their target audience. "The Bottoms" was the meanest of Nottingham's slums. Its people were unemployed, destitute, and desperately poor. It was to these that William and his friend went with the message of God's love.

Standing on a chair or barrel in an alley or on a street corner, William would invite people to attend a meeting in a nearby cottage where he preached his heart out to anyone who cared to listen. Booth's natural flair for relating to people enabled him to communicate the gospel message in a way his uneducated audience could understand. With passion and love he preached the way of salvation, urging his hearers, be they only a handful, to make their response to God.

One early success came with a preaching venture that found him in Kid Street with Will Samson. Expectantly, they had positioned themselves on the street edge, outside the home of a notorious drunk, Besom Jack. Their open-air meeting commenced with a hymn that seemed to be appropriate for the occasion. It was from the Methodist songbook:

Outcasts of men, to you I call,
Harlots and publicans and thieves!
He spreads His arms to embrace you all;
Sinners alone, His grace receives:
No need of Him the righteous have,
He came the lost to seek and save.[10]

They had no sooner raised their voices than a large, boisterous crowd encircled them. Young William was on his chair in an instant. "Friends," he cried as he dodged a well-aimed, overripe missile, his large hooknose having a somewhat magnetic appeal to the tomato-launching public. "I want to put a few straight questions to your soul," he declared passionately. "Have any of you got a child at home without shoes to its feet? Are your wives sitting now in dark houses waiting for you to return without money? Are you going away from here . . . to spend on drink, money that your wives need for food?"[11]

At that moment the front door behind him flung open and out stumbled Besom Jack, eyes aflame and heading straight for the preaching duo, shouting abuse and lunging at them while still six feet away.

"Jack, God loves your wife, and so did you once," said William steadily, looking the broom-seller in the eye. Jack stopped in his tracks and immediately became quiet. "Can you remember how much you loved her and cherished her when first you met?" the teenager asked tenderly. Jack nodded; his eyes fixed on the ground. "Well, Jack, God loves you with a love like that, with a love far deeper and greater than that." The hushed crowd strained to catch what the boy-preacher was saying, amazed at the change that had overcome the drunkard.

Jack lifted his eyes and blinked sheepishly. "Me?" he asked in wonderment.

"Yes, Jack, you," said William as he stood down from the chair and took hold of Jack's arm.

Jack's wife recounted the end of this meeting to Mr. Eames, the pawnbroker, the following week, saying,

> And 'e said to 'im, "Come Jack, just kneel down 'ere and tell the Lord you love 'im too. And ask 'im to forgive yer." And 'e did! My Jack knelt there in the gutter and 'e's bin a different man ever since; 'e says 'e's a Christian now![12]

Young William's heart beat for souls! His desire to help the poor had grown into a desire to see them saved. Gone were his notions of joining the Chartists, whose policies could only address the outward, political symptoms of poverty but never affect the heart of a person caught in alcoholism or despair. He had found his calling as a preacher of the gospel, the only true agent of inward change.

Although excited by their attempts at open-air preaching, William realized the people needed more. They needed to be taught the ways of God. They needed, he decided, to attend chapel. Heading down to the slums of "The Bottoms" one cold Sunday, he drew together a crowd and persuaded them to accompany him to the chapel service.

As the comfortable congregation concluded the fourth hymn of the morning, the chapel doors were flung open, and following the icy-cold blast of air came the shabbiest, dirtiest, smelliest procession of people the church had ever seen. To the dismay of the Rev. Samuel Dunn, William Booth ushered them into the very best seats. Rev. Dunn's heart sank as he thought of the pewholders and sank further as he felt the piercing stares of the respectable congregation.

On the side of the chapel, behind a partition, sat a few rows of empty benches. These were the seats reserved for the poor. They could come unnoticed through the side door, and although they could not see the pulpit, the service could be clearly heard. Today, despite the record number of poor in attendance, these benches remained empty.

William Booth, totally oblivious to the stir his actions were causing, joined in heartily with the singing. As he listened to the message he wondered if he might even be commended for bringing so many to chapel. Nothing could have been further from the truth! At the conclusion of the service, he was summoned to an impromptu meeting with the deacons, and Rev. Dunn sternly instructed him to follow protocol next time he intended on bringing any such people to church. They were to enter via the side door and be seated on the benches appointed for them.

William accepted this rebuke and many more like it. As he pursued his passion to see lost souls saved, he received little encouragement from his church leadership to inspire his efforts. While this made things hard, in a sense it did not matter to William. As a young man, he had made his choice. He chose the salvation of souls and the extension of the kingdom of Jesus Christ as the supreme object for which he would live and work. Like Moses, he had grown to maturity and chosen to forgo the pleasures of this life, preferring to share the oppression, suffer the hardships, and bear the shame of the people of God rather than have the fleeting enjoyment of a sinful life. (See Hebrews 11:25.)

This object of salvation, this purpose of the kingdom, continued to shape and master William's thoughts, ambitions, and activities throughout his adolescence and in fact for his whole life. All that he accomplished was governed by his desire to live and work to see salvation come to all men and the kingdom of God extended in the world in which he lived. William knew what he was about. As he matured, his church leadership and close acquaintances began to recognize the gifting of God on his life. When he was seventeen his minister appointed him as a local preacher, and he began to speak on a regular basis at the Broad Street Chapel as well as the chapels in the smaller villages around Nottingham. In addition to this, William also continued to hold open-air meetings, preaching and praying as often as he could.

As he neared the end of his apprenticeship in 1848, at the age of nineteen, William began to think more of the future. His minister suggested he should offer himself for ministry in the Methodist church. William hesitated over this decision for many months. His health had been poor for some years, and this discouraged him from taking such a step. When he sought his doctor's opinion he was firmly told that not only was he totally unfit for such strenuous work but "that twelve months work in the ministry would land him in the grave, and send him to the throne of God to receive punishment for suicide!"[13] The final choice was made when his apprenticeship ended and he found himself out of work. Mr. Eames could no longer afford to keep him. While William was thrilled to at last leave the hated shop, he was not so thrilled to be unemployed. His dire financial situation seemed to make certain his inability to enter the ministry.

When twelve months of seeking employment in Nottingham yielded no results, William decided to move to London. The year was 1850. Arriving by train, he hoped to stay with his sister and her husband until he got himself on his feet. These plans were quickly swept away when he discovered both had turned to drink and were neither able nor willing to take him in. London's first impression upon William's heart was one of great loneliness. His hopes of finding work grew dimmer by the day, and with no family, no friends, and little money, he realized he would have to fall back upon his despised trade. The only employment he could find was in a pawnbroker's shop at Kennington Common, Walworth, in London's southeast.

His hours of work were seven in the morning until late at night, with only Sundays and two hours on one weeknight free. The shop provided him with a small attic bedroom, the door to which was locked at precisely ten o'clock each evening. The work and pay conditions were very poor, but William was grateful for employment and delighted that he would be able to use his free time for church work. Writing to a friend at that time, he said, "I am decided for God to live and for God to die."[14]

He began to attend the Methodist chapel in Walworth, and his new circuit minister was soon happy to add William's name to the preaching plan. His only free day then became filled with meetings, sometimes as far away as Greenwich, eight miles to the south of his home. His weary body struggled to keep up with the pace required to travel this distance, preach, and return before lock-up time. Before long the physical demands of his long working hours and the ministry took their toll on his already poor state of health. He developed nagging stomach pains that were to remain with him throughout his life.

Despite his great enthusiasm, William received little encouragement from his circuit minister. His passionate preaching was not always well received by the middle-class congregations he addressed. He continued to preach in the open air whenever possible, often enjoying the interaction with those outside the church more than those within. William's circuit minister began to suspect he was more akin to the expelled reformers, and he chose to limit William's opportunities to preach. When William asked to be withdrawn from the preaching plan altogether in order to devote more of his time to open-air preaching, his minister became even more suspicious of his motives. Although William requested to remain a member of the Walworth church, the renewal of his ticket of membership was declined. The loneliness of London was suddenly compounded as William was expelled from fellowship.

The young man felt the sharp sting of rejection as he was stripped of his mentors and the opportunity to preach. The pain seemed all the greater as it came from the very denomination in which he longed to serve. "To me," he later said, "there was one God, and John Wesley was His prophet."[15] William searched tirelessly for new avenues of ministry, and at one stage he seriously considered paying passage to Australia on a convict-laden ship bound for the colony. The chance to "face the storm and the billow, and the tempest's rolling wave, and to preach to the very worst of men Christ's salvation"[16] appealed immensely to William's adventurous nature. This was not to be, however, for God had His own blueprint to fulfill for William's life.

His preaching style, although not popular with every congregation, had won him at least one admirer from the Methodist Church. Edward Rabbits, a bootmaker who lived in Walworth, had listened to William preach on a number of occasions and he liked what he heard. Mr. Rabbits was a man of influence, due in part to the wealth he had accumulated as owner of a chain of successful boot stores in South London. He had rebelled against the Methodists' resistance to change, aligning himself instead with the reformers.

The fire, passion, and bluntness of William's messages stood in stark contrast to most other sermons of the day. Mr. Rabbits recognized the potential in the zealous young evangelist. Upon hearing of his expulsion from the Methodist movement, he invited William to join the reformers. Before long William was given opportunity to preach in their chapels. In the midst of his loneliness and despair, William found a friend and confidant in Rabbits. A letter written to a friend by William talked of his frustration:

> In my present position I am unsettled—unhappy—my occupation is so contrary to my views that I am continually desiring something different—I feel it in my heart—on my soul from day to day that I would be a missionary of God.[17]

William's passion to preach the gospel was no longer satisfied by the opportunity to preach from time to time in chapels or the open air. Within him grew the desire to commit all of his time and energy to seeing souls saved. Mr. Rabbits also believed William should be in the ministry, and he wasted no time in telling him so.

Early in 1852 he invited William to dinner. At the conclusion of the meal he looked directly at his young friend and insisted, "You must leave business and wholly devote yourself to preaching the gospel."

William shook his head, surprised at the sudden outburst. His friend obviously had no idea how hard William had looked for opportunities to preach. It seemed the only work open to him was that of the open air and, as he knew from experience, this would put neither a roof over his head nor food in his stomach. "There is no way for me. Nobody wants me," William replied. The words seemed to cut into his heart, increasing the depression he already felt. He was surprised to hear his friend disagree. He was even more surprised to hear from him that the reformers wanted to take him on as an evangelist! But there was still the question of survival. How could he pay his way?

"How much can you live on?" asked Mr. Rabbits.

William thought for a moment, adding up the essential expenses of food and lodgings. "I would say about twelve shillings a week," he replied, curious to know where the conversation was heading.

"Nonsense," came the reply. "You cannot do with less than twenty shillings a week, I am sure. I will supply it, for the first three months at least."[18]

William was elated. With joy he accepted the proposal. Within days he had quit his pawnbroking job and secured a couple of rooms in a widow's house. In time his name was added to the reformers' preaching plan and he was appointed to deliver sermons in their Binfield Road Chapel. At last William could devote all of his time and energy to what had become his one ruling passion: preaching the gospel.

This passion for souls governed William's life from the moment of his conversion at fifteen until his death at the age of eighty-three. The conviction that ruled his life was the salvation of souls and the extension of the kingdom of God. Reiterating the courageous words of Jesus' apostles to those who sought to silence them, he staunchly proclaimed, "I cannot but speak of the things I have seen and heard." (See Acts 4:20.)

For William, following Christ meant having the same purpose as his Savior. Later he would pen these words that captured the very essence of his passion for saving souls.

> How can a man follow Christ if he is not moved by the same purpose? What was His purpose? The salvation of the world. Not the humiliation and the suffering and the agony and the death. These were the means by which only the end could be reached; if the end could have been gained by any less agonizing way, doubtless it would have been followed. He wanted to reach the dying millions and, by living a divine life before them, and pouring forth His divine Blood for them, to make the salvation of all possible, to make the salvation of multitudes sure.
>
> This was his purpose. To this every thought and feeling and effort were offered up. His whole being was consecrated to its accomplishment.
>
> My comrades, here is our pattern. What are you living for? What is the deep secret purpose that controls and fashions your existence? What do you eat and drink for? What is the end of your marrying and giving in marriage—your money-making and toilings and plannings? Is it the salvation of souls, the overthrow of the kingdom of evil and the setting up of the Kingdom of God? . . . I must push this question. Have you the assurance that the ruling passion of your life is the same as that which brought Christ to the manger, led Him to fight the foul fiend of Hell in the wilderness, bore Him onward on the back of suffering and tears and ignominy and shame, sustained Him in drinking the cup of anguish and enduring the baptism of blood, bore Him through Gethsemane, nailed Him to the Cross of Calvary and enabled Him in triumph to open the gate of the Kingdom? Is this what you are living for? If not, you may be religious—a very proper person amongst religionists—but I don't see how you can be a Christian.
>
> What is the value of a shell without a kernel? What is a body without a soul? What is a Christian without a Christ inside? If any man have not the spirit of Christ, he is none of His, and the supreme purpose of Christ's spirit was, and still is, and ever will be, to save the world.[19]

William's mission was clear; his mind was set. He knew what he was about. His life's battle cry was unmistakable: "Go for souls! Go for the worst!"

The great Army William Booth was to raise up beneath him was still a long way off. As he set about his work of preaching for the reformers, he had little inkling of the path God had chosen for him. All he knew was what he had experienced of God. All he could do was respond to the overwhelming desire in his heart to preach and to see souls touched, saved, and transformed by the power of his God.

However, the call of God on William's life was not a call to be filled alone. For such a task, he required a partner. Not just any partner would do. William needed an equal, one whose heart was charged with the same fervent passion for souls and with the same unrelenting commitment to God. Together such a partnership would achieve so much more than either individual alone. Together such a partnership would strive to raise the Army of God in their day. It was time for William to meet his match.

CHAPTER 3

And the Two Shall Become One

WILLIAM AND CATHERINE'S COURTSHIP (1852–1855)

What follows is one of the most remarkable and charming love stories in the world—the love story of a man and a woman in whose hearts an extraordinary sense of religion had the uppermost place, to whom everything secular and human had a divine relativity, for whom God and His worship were the sovereign ends of existence.

—HAROLD BEGBIE, DESCRIBING WILLIAM AND CATHERINE'S ENGAGEMENT[1]

William knocked forcefully on the heavy wooden door and stood back to catch his breath, wondering if he were the last guest to arrive. The door swung open and he was ushered into a dark hallway. Muffled tones of conversation echoed in the hall and increased in volume as he entered the parlor.

"Ah, William," declared Mr. Rabbits as he strode to the door, hand outstretched in greeting. "Glad you could make it—come in," he continued, escorting William into the lavishly appointed room. William recognized most of the reformers who had been invited for afternoon tea and conversation. They greeted him warmly as Mr. Rabbits made the introductions.

"Good day, Mr. Booth," said one dark-haired young lady, her smiling eyes welcoming him. William's heart skipped a beat, and he immediately recalled meeting Miss Mumford only a fortnight before. He had just completed his first message at the reformers' Binfield Road Chapel in Clapham. The congregation had been enthusiastic and responsive as he preached from the text, "This is indeed the Christ, the Saviour of the world" (John 4:42). After the service Mr. Rabbits pulled him aside and introduced him to Miss Catherine Mumford. They had spoken only briefly. A few days later, Mr. Rabbits confessed to William that he had asked Catherine for her opinion of the message. Her answer, relayed to him by his friend, had surprised William. "One of the best I have heard in this chapel," she had said emphatically. Although William couldn't appreciate the value of the young woman's critique, Rabbits certainly did. He spoke very highly of Catherine, declaring to William that she was the best judge of a sermon he knew![2]

William sat down and was quickly drawn into the conversation that continued among the young reformers. As they talked, his gaze rested momentarily on Catherine. She was petite with simple, elegant features, her soft black curls framing her sweet face. Her dark eyes sparkled as she spoke with the young lady sitting next to her. Everything about her seemed so alive.

"William does an excellent recital," said Mr. Rabbits, interrupting his thoughts. "Will you share a piece with us now?" he asked. "How about that American temperance poem?"

William's heart sank. Although he felt at home preaching in front of great crowds, he had never been one for social performance. Looking around the room he realized that many of those present were likely to enjoy the occasional drink. William himself was not a zealous advocate for total abstinence, but he did not want to make any of the guests feel uncomfortable. He shook his head and politely refused the invitation, wondering where Miss Mumford stood on the temperance issue as he did so.

"Oh, but we insist, William, don't we, friends?" replied Mr. Rabbits, rallying support for his suggestion. Seeing that he was not going to be able to escape this time, William sighed lightly and stood. All eyes rested upon him, but none more beautiful or calming than Catherine's. Taking a deep breath, he began.

"The Grog-Seller's Dream"
A grog-seller sat by his barroom fire,
His feet as high as his head and higher. . . .
Foolish and fuddled, his friends had gone,
To wake in the morn to a drunkard's pain,
With bloodshot eyes and a reeling brain. . . .

William lost himself in the dramatic poem that described the troubled dreaming of the drunken grog-seller. His expressive voice and lively gestures brought the sobering poem to its climax as he approached the conclusion:

For to pamper your lust with the gold and pelf,
You rival in mischief the Devil himself.[3]

William's fears were realized as he sat down, applauded only by an awkward and uncomfortable atmosphere. After what seemed an eternity, the silence was broken. A number of the young men present were moderate drinkers, and they launched their attack, strongly defending their position. A noisy debate arose within the group. William was astonished when from the demure Miss Mumford came the most fierce and logical argument for total abstinence that he had ever heard. His admiration for her grew as he realized she was more than a match for the protesting men. Mr. Rabbits finally brought the heated discussion to a conclusion and invited the group to adjourn to the dining room for refreshments. William farewelled the party a short time later, smiling privately with Catherine as they noted together that the wine had remained untouched.

Mr. Rabbits had been instrumental in arranging William's first and second meetings with Catherine. Their third meeting, some months after the tea party, was also the result of Mr. Rabbits' plans. It was Good Friday, April 9, 1852, and William was on top of the world. He'd just quit the pawnbroking trade, thanks to the three months of support offered by Mr. Rabbits. The previous day he had moved into his new lodgings, and tomorrow was his twenty-third birthday; life was looking up.

Good Friday, he thought to himself as he strolled through the streets of Walworth, *What a good day!* William was intending to visit a cousin, a plan that was soon put aside when he met his friend Mr. Rabbits. After inquiring as to his arrangements for the day, Mr. Rabbits insisted that William accompany him to a meeting in a schoolroom on Cowper Street. William was happy to change his mind and talked excitedly with his friend as they walked to the meeting.

To make a good day even better, Miss Mumford was attending the meeting. She and William spoke briefly together before the service began. It proved to be a long one, and Catherine, who was feeling unwell, decided she was unable to stay until it finished. William's heart sank momentarily, only to soar again when he was asked by Mr. Rabbits to escort her to her home in Brixton.

The hackney carriage rattled over the rough London streets. William and Catherine, alone for the first time, began to talk. The conversation flowed easily as they shared from their hearts with freedom and excitement. The sweet presence of God filled the carriage as they talked, and in the depths of their hearts they both realized His favor was upon them. To William and Catherine, that journey became a precious memory of the moment they fell in love. Although neither spoke of it initially, they both knew from that time on that they belonged together.

Catherine Mumford shortly before her marriage to young William Booth, in 1855.

Catherine later wrote,

> That little journey will never be forgotten by either of us. . . . We struck in at once in such wonderful harmony of view and aim and feeling on various matters that passed rapidly before us, that it seemed as though we had intimately known and loved each other for years and suddenly, after some temporary absence, had been brought together again. Before we reached my home we both . . . felt as though we had been made for each other. . . .
>
> It was curious, too, that both of us had an idea of what we should require in the companion with whom we allied ourselves for life; if ever such alliance should take place . . . and here we were, thrown together in this unexpected fashion, matching those preconceived characters, even as though we had been made to order! We felt that henceforth the current of our lives must flow together.[4]

Although Catherine was feeling weak and tired, their lively conversation continued when they arrived home, Catherine's mother joining in. The hours passed quickly, and it was soon much later than they realized. Given the time and the distance William would have to travel home or to his cousin's, Mrs. Mumford invited him to stay the night. William left early the next morning but returned just a few hours later and soon began to visit Catherine almost every day.

The sweetness of the affection he had found disturbed William. He had not been looking for love. At twenty-three years of age, he was not a bit concerned about finding a wife or starting a family. His heart was focused entirely on his work as an evangelist, and he planned to give everything he had—time, money, and effort—to the work of God. For the eight previous years he had longed for the opportunity to devote himself wholeheartedly to the work of saving souls. Now that this opportunity was his, he was determined not to allow any other passion, pursuit, or purpose to distract him from this task.

Overnight, and quite against his will, however, a new love had captured his heart. Talk of becoming engaged was almost immediate, but the more they discussed it, the more unreasonable it seemed. Yet Catherine appeared to be everything he could hope for in a soulmate. Her devotion to God, her keen intellect, her purity of heart, and the beauty of her spirit drew from William an affection he seemed powerless to resist. He had stumbled across one who perfectly fulfilled his criteria for a life-partner. Catherine was a godly woman, one who had yielded her life to the work of the Holy Spirit, to holiness, and to living for Christ and for souls. Her conversation was both stimulating and intellectual. He had never met a woman with whom he felt so comfortable, so alive, and so complete. Yet as a man who planned to live as a traveling evangelist, what kind of a future did he have to offer her?

With his heart in turmoil, William turned to prayer, pleading with the Lord to take away the disturbing feelings of love and attraction that grew stronger with each passing day. The more he prayed, however, the more deeply he fell in love with Catherine. He found himself wondering how something that seemed in his heart to be so right could at the same time be judged by his mind as being wrong. How could he possibly consider engagement and marriage when his future and financial security were so uncertain? As he battled with this dilemma, it was as though the control he had only recently gained over his life had suddenly been stripped away.

Day after day William and Catherine talked together, sharing from their hearts, revealing their love for one another, and kneeling to pray for their concerns. While they both believed it would be foolish to rush into an engagement, this seemed to be the most natural step for them to take. Catherine understood William's fears, and rather than pressuring him toward marriage, she insisted she would not even consider an engagement unless he were convinced in his own mind that it was God's will. They agreed to earnestly seek God's guidance on the matter.

William's passionate personality also caused him to swing between extremes. As he thought and prayed about the engagement, he experienced every conceivable emotion, from elation to despair, from enthusiasm to fear. At times his mood was depressed and melancholic when he was with Catherine as he struggled to reconcile his passion for her with his passion for souls. He expressed this to her honestly, but impossible to ignore was the joy that had come into his heart from having met her. In one of his first letters to her, he wrote:

My own dear Catherine,

I know you will, at least I will presume you will, forgive the liberty I take in writing you a line, although it is not so long since we met, but for some reason or other I am happier than I have been for some time back and when there is a ray of sunshine in my heart I conceive you have a right to know it especially seeing you have been made too minutely acquainted with every dark cloud that has flitted across the horizon of my soul of late. I have been thinking of you very much yesterday and this morning, I feel that the affection I entertain for you is a growing, deepening, expanding, and extending feeling I trust that on both sides it shall be ever and ever thus. To love as one, live as one, with *one*, only *one* clap of cares and anxieties . . . what is thine in this respect shall be mine, and what is mine shall be thine. . . .

My love to your dear mother, her kindness is indelibly graven on my heart, a heart Catherine which is all yours now, may your influence I compassionately hallow, soften, and imbue it with more of your own gentleness, and sweet meekness. Until we meet be assured that I am forever, your dearest and most sacred friend, . . . William.[5]

Though he was obviously smitten with Catherine and longed to be able to give with his love the best that life could offer, William knew the life he had chosen would not allow him to do so. When he inquired of his friends, they confirmed his doubts—Miss Mumford was a young lady who deserved much better prospects than he could hope to provide. William's only encouragement came from the times he spent with Catherine. In her company, fear and doubt were pushed aside by the overwhelming rush of joy and love that welled up within his heart, yet she sensed his moodiness, the struggle in his soul. In a fit of emotion and low self-esteem that betrayed his youth, he even declared on one occasion he could never be a blessing to her because of his circumstances and uncertain future. In fact, perhaps it would have been better if she had never met him at all!

Catherine would have none of this. As she sensed the doubt that plagued his mind, she urged him not to take any step that he might later regret, not to get caught up in the emotions that were clouding God's simple guidance. With incredible wisdom and insight, she recognized the crippling power of such intense love and passion if pursued in opposition to the will of God. Circumstances and the future were ultimately in God's hands. It was not a question of having everything worked out ahead of time but of walking in His will obediently. She expressed her concern and loving correction for William in one of her letters as she wrote:

My dear Friend,

I have been spreading your letter before the Lord and earnestly pleading for a manifestation of His will to your mind in some way or other . . . my heart feels for you far beyond what I can express. Oh, that I knew how to comfort you in an indirect way. . . .

You do grieve me by saying you fear you "have blocked up every way of being a blessing to me." *I tell you it is not so.* Your kindness and character will ever give weight to your advice and teachings and creates sympathy with your prayers which cannot fail to benefit me.

71

If you wish to avoid giving me pain, don't condemn yourself, I feel sure God does not condemn you, and if you could look into my heart you would see how far I am from such a feeling. *Don't pour over the past.* Let it all go. Your desire is to do the will of God and He will guide you. Never mind who frowns if God smiles. Though you are surrounded by a host of foes, He is *able* to deliver and He *will* deliver, only trust in Him and don't be afraid. The darkness and gloom that hangs about your path shall all flee away; when you are tried you shall come forth as gold! The words gloom, melancholy, and despair lacerate my heart—don't give way to such feelings for a moment. *God loves you.* He will sustain you.

The thought that I should increase your perplexity and cause you suffering is almost unbearable. Oh, that we had never seen each other. Do try to forget me as far as the remembrance would injure your usefulness or spoil your peace. If I have no alternative but to [either] oppose the will of God or trample on the desolations of my own heart, my choice is made: "Thy will be done" is my instant cry. I care not for myself, but oh if I should ever cause you to err I shall never be happy again. Don't, I beseech you, take any step without some evidence *satisfactory* to your own mind of the will of God; think nothing about me.[6]

Then, when William suggested they agree on an engagement and wait to see how things turned out with his evangelistic work, Catherine refused. The following day William wrote,

My dear Friend,

I promised you a line. I write. I know no more now than I knew yesterday. I offered, as you know full well then and there, to make an engagement. You declined on what without doubt are good grounds, but still I cannot do more. . . . You know the inmost feelings of my heart, and I can say no more than that I have not, as I could have wished, seen anything to intimate the will of God. If my circumstances had not been so benighted I might not have desired this. . . . As I said yesterday, I offer now a step in the dark. I will promise you anything you wish for your own dear sake.[7]

Catherine's reply was clear. Writing once more on the thirteenth of May, she replied,

You say, if your circumstances were not so benighted, you would not desire so striking an indication of God's will. I answer, if you are satisfied of His will, irrespective of circumstances, let circumstances go and let us be one, come what will, but if there is anything in me which you fear, anything which you think would mar your complete happiness, banish the thought of any union forever, and let us regard each other as true and tried friends. But if you feel satisfied on these two points, first, that the step is not opposed to the will of God, and secondly, that I am calculated to make you happy, come on Saturday evening and on our knees before God let us give ourselves afresh to Him and to each other for His sake, consecrate our whole selves to His service, *for Him to live and die.* When this is done what have we to do with the future? We and all our concerns are in His hands.[8]

There was no way Catherine would accept a proposal of engagement that was to William a step in the dark. Surely such a blind decision was not God's way. However, she realized from his letter that his hesitation was still based on what he could and could not give her—on his circumstances. As she wrote to William, she endeavored to help him understand that they had to discover God's will, irrespective of their circumstances. After all, God was far greater than any circumstances they would face in the present or the future! As they worked their way through their emotions and faced their fears concerning the future, William and Catherine were learning what it means to be obedient to the will of God, regardless of the consequences. This principle of guidance became a vital foundation for the work God would later call them to pioneer.

Catherine's last letter seemed to settle the matter, for on that Saturday, May 15, 1852, William and Catherine, having obtained her parents' blessing, knelt down solemnly beside the sofa in her home. It was little over a month since their carriage ride home together from the Cowper Street meeting, but the will of God was now clear in their hearts. Hand in hand they prayed together, dedicating themselves to God and to each other. As they stood to their feet their lives had already begun to flow together as one. Overwhelmed by joy, they embarked on a three-year engagement that would later be described as

a Methodist love story. Passion was there, deep and abiding, but passion restrained by duty and consecrated by devotion. An immense reverence for the woman characterized by the love of the man, and a deep, self-sacrificing faith in the man and his destiny characterized the love of the woman.[9]

Catherine's first letter to her fiancé revealed the feelings she had resolutely set aside until William was convinced their engagement to marry was God's perfect will for them. "My dearest William," she wrote,

I fancy I see a look of surprise . . . at the reception of this after such a recent visit. You will think it unnecessary and so it is. . . . The evening is beautifully serene and tranquil according sweetly with the feelings of my soul, the whirlwind is past. . . . All is well. I feel it is right and my soul praises God for the satisfying conviction. Most gladly does my soul respond to your invitation to give myself afresh to Him and to strive to link myself closer to you, by rising more into the likeness of my Lord; the nearer our assimilation to Jesus, the more perfect and heavenly our union. Our hearts are now indeed one, so one that disunion would be more bitter than death. . . . The thought of our walking through life together perfectly united, together enjoying its sunshine and battling with its storms, by softest sympathy sharing every smile and every tear, and with thorough unanimity performing all its momentous duties, is to me exquisite happiness, the highest earthly bliss I desire. . . . We have acknowledged God from the beginning, we have sought His will . . . and we do now love Him more for the love we bear each other. . . . You are always present in my thoughts. Believe me, dear William, as ever your own loving Kate.[10]

By now, through the influence and perseverance of Mr. Rabbits and some others, William's name had been added to the reformers' preaching plan, and he was getting some notice. With the decision of his future with Catherine finally settled, William was able to return his thoughts more fully to his evangelistic work.

As he spent more time working with the reformers, he began to be alarmed by some of the actions and decisions of those leading the new organization. He struggled to work under a leadership that appeared, to him, to be lacking in integrity and out of tune with the Spirit of God. He soon concluded that the troubles among the reformers would only result in instability. After discussing it at length with Catherine, they both decided that the agreement made with Mr. Rabbits should not be extended at the end of the three months. Neither wanted William to feel obligated to a system because of finance. Catherine was not perturbed by the fact that her fiancé was now completely without income or support. Instead she encouraged William, believing with a certainty that God would intervene on their behalf. Her maturity and faith were immediately a great source of strength to William. "Never mind," she used to say, "Do not give way. God loves you. He will sustain you."[11] She believed unswervingly in the call of God upon William's life, and she always sought to encourage him concerning his destiny. As is the case with any relationship, Catherine's admiration and respect for her fiancé empowered William to achieve more than he ever could have accomplished alone.

While at this time we may see in Catherine a quiet and confident wisdom to put things in their proper order, it is also evident that she was hungry for more of God and dissatisfied with the spiritual norm of her home church and its congregation. In a diary entry of this time she wrote:

> I went to Deverel St. in the evening, enjoyed the sermon, but felt pained to perceive such a manifest deadness among the people. They seem almost at the freezing point. The preacher evidently felt the depressing influence and labored hard to rise above it. My soul *deeply sympathized* with him. It must be hard work to preach to a people destitute of the *true spirit of prayer*. This seems to me the desideratum [great need and desire] of the church.[12]

This passionate desire for more of God may well have been the conviction that drew quiet, demure Catherine so quickly to her fiery, impulsive fiancé. She wanted more of God, and this is exactly what William preached and lived. Theirs seemed literally a match made in heaven.

Catherine believed it would benefit William to spend some time at college. At her suggestion, he applied to join the Congregationalists. This was also appealing because the Congregationalists believed each individual church had the right to govern itself. Late in her life, Catherine explained it this way:

> It was at this time, when the way to the Ministry seemed totally closed in the Methodist direction, that William's attention was turned to the Congregational Church. I think this was my doing; indeed, I know it was; but, until he came to this dead stop, he would never hear of it, and even now his difficulties appeared almost insurmountable. To leave Methodism seemed an impossibility. . . .
>
> Although I could sympathize with all this, and had a fair share of love for the Church to which I also owed much and in which I had experienced a great deal of blessing, still, I had nothing like this blind attachment. For one reason, I had not been actively engaged. Mine had been more the position of a spectator; and moreover, I argued, that once settled in a Congregational pulpit, he could impart into his services and meetings all that was good and hearty and soul-saving in Methodism, at least, I thought he could, and consequently, I pressed him strongly to seek an open door for the exercise of his Ministry among the Independents.
>
> He was slow to accept my counsel.[13]

William's largest concern about the Congregationalists was their Calvinistic view on predestination. He was also concerned about the "intellectual and literary status of the Body."[14] However, in reasoning together with Catherine, he was convinced that the open door to minister was more important than the doctrinal differences that probably wouldn't matter down the road when he had his own pulpit. It is also likely that Catherine, in her eagerness for his success, was pushing to get him to be the student she felt he should be; she had yet to recognize his true reluctance to play the scholar. Despite their reservations, William and Catherine began attending Stockwell Congregational Church, a church Catherine had previously enjoyed visiting to hear its excellent preacher, Reverend Dr. David Thomas.

For William, the next step was a series of meetings with ministers of the Congregationalists where he was, as Roy Hattersley put it in his recent book, "passed from minister to minister like a package that nobody wants to keep."[15] Certainly such treatment would have discouraged all but the most determined, yet William persevered. Reverend Thomas, no doubt with Catherine's encouragement, came to William's aid and convinced Dr. James Campbell to accept William as a student in their Cotton End College. On the eve of his first day, a dispute arose over the doctrine of divine election. Although William had been assured that he would not be required to preach any doctrine he did not honestly believe, he was informed that by the end of the first term he should be willing to conform to the Calvinistic doctrine of the church. The Congregationalists believed that God by His foreknowledge had chosen those who were to be saved and that the atonement of Christ applied only to them. William's fiercely evangelistic nature would not allow him to limit in his mind the saving power of the blood of Jesus to a select group. He strongly believed that Christ died on the cross for all of humankind and that this meant it was possible for all to be saved. When he discussed it with Catherine, they were in agreement. Their understanding of the extent of the love of God and the effect of the sacrifice of Jesus would not allow them to adopt, let alone teach, this doctrine. William withdrew from the college immediately.

Here we see a pattern that lasted the length of their engagement and perhaps their lives. William was a reluctant scholar at best, Catherine an ardent intellectual. Just as he loved all that had to do with soul-winning, he detested anything that might complicate the process of salvation or take his attention away from getting people saved. Where Catherine was the timid, cautious planner, thinking everything through in great detail before acting, William was the bold pioneer, rushing in with the basics and relying on the Holy Spirit to direct and make things happen. Catherine understood and skillfully debated the doctrines fundamental to the movements of their day. William cared for little but the elementary doctrines concerning salvation and holiness.

Yet God knew exactly what He was doing in bringing them together. Theirs was to become a union of thoughtful biblical conviction with evangelistic charisma, fervor, and boldness. Their relationship would become one where neither served the other as subordinate, neither as man and woman nor as differing ideologies, and so they immediately and naturally began to shoal up one another's weaknesses and gave each other greater confidence in their strengths. Each submitted to the other in love and seemed to take no steps in which they did not completely agree. By fusing their hearts together, God was creating the balanced leadership that would eventually revolutionize spiritual and social reform on a world scale.

William's reluctance for scholarship and schooling or study of heavier doctrine and theology had been evident from the start. In a letter dated June 9, 1852 (less than a month into their engagement), William wrote,

> In accordance with my promise I write you a line—do not complain if the composition of the penmanship are not just what you could desire as I feel satisfied that other matters of a more important view and character demanding my attention—Finney's Moral Theology for instance. And then I know not what to say as I really exhausted my stock last night, and as I abhor all things I abhor the talking or writing of rubbish. I feel it a difficult matter to fill this sheet. You wish it. Your wish as a matter of course is law.
>
> I feel uncomfortably dull this morning, returning to bed, as I suppose it was twelve o'clock and that perhaps has something to do with it. When shall I learn better? When shall I acquire the student's habits? Never, I fear, never.
>
> Jesus' religion is a grand remedy for everything. All duty is easy when we are brought fully and delightfully under the perfect influence of the Gospel of love. . . .
>
> Our meetings *must* and *shall be* salvation meetings. . . .
>
> I tell you that nothing can afford me lasting and satisfactory and complete enjoyment but the hunt of winning souls—and how little I am doing of that just now.[16]

William saw little use for the discipline of intellectual learning when there were so many out there that needed only the simple gospel of love so evident throughout the Gospels. He longed to be back in the pulpit preaching salvation.

Upon leaving the Congregationalists, William again faced what appeared to him to be a desperate situation. He was penniless, having sold most of his furniture just to survive. A room was offered to him in the Mumfords' home. Catherine's unyielding faith in the provision of God was soon rewarded. Earlier a friend had recommended William as a preacher for a small group of Reform churches in the Spalding district, about a hundred miles north of London. In November of 1852 he was appointed to take charge of these churches. His salary was set at eighty pounds per year. This was a significant raise from his support of twenty shillings a week from Mr. Rabbits—this annual salary afforded roughly thirty shillings a week.[17]

William left London and took on the work of preaching and evangelism in the churches under his care, while Catherine continued her work as class leader in her local church. They missed one another intensely, and the separation served as a catalyst, turning them to letter writing to share their lives and their love. Things often come out on paper that would have never been mentioned in conversation.

Although they agreed initially to write once a week, letters were soon written daily, especially by Catherine. She began a routine of starting a letter before breakfast and adding the last few lines before dropping it in the post that evening. Her aspirations, dreams, and disappointments poured forth from her pen at a rate of up to two thousand words a letter.

The passionate letters written during their engagement reveal not only their growing love for one another but also the development of the foundational principles of ministry that were pivotal to the movement they would later pioneer. They determined to communicate honestly on every subject that seemed important to their lives, their relationship, and their ministry. In doing so, though separated by distance, their unity of heart and spirit became both intimate and strong.

Catherine herself expressed the value of the separation when she wrote,

> This long correspondence should have developed our character to each other, for my part I am sure I have written the very workings of my soul and I am sure you know me *far better* than you could have done by personal [conversation] of twice or thrice the length of time.[18]

God's method of preparation for His servants was perfect.

As each went about their work for the kingdom, they shared together an increasing passion for souls. Catherine wrote,

> My dearest William . . .
> This afternoon I went to school, and enjoyed a few moments *sensible*

access to God before I commenced the duties of the class. I felt as I sometimes used to feel in brighter happier days, as if self were sinking, expiring, and for the moment, the glory of God only seemed to engage and rivet the eye of my soul, as the sublime object at which I must aim. Need I tell you that I had special liberty and pleasure in speaking to the children. . . . It is a glorious work in any way to be instrumental in winning souls. Oh, for *wisdom* and *grace* to do it in the best way and having done all, to *feel* in our inmost souls our insignificance, and adore the condescending love which deigns to use *such* instruments for the accomplishment of so great a purpose.[19]

Simultaneously they grew more and more unsettled in the environment of comfortable Christianity that characterized the churches of the day. Catherine expressed the desire of their hearts when she wrote, "Oh, my Love, let us live to purpose while we do live. Oh, to be indeed 'light and salt' in our influence on all around us, right through life. Oh, to rise above the common beaten track of professed Christian life."[20] And again,

Others may trim and oscillate between the broad and narrow path, for us there is but one straight, narrow, shining path of perfect devotedness and if we walk not in it we are undone. . . . You acknowledge the possibility of "going round the circuit and satisfying the people, without winning souls to God, to peace and heaven." Yes . . . it is awfully possible and especially in your case; but to live a *holy life* without winning souls is just as *impossible*. Oh, be determined to know nothing amongst men but Christ, seek nothing amongst them but His exaltation.[21]

It would seem, however, that William's sermons could rarely have been classed as comfortable. Soon after he arrived in Spalding, he began to conduct regular revival meetings that saw many souls saved. His reports to Catherine on the excitement and spiritual manifestations that were occurring in some services became a topic of discussion between them. Catherine wrote,

I *rejoice exceedingly* to hear how the Lord is blessing your labors, but as I stand at a distance and contemplate the scene of action and all the circumstances attending it, I tremble with apprehension. . . . I know how popularity and prosperity have a tendency to elate and exalt *self*, if the heart is not humbled before God. Try to get into that happy frame of mind to be satisfied if Christ be exalted, even if it be only by compelling you to lie at the foot of the Cross and look upon Him. . . . Watch against mere *animal excitement* in your revival services. I don't use the term in the sense in which anti-revivalists would use it, but only in the sense in which Finney himself would use it. Remember Caughey's silent, soft, heavenly carriage; *he* did not shout. There was no necessity. He had a more potent weapon at his command than *noise*. I never did like noise and confusion—*only so far* as I believed it to be the *natural* expression of deep anxiety wrought by the Holy Ghost, such as the cries of the jailer, etc. Of *such* noise, produced by *such* agency, the more the better. . . . I should not have troubled you with my views on the subject . . . only that you have been wondering how I shall enter into it with you. . . . I believe in instantaneous conversion as firmly as you do, at the same time I believe that half of what is called conversion is nothing of the kind. . . . Great caution is necessary in dealing with inquirers, especially the young.[22]

William's response to her letter was obviously not all that positive. The length of their separation and the restrictions of written communication led to some misunderstanding between them. What was intended as constructive advice was received as negative criticism. Catherine's next letter reveals her distress.

One thing you said pierced my soul. It was this, "if you cannot bear the hearty responses and Alleluias of *God's people* our fellowship will not be in prayer meetings," as though you excluded me entirely from their number. . . . I *cannot bear it*, it *breaks my heart*. . . . I have tried to recall what I wrote in that letter, I am sure no feeling but pure love dictated one word. . . . Would that I could see you. My heart is almost bursting, but you think me extravagant, too extravagant for this world. Perhaps I am, but my Heavenly Father knows all about my heart. . . . I thought you would understand me. . . . Oh, my dearest William, let us be one, do not allow a cloud to pass over your brow, and angry feelings to rise in your heart when you peruse my letters. . . . Do not let *any thing* come between your soul and mine—neither God's people, Methodism, nor anything else. We are one in *all things*. . . . I hope, dearest, my soul will always be in tune not merely to hear "a shout *inspired by God* and accompanied by *His* power," but to join in it. I never did shout, but I *have felt* enough of His power to have made me do so. . . . Do not fear that anything of this kind will ever come between me and thee if I can help it.[23]

The matter continued to dominate Catherine's mind, and a few days later she wrote,

Don't imagine "confusion" would frighten me if it was the consequence of the shaking of dry bones. I hope never to resist God's own work, let Him adopt what means He may to accomplish it; indeed, the enthusiasm of my nature would soon lead me to mistake feeling for grace than to oppose feeling the effect of grace. Perhaps it is this knowledge of my own danger which makes me apprehensive of it in others.[24]

Whenever they did not initially agree on the matters they discussed in their letters, they communicated openly until they were of the same heart and mind. This invaluable skill of communication was keenly developed between them due to their separation.

In May of 1853, six months after he had left for Spalding, William traveled to London to spend a few days with Catherine. While in London, he spent time with Mr. Rabbits and others, including Dr. Cooke, a prominent minister with the Methodist New Connexion. There was talk at the time of a possible amalgamation between the reformers and the New Connexion. Dr. Cooke offered William work within the New Connexion, an offer that was initially declined.

Neither Catherine nor William knew much about this splinter group of the Methodist church, so Catherine set about researching its history. One condition of joining the New Connexion was a four-year probation period prior to marriage for new ministers. William and Catherine hoped to marry at the end of the year. The thought of waiting another four years was enough to make up their minds that this new group was not for them.

William returned to Spalding but continued to discuss the proposal with Catherine as an option for their future. After their brief visit together, the distance between them seemed even more unbearable. Another visit in August involved further discussion with Dr. Cooke and Mr. Rabbits. It was proposed that should he join the New Connexion, the probation period would be dropped to two years.

William returned once more to Spalding, feeling torn between his options. Should he stay in Spalding and marry at the end of the year or join the New Connexion and wait another two years before they married? The future of the Reform movement was still very uncertain, while the New Connexion offered the chance of greater long-term security. Once again Catherine insisted that he pray and make up his own mind. She did not want the timing of their wedding to be the deciding influence on William's ministry. The people of the Spalding circuit begged him to stay. His revival meetings were also seeing many souls saved, and this made the thought of leaving even more difficult.

Finally he made his choice. In February of 1854 William returned to London to study under Dr. Cooke in preparation for ministry in the Methodist New Connexion. It didn't take his mentor long to realize that William Booth was not a student to bury in books and theological study. On his first day of enrollment, William saw fifteen new converts saved when he preached at the Brunswick Chapel. Dr. Cooke was impressed by the young evangelist's unorthodox preaching methods. While the refined London congregations were often taken aback by his antics, his passion, and unscholarly style, he still powerfully communicated the truths of the gospel. Dr. Cooke recognized the anointing and call on William's life as an evangelist and a preacher, and he endeavored to tailor his training to help rather than hinder his progress in these. He provided William with opportunities to preach in churches around London even at the expense of time spent in the classroom.

Dr. Cooke's assessment of William's abilities as a minister were more fully revealed when, at the New Connexion Conference in June of 1854, he put his name forward to fill the position of Superintendent of a large London circuit. Twenty-five-year-old William was astounded. He refused to accept the appointment, believing himself to be too young and far too inexperienced for such responsibility. A compromise was made, and William was appointed as resident minister of a new chapel on Packington Street, Islington, under the authority of an older minister. Mr. Rabbits supplied the funding for his salary. The Conference also agreed to grant William permission to marry Catherine after he had completed his first year in the ministry.

Although the physical distance between William and Catherine was now much less, the demands of William's training restricted the amount of time they were able to spend together. Their brief time with one another in London soon came to an abrupt end. Shortly after his appointment to the London circuit, Catherine fell ill. In light of the cholera epidemic sweeping across the city, she went to stay with friends in Burnham. It would not have been any different should she have remained in London, however, for William's reputation as an evangelist had brought him invitations from all over England. He was soon as busy traveling and holding revival campaigns as he was with his Packington Street congregation.

William and Catherine were once more left to build their relationship long distance. Their letter writing resumed, and they continued to grow in love and unity. As before, whenever an issue arose on which they did not see eye to eye, it became the topic of their letters. One particular matter that took some time to resolve was a matter certainly worth resolving. The issue in question was the role of women in ministry. When their discussions via mail finally came to a conclusion on this matter, they had agreed upon a radical principle that was instrumental to the success of the movement God would later lead them to begin.

The Victorian woman's world was one of needlework, reading, and polite conversation. There was little or no room made for women in education, medicine, science, politics, or the public work of the church. It was, in fact, a commonly held belief that women were intellectually inferior to men. Their lives were given meaning only by relationship with their husband and children. Consequently the woman's world was narrow and restricted, revolving predominantly around home, family, and their social circle. The obvious exception was the plight of the poor working-class women who had no option but to find employment in factories or as domestic laborers. For the most part, the church of the day merely reinforced society's subjection of women.

Through her years of studying the Bible and other books, Catherine had adopted a radical view of the equality of women and men before God. As a twenty-one-year-old, she had written a lengthy letter to Rev. Dr. David Thomas after hearing him speak of women in a derogatory manner during a sermon in the Congregational church she occasionally attended. She wrote,

> I had the privilege of hearing you speak on Sunday morning . . . and it is for a few remarks in that discourse that I would ask your second consideration. . . . Your remarks appeared to imply the doctrine of women's intellectual and even moral inferiority to man. . . . Permit me, my dear sir, to ask whether you have ever made the subject of women's equality as a *being*, the matter of calm investigation and thought?[25]

By this time in her life, Catherine had! She wrote logically and passionately, presenting sound scriptural evidence for the equality of the sexes before God. Her points were illustrated with Jesus' teachings and the love and respect He had for the women He met. She concluded her letter with a biblical description of submission and signed it anonymously by describing herself simply as "an attentive hearer."

Early in their engagement Catherine had made her views clear to William. To her dismay, he had at first argued with her, stating that while women were superior to men in areas of affection, men were superior to women in the way of intellect. He even had the audacity to quote to her an old saying: "A woman has a fiber more in her heart and a cell less in her brain!" Catherine protested immediately, but she quickly realized that William had merely adopted the common view and had not given much sincere thought to the matter for himself. In her letters she described her understanding of the scriptural view of women.

> I am ready to admit that in the majority of cases the training of women has made her man's inferior . . . but that *naturally* she is in any respect, except in physical strength and courage, inferior to man I cannot see cause to believe, and I am sure no one can prove it from the *Word of God.*[26]

As the time drew near for them to be wed, Catherine wrote extensively to William on this issue, using Scripture to present her case. She described to her fiancé how she had "tried to deal honestly with every passage on the subject, not forgetting to pray for light to perceive and grace to submit to the truth, however humiliating to my nature."[27] Her arguments were clear, well presented, and biblically sound.

William's reply reflected once more the depth of their relationship and their ability to communicate in a forthright and honest manner. It was clear he needed to give it more thought. He wrote,

> Thy remarks on woman's position I will read again before I answer. . . . I would not stop a woman preaching on any account. I would not encourage one to begin. You should preach if you felt moved thereto; felt equal to the task. I would not stay you if I had the power to do so. Although I should not like it. I am for the world's salvation; I will quarrel with no means that promises help.[28]

Although hesitant at first, he eventually became as adamant as Catherine about the equality of men and women in ministry. William's initial indecision on the matter of women preachers did not disturb her. She had been careful in her letter to emphasize that nothing she had said was to be interpreted as referring to her personally. To Catherine, the very thought of standing before a congregation to preach was terrifying. She was content to send William copies of sermon outlines, provided of course that he promised not to tell anyone they were hers!

William's successful evangelistic campaigns prompted the New Connexion Conference of 1855 to alter his ministry position. He was soon released from his duties at Packington and appointed as a full-time traveling evangelist with the New Connexion. Any hopes William and Catherine may have had of setting up a permanent home together after their impending marriage were quickly set aside. Invitations continued to flood in from all across England, and it was obvious that travel and transient lodgings were to be part of their marriage from its outset.

As the date set for their wedding approached, William and Catherine continued to communicate through their letters. The love they shared had matured and deepened throughout their three-year engagement and was now expressed in writing without reservation.

Catherine wrote of her ideal of the love between husband and wife in her letters written from Burnham.

William and Catherine were married on June 16, 1885, at Stopwell Green Congregational Church, England.

Your *words*, your *looks*, your actions, even the most trivial and incidental come up before me as fresh as life. . . . Oh, my Love, if you knew the ecstasy my spirit feels when resting in satisfied confidence on your affection, you would think [it] no mean work to kindle such a joy. My soul is capable of the most heroic devotion and when uncrushed and unalloyed by distrust can mount up as on the wings of an eagle far above the damps and fogs of melancholy and sadness and I doubt not will some day, when all restraints are removed, bear you with it to regions of purest bliss. . . . God bless us and crown our fellowship with *His* smile and let it approach as near the bliss of angels as mortals have on earth. Oh, why should we not be fully and truly happy? Life is so short and so uncertain! Let us make it as sweet and as bright to each other as we can—if you were to die the thought of ever having spoken to you unkindly would be intolerable. I do see and feel more than ever the importance of kindness. If ever God gives us children their young hearts shall expand under its full and gentle influence. . . . If we truly love each other and feel perfect childlike confidence in each other's sincerity, integrity, and fidelity, a oneness of sentiment, aim, and interest, a perfect transparency of soul, what a home ours may be![29]

William also poured out his devotion to his bride-to-be:

My dearest and most precious Kate . . . I am yours, willful, impulsive and fitful as I am, I am yours in an affection *enduring* and tender and *faithful*. . . . I hope you are very well and *very, very* happy. Bless you, I am more so . . . for two reasons, first, our union is more perfect . . . and my love for you more calm and tender. My thoughts stray to you much when alone, and after times of excitement and effort I fall back upon you in thought and imagination, as I shall do in reality in the future, for repose and peace and happiness.[30]

And again,

I will love you as few are loved and watch over you as few are watched over, and we will live for each other and every sinew and every nerve shall be strained to save thousands and tens of thousands of perishing souls . . . and when we meet I will look the love I cannot speak. Farewell; never more fondly did I press an epistle to my lips before posting than I do this. . . . God bless you—remember me as your own.[31]

Finally their wedding day dawned. On June 16, 1855, in a simple private ceremony conducted at the Stockwell Chapel by Rev. Dr. David Thomas, Catherine and William pledged their lives to each other. The vows they exchanged reflected the views they had formed together on the ideal relationship between husband and wife. To William and Catherine, marriage was a partnership between equals, with obligations and privileges for both husband and wife. With selfless love as their foundation, they pledged to live in partnership for the rest of their lives—to partner in their work for God, in their home life, in the raising of their family, in the joys and pains, the smiles and tears, the rewards and triumphs, as well as the hardships and losses life would bring their way.

As he led the happy couple through their marriage ceremony, Rev. Dr. Thomas was moved by the unity of heart, mind, and spirit so evident between them. With mutual submission to God and to each other so clearly the intent of both bride and groom, this was to be no ordinary marriage. Perhaps he recalled the anonymous letter he'd received some years ago with its biblical description of the equality of women and submission and its brief but beautiful insight into the marriage relationship as God intended it to be. It stated,

> The glorious provisions of Christianity come to those who are united in Christ. . . . The wife may realize as blissful and perfect a oneness with her husband as though it (the curse) had never been pronounced. For while the semblance of it remains, Jesus has beautifully extracted the sting by making love the law of marriage, and by restoring the institution itself to its original sanctity. What wife would not be careful to reverence a husband who loves her as Christ loves His church?[32]

In the couple standing before him, Thomas caught a glimpse of the perfect love and unity intended for every marriage relationship. There was no doubt: Love was the law of this marriage.

Under the loving guidance of the Lord, William and Catherine had found in each other unity of heart and unity of purpose. They were perfectly matched in their passion for souls and completed each other in the areas where they differed. Their total dedication to God paved the way for their empowering for ministry. God had drawn them together and then united them so completely in a dynamic and powerfully effective partnership that would sustain them both through the many battles that lay ahead.

CHAPTER 4

One in Marriage, One in Ministry

A YOUNG MINISTER AND HIS WIFE (1855–1861)

Could a mariner sit idle if he heard the drowning cry? Could a doctor sit in comfort and just let his patients die? Could a fireman sit idle, let men burn, and give no hand? Can you sit at ease in Zion with the world around you damned?

—LEONARD RAVENHILL

Catherine's eyes could hardly take in the full beauty of the magnificent Guernsey coastline as she strolled arm in arm with William along the boat deck. Rugged rocky cliffs rose majestically out of the azure waters, interspersed with small, sheltered bays of golden, sandy beaches. The warmth of the afternoon sun was like a tonic to the soul. Gratitude to God arose spontaneously in Catherine's heart as her thoughts drifted back over their first week of married life.

They had chosen the Isle of Wight, a picturesque island just off the southern coast of England, as the destination for their honeymoon. It was perfect. To Catherine's delight, the week had passed slowly and William had completely relaxed, for a time leaving behind the pressures of ministry. Together they had enjoyed the natural beauty of the island, strolling through its rolling farmland and quaint villages and lazing on its glorious sandy beaches.

After a week they embarked for the Channel Island of Guernsey. Catherine pushed aside her dread of sailing with the anticipation of what lay ahead. William had visited the island a few months before, conducting a revival campaign that had resulted in a great number of converts. He had made many friends on the island and had accepted their invitation to return, this time with his bride.

"We'll be coming into port soon," William said excitedly. "I expect there will be quite a crowd to meet us." Catherine's heart leaped as she thought of the meeting her husband would hold in a few hours. Finally, after three years of supporting him in prayer, her heart's desire to join William in a revival campaign would be met. Her expectation grew as the ferry entered St. Peter Port. She began to think about the people they would meet as the boat drifted past their homes, carved into the cliffs surrounding the market town.

William was right. As the large ferry edged its way closer to the pier, he spotted some familiar faces waiting in the crowd. He waved from the deck and pointed them out to Catherine. When they finally disembarked, the enthusiastic welcoming party greeted them warmly. William was delighted as he recognized many converts from his previous visit.

There was little time to rest and freshen up before Catherine and William were escorted to the chapel for the evening service. They were ecstatic to hear how the church doors had to be opened early to allow those who had purchased tickets to get a seat before the expected throngs arrived. When they reached the little chapel, it was full to capacity and overflowing! The grace and anointing of God rested powerfully on William as he preached during the meeting, and many new souls were added to the kingdom.

Catherine quickly found her place alongside her husband. She prayed for individuals while William preached, pleading with God for the salvation of different ones as He pointed them out. With her own experience of conversion indelibly imprinted upon her mind, she knelt beside those who came forward seeking salvation, leading them whenever possible, through prayer and counsel, to the experience of true conversion. She chose to come alongside them in much the same way she had done with the drunkard when she was a child. She knew every sinner had to realize sin's penalty and come to the Cross of Jesus in true repentance, but there was no need for them to do it alone or in ridicule, without a compassionate hand to counsel and guide them during the journey. She wept with the repentant until together their tears turned to joy as the miracle of salvation took place.

Night after night, meeting after meeting, the chapel was packed full of people eager to know more of God. When their campaign in Guernsey concluded, they moved on to the nearby island of Jersey and held meetings there before returning to London for a short break.

Catherine had been concerned in the past by the intensity of William's work schedule. Now, seeing firsthand the enormous pressure of preaching daily and praying for hours for new converts, she was amazed at his stamina. He seemed to be sustained by an endless source of energy. The meetings were a great strain on Catherine. Her body, with its continual weakness and bouts of poor health, could hardly keep up. After a particularly rough voyage back to London, Catherine admitted that she was not fit to join William for his next campaign in York. She rested at her parents' home, hoping to recuperate enough to join him in Hull for his next series of revival meetings.

Upon leaving for York, William wrote the first letter of their marriage, probably while still on the way:

> My precious wife (the first time I have written you that endearing appellation) . . . how often during my journey have I taken my eyes off the book I was reading to think about you . . . about our future, our home. Shall we not again commence a new life of devotion and by renewed consecration begin afresh the Christian race?[1]

William was constantly resolved to forget those things which are behind and reach forth unto those things which are before, pressing toward the mark for the prize of the high calling of God in Christ Jesus. (See Philippians 3:13–14.) He was ever ready to take any circumstance as an excuse for a new beginning. This continual refocusing of his life spilled over into his ministry, and he was always eager to have men and women "start afresh" in their own lives, regardless of whatever lay in their pasts. One could never sink so low as not to be able to begin anew. In these early years, this attitude would mark his enthusiasm to minister as they went from one denomination to the next looking for an open door to evangelize. Later, as they ventured forth to begin the work among the poorest of East London, it would bring the inner strength to persevere in the face of bitter disappointments, times of toil with little fruit, persecution, limited resources, and the incessant needs of poverty.

For now, though, their thoughts turned to more domestic matters: their home and, eventually, their children. Catherine was expecting their first child in March of 1856—a honeymoon baby! In a letter she responded to something William must have written of these issues:

> Bless you, that little study shall be a beauty, and thou shalt come out of it as often as thou wilt to greet little sunny faces and to bless thy loving wife with one of thy brightest smiles. . . . I find myself thinking more about a nice home than ever I did before. I should like to make it a neat, tasty,

clean little place. I can just picture it to myself sometimes, the best bed-room—that room where our firstborn is to be ushered into the world. O my precious one let us pray about it. Bless thee. How I long to see thee.[2]

However much they wanted to settle in one locale, William's schedule of moving from place to place in response to invitations to minister would soon be established as normal life for them. They had to come to a decision about either being together or establishing someplace as home, which would even-tually mean William traveled while Catherine was with the children. Their love for each other and their desire to labor together left them little choice: If William was going to be an evangelist, they would have to take their family on the road.

They refused to despair in this. Concerning having a home of their own, Catherine wrote to her mother later in November of that year,

We have quite given up the idea of having one; even after I have a baby, we intend to travel together and carry it with us and take apartments with attendance in every place. This is one thing which has made me so much happier of late, the dark cloud of separation which has always hung over the future having been dissipated. It was at Caister the idea first struck us and we were not long in deciding it.[3]

She also said,

Much as I should like to have a settled home, you know my objections to leaving William and they get stronger as I see the constant need he has of my presence, care, and sympathy. Neither is he willing for it himself. He says that nothing shall separate us while there is any possibility of our trav-eling together.[4]

Wherever they went, they would make the most of the accommodation they were given, turning their room into their home for a short time. Their personal belongings were kept to a minimum to make traveling as simple as possible. They accepted this as part of the cost they must bear as they obeyed the call of God on their lives. Their marriage relationship did not suffer from this lack of a secure and stable home. They were so caught up in growing closer to each other that little else besides the work of God mattered.

Long before Catherine met William, she had determined the four princi-ples she would live by when married. These principles became the unwritten rules adopted by the couple to ensure happiness for their marriage and their family.

First, they determined never to keep anything secret from each other that affected their relationship or their family.

Second, they decided never to keep individual money supplies.

The third rule described the way they would deal with disputes. Catherine wrote,

> My third principle was that, in matters where there was a difference of opinion, I would show my husband my views and the reasons on which they were based, and try to convince him in favor of my way of looking at the subject. This generally resulted either in his being converted to my views, or my being converted to his.[5]

Finally, they determined never to argue in the presence of their children.

The same passion with which they had worked on their relationship during their long engagement was now poured into their marriage. Theirs was a partnership soaked in prayer. They prayed for one another constantly and knelt together to seek God every day.

For all their seriousness, it would be natural to picture William and Catherine as solemn, prudish puritans—but nothing could be further from the truth. They both had a marvelous sense of humor, and they thoroughly enjoyed life. It was not uncommon for William to sing cheerfully as he went about his chores. Laughter came to him quickly, and he rarely missed an opportunity to make others laugh when in private. In one letter to her mother, Catherine wrote,

> William often says, "Your mother would say so-and-so," and then we laugh and wish we could see you. William has got lots of funny things to tell you, he is hoarding up lots of tales about me and my doings to be made the topic of future conversation and a bit of fun.[6]

Both were able to disperse a tense or gloomy atmosphere with laughter, and they often saw the funny side of even the most difficult or mundane circumstances. This ability to enjoy life, and to experience the vibrant joy that is so much a part of God's kingdom, proved to be a great strength throughout their lives, not just for them but also for those who would follow in their footsteps.

Catherine did eventually join William in Hull, and in September of 1855, the Booths moved on from Hull to Sheffield. In a letter home to her parents, Catherine describes the success of their meetings. "My dear Parents," she wrote,

> I am at home alone this evening having had rather a fatiguing day yesterday. . . . We had a mighty day at the chapel, a tremendous crowd jammed together like sheep in a pen, one of the mightiest sermons at night I ever listened to. . . . The chapel continued crowded during the prayer meeting and before half past ten o'clock seventy-six names were taken. All glory to God. My dearest William has been very prostrate today but he is preaching tonight.[7]

Despite Catherine's constant illnesses, life traveling with William was not without its small pleasures.

Catherine's tiredness at this time was due in part to her pregnancy, but this had not changed their plans to continue with evangelistic work. They moved on to conduct fruitful campaigns in Dewsbury and then held eight weeks of revival services in Leeds. Everywhere they went they witnessed the excitement of a great spiritual awakening within the people. Whole towns and cities were stirred by the work of God in the lives of so many everyday people.

In a letter at this time from Catherine to her mother, we catch a glimpse of the playful bantering exchanged by the young lovers. William, snatching the letter away from Catherine as she wrote, added his own comments on the situation she described:

> The finish up at Leeds was glorious, triumphant! My precious William excelled himself, and *electrified* the people. You would indeed have participated in my joy and pride could you have seen and heard what I did. (W. B.) I have just come in the room where my wife is writing this precious document, and snatching the paper have read the above eulogistic sentiment. I just want to say that the very same night when snug and cozy in the certain place she gave me a curtain lecture on my "block-headism" stupidity, etc., and lo! she writes unto you after this fashion. However, she is a *precious*, increasingly a precious treasure to me with all her eccentricities and oddities. (C. B.) I had a scuffle over the above, but I must let it come for I have not time to write another having an engagement at two o'clock and it is now near one and I have to dine, but I must say in self-defense that it was not about the speech or anything important that the said curtain lecture was given, but only on a point which [in] no way invalidates my eulogies.

By leaving his comments in and countering with her own, Catherine must have wanted her parents to see something of the way they related to each other: each playfully stubborn in their convictions; each yielding to the other in love. Catherine finally hands over to William to conclude the letter:

Kate has not time to write more this time so I must conclude for her and put it into the post. I hope you are both better. Kate keeps up delightfully all things considered and is better looking than ever she was in her life. Farewell. Believe us, dear Parents to remain Your affectionate son and daughter William and Catherine.[8]

In February of 1856 they moved once more, this time to Halifax to conduct four weeks of services, with meetings held daily. This campaign was exceedingly successful, and at the end of the month, 640 converts were counted. It was here on the evening of March 8 that William Bramwell Booth was born. As Catherine nursed him, William lifted his hands to God and prayed, dedicating their firstborn to the Lord and praying that he might be used as a preacher of the gospel.

William and Catherine continued on the campaign trail, traveling to Macclesfield, Yarmouth, back once more to Sheffield, and on to Birmingham before the end of the year. In December and January they spent six weeks in William's hometown of Nottingham. The city was buzzing with excitement at his visit; even the mayor's family attended the meetings. Once again Catherine wrote home to her mother, describing one meeting:

> Yesterday the chapel . . . [seating 1,200] was so packed that all the windows and doors had to be set wide open.[9]—and this was in the middle of December! In these six weeks 740 persons came forward giving their names and addresses.[10]

William had begun to experiment with a new technique of dealing with those who responded in his meetings. Although evangelistic to his core, he felt a great responsibility for the souls birthed into the kingdom through his ministry. He appointed two officials in each service to take down the names, addresses, and personal details of every person who responded. Once these were attained, a proven convert was given charge of each new believer. William did all he could to ensure these new lives were not left to struggle alone.

After a brief two-week holiday in London with Catherine's parents, William was off again, this time to Chester. Catherine, who was once again pregnant, stayed on with her parents until her husband returned. Bristol, Cornwall, and Stafford were their next ports of call. Each place saw hundreds more give their lives to Christ. William and Catherine were excited and encouraged by the ongoing fruitfulness of their ministry, and they were careful to give glory to God for His work. Invitations continued to flood in from around England,

and with the birth of their second child drawing near they had every intention of continuing their traveling.

In June of 1857 the annual New Connexion Conference met in Nottingham and unexpectedly terminated William's work as an evangelist. Leading ministers spoke out against Booth during conference, decrying the disorder and chaos caused in churches as a result of the revival services. They objected to his whirlwind meetings and complained of the amount of follow-up left to the local ministers when each campaign finished. Some felt William was receiving far too much prominence and recognition. One critic summed up their protests, saying, "He is taking the cream and leaving the skimmed milk for others."[11] After much heated discussion, the matter was put to a vote. With a difference of four ballots, the conference resolved to end William's campaigns. He was appointed for one year to the run-down mill town of Brighouse, Yorkshire. It was one of the New Connexion's least-promising circuits.

When the news of this reached William and Catherine, it came as an incredible shock. There had been no warning, no caution, no hint that such sentiment had arisen against their work. They faced one of the greatest tests of their character and their ministry. In the face of personal criticism, and although the decision went against the very purpose of their souls, they submitted in obedience to their leadership and accepted the appointment to Brighouse. William's heart response is shown in a letter written at the time:

My concern is for the Connexion—my deep regret is for the spirit this makes manifest, and the base ingratitude it displays. However, I leave the matter with the Lord. My work and reputation are in His hands. I wait the manifestation of His will, and wherever He points there will I try to go.[12]

Catherine expressed similar sentiment in a letter to her mother:

I have felt it far more keenly than I thought I should. Great interests are involved, far more than are seen at first sight but it is God's cause. I believe He will order all for the best. I have no fears for the future. I have confidence in my husband's devotion and capacity for something greater yet.[13]

Her faith in God was unshakable. Later, as they settled into their new home, she wrote again, saying,

It is very nice to be in a home of one's own and I think we shall be very happy and useful in the Circuit tho' I shall never alter my opinion with reference to the spirit and motives which brought us here.[14]

The move to Brighouse brought great change to the Booth family. For the first time they had a home they could call their own. For the first time, too, they had the responsibility of the nurture and equipping of those under their care. Although they felt confined by their new position, God continued His work of preparation in their lives. They couldn't see it yet, but His purpose for them extended far beyond the scope of itinerant evangelists.

Shortly after the birth of their second son, Ballington, William encouraged Catherine to take on the leadership of a class of female church members. Catherine hesitated at first, but then she accepted and began to teach thirteen girls on Sunday afternoons in her home (as well as a group of twenty-nine older women). By early 1858 they were both busy within the life of the church, holding meetings almost every night. All this with two young children and another soon on the way. Catherine's frail body gave way under the strain of the work and she was forced, due to back trouble, to slow down and rest.

Brighouse was a dismal working-class town of smokestacks and coal-blackened buildings. The atmosphere was depressingly dreary; a haze of smoke perpetually enveloped its grimy streets. Since the commencement of his ministry in London, William and Catherine had worshiped and worked mainly among middle-class congregations. In Brighouse, however, they were once again in contact with the poor masses that had so stirred their hearts during childhood. Appalled by the work conditions in the factories and mills, they did all they could to bring change. Together they pressured authorities to address the issues of child labor and the appalling conditions under which they worked. Children as young as six and seven were forced to work in the mills for up to fourteen hours a day. They had no more than one half-hour break throughout the day and were often kept awake only by the lashing of the overseer's whip. The Booths fought to see such injustices end, their compassionate hearts breaking once more over the terrible inequalities of society.

As the time drew near for the annual conference, William and Catherine cautiously began to dream of being released again to the revival work they loved so much. Shortly before the conference was due to meet, Dr. Cooke visited the Booths in Brighouse. Any hopes they had of the conference releasing them from circuit work were dashed. Their friend and mentor, who had been so supportive of William's evangelistic work, was much less encouraging now. In a letter to her mother, Catherine wrote, "We don't anticipate William's reappointment to the evangelistic work. All the whispers we hear on the subject seem to predict the contrary."[15]

In May of 1858 the conference met in Hull. William, having served his four years of probation, was ordained as a minister of the Methodist New Connexion. However, his request to return to evangelistic work was refused. Instead it was resolved "that he should spend one more year in a circuit and at its close be recalled to revival work."[16] He was appointed to the Gateshead circuit and, once again, William submitted to the leadership and accepted their appointment.

Gateshead was an industrial suburb of the northern city of Newcastle-Upon-Tyne. The bleak expanse of drab houses beyond the chapel walls beckoned to William as he wondered,

> In how many of those houses is the name of Christ never mentioned? Why am I here, with this crowded chapel of people who want to hear the message? Why am I not outside, bringing the message of God to those who don't want it?[17]

William's unrelenting passion for souls caused his heart to ache as his time was filled quickly with the concerns of his circuit. He longed to be able to spend more time and energy seeking the lost souls who so needed to hear the message of salvation.

Soon after their arrival, Catherine was again invited to take on the leadership of class meetings for women. Once more she happily took on this task, meeting weekly with them in their home. Even though she loved teaching and encouraging the Christian women, she, too, was drawn with compassion to the helpless crowds who did not know God. It was in this industrial setting, in this place not of her own choosing, that God began to speak to Catherine, compelling her to step out in ministry. She was comfortable in her role as a teacher in a small-group setting, but she still shied away from public ministry. As mentioned previously, the freedom she had known when first converted, to speak to people about Jesus, had long since given way to timidity and shyness. This was to change while she was in Gateshead.

The first breakthrough came as she walked alone one evening to chapel. William had left earlier while she settled the children for the night with their nursemaid. She tells her own story:

> One Sabbath I was passing down a narrow, thickly populated street on my way to chapel, anticipating an evening's enjoyment for myself and hoping to see some anxious ones brought into the kingdom, when I chanced to look up at the thick rows of small windows above me, where numbers of women were sitting, peering through at the passers by, or listlessly gossiping with each other.

It was suggested to my mind with great power, *Would you not be doing more service and acting more like your Redeemer, by turning into some of those houses, speaking to these careless sinners, and inviting them to the service, than by going to enjoy it yourself?* I was startled; it was a new thought, and while I was reasoning about it, the same inaudible interrogator demanded, *What efforts do Christians put forth, answerable to the command, "compel them to come in, that My house may be filled"?*

This was accompanied by a light and unction which I know to be Divine. I felt greatly agitated. I felt verily guilty. I knew that I had never thus labored to bring lost sinners to Christ; and, trembling with a sense of my utter weakness, I stood still for a moment, looked up to heaven, and said, "Lord, if Thou wilt help me, I will try," and without stopping further to confer with flesh and blood, turned back and commenced my work.

I spoke first to a group of women sitting on a doorstep; and what that effort cost me, words cannot describe; but the Spirit helped my infirmities, and secured for me a patient and respectful hearing with a promise from some of them to attend the house of God. This much encouraged me; I began to taste the joy which lies hidden under the Cross, and to realize, in some faint degree, that it is more blessed to give than to receive. . . . I went on to the next group who were standing at the entrance of a low, dirty court. Here again I was received kindly and promises were given. No rude repulse, no bitter ridicule, were allowed to shake my newfound confidence, or chill my feeble zeal. I began to realize that my Master's feet were behind; nay, before me, smoothing my path and preparing my way.

This blessed assurance so increased my courage and enkindled my hope that I ventured to knock at the door of the next house, and when it was opened to go in, and speak to the inmates of Jesus, death, judgement, and eternity. The man, who appeared to be one of the better class of mechanics, seemed to be much interested and affected by my words, and promised with his wife to attend the revival services which were being held at the chapel.

With a heart full of gratitude and eyes full of tears, I was thinking where I should go next, when I observed a woman standing on an adjoining doorstep with a jug in her hand. My divine teacher said, *Speak to that woman.* Satan suggested, "Perhaps she is intoxicated" but after a momentary struggle I introduced myself to her by saying, "Are the people out who live on this floor?" observing that the lower part of the house was closed. "Yes," she said, "they are gone to chapel." I thought I perceived a weary sadness in her voice and manner. I said, "Oh, I am so glad to hear that; how is it that you are not gone to a place of worship?" "Me," she said, looking down upon her forlorn appearance; "I can't go to chapel, I am kept at home by a drunken husband. I have to stop with him to keep him from the public house, and I have just been fetching him some drink." I expressed my sorrow for her, and asked if I might come in and see her husband. "No," she said, "he is drunk; you could do nothing with him now." I replied, "I do not mind his being drunk, if you will let me come in; I am not afraid; he will not hurt me." "Well," said the woman, "you can come in if you like; but he will only abuse you." I said, "Never mind that," and followed her up the stairs.

I felt strong now in the Lord and in the power of His might, and as safe as a babe in the arms of its mother. I realized that I was in the path of obedience, and I feared no evil.

The woman led me to a small room on the first floor, where I found a fine, intelligent man, about forty, sitting almost double in a chair, with a jug by his side, out of which he had been drinking. I leaned on my Heavenly Guide for strength and wisdom, love and power, and He gave me all I needed. He silenced the demon, strong drink, and quickened the man's perceptions to receive my words. As I began to talk to him, with my heart full of sympathy, he gradually raised himself in his chair, and listened with a surprised and half-vacant stare. I spoke to him of his present deplorable condition, of the folly and wickedness of his course, of the interest of his wife and children, until he was fully aroused from the stupor in which I found him. I read to him the parable of the Prodigal Son, while the tears ran down his face like rain. I then prayed with him as the Spirit gave me utterance, and left, promising to call the next day with a pledge-book, which he agreed to sign.

I now felt that my work was done. Exhausted in body but happy in soul, I wended my way to the sanctuary, just in time for the conclusion of the service and to lend a helping hand in the prayer meeting.

On the following day I visited this man again. He signed the pledge, and listened attentively to all I said. Full of hope I left him, to find another similarly lost and fallen. From that time I commenced a systematic course of house-to-house visitation, devoting two evenings per week to the work. The Lord so blessed my efforts that in a few weeks I succeeded in getting ten drunkards to abandon their soul-destroying habits, and to meet me once a week for reading the Scriptures and for prayer.[18]

As Catherine nervously stepped out in response to the prompting of the Holy Spirit, she pioneered an area of ministry that would prove to be a vital element in the work of The Salvation Army. She later declared, "I esteem this work of house-to-house visitation next in importance to the preaching of the Gospel itself."[19]

The year passed quickly and fruitfully. Three months after their arrival in Gateshead, Catherine gave birth to their third child—Little Catherine, or "Kate," as she was quickly nicknamed, was born on September 18, 1858. The Booths' nursemaid now had her hands full with three youngsters to watch over.

In addition to caring for their growing family, William and Catherine were kept busy with their growing congregation. During their first year at Gateshead, they saw the membership rise from thirty-nine to three hundred. Their work was thriving. The spiritual atmosphere in the city changed so much that the chapel in Gateshead was nicknamed by locals as "The Converting Shop" because of the great numbers of people who were being saved.

Catherine, thinking ahead to the campaign trail once more, wrote of her plans to her mother.

> I have fully and formally consented to let William go forth as an evangelist on condition that he concentrates on one district at a time, making his home in some central town . . . so that I shall see him at least once a week.[20]

As the annual conference drew near, however, it became obvious to William that the leadership of the New Connexion was still opposed to his work as an itinerant evangelist. The stipulation that he be reappointed to revival work after one more year of circuit work did not even appear in the records from the last conference! The officers from his Gateshead circuit appealed to conference that William remain for a second year as superintendent. In light of the large number of new converts, he was reappointed to Gateshead for a further year, to consolidate the work.

William still longed to be able to focus more on the task of taking the gospel throughout the nation. His passion for souls could no longer be curtailed by the restrictions of circuit work. He determined in his heart to set aside some of his "required" duties that Gateshead might be saturated with the gospel message while under his leadership.

Out of this determination, William introduced new methods of ministry to traditional circuit work. As his first year came to a close, he began a series of revival services with a day of prayer and fasting. A list of names was drawn up of the people who would be specific recipients of intercessory prayer during the ten-week campaign. On this list were the names of some of the most notorious sinners in Gateshead. Members spread out across the town, distributing flyers and personally inviting people to the daily revival meetings. Catherine and others went door to door, talking with people and urging them to attend.

As part of the campaign, William reinstituted the open-air meetings he had begun as a teenager in Nottingham. People gathered together in public areas to sing and share a testimony, and then the joyful procession made their way to the chapel, inviting onlookers to join them for the meeting. By the end of the ten-week period, most of the people on the list prepared beforehand had attended services and been converted. Many others also responded and gave their lives to Jesus.

William's spirits soared. Nothing could dampen the enthusiasm he felt as he witnessed God moving by His Spirit and drawing many to repentance. Well, almost nothing. Catherine had continued her weeknight visitations to the poor until she caught a cold that quickly developed into a serious chest infection. She had become pregnant again and was forced to slow down to allow her body to recover. Her constant bouts of sickness brought great concern to William.

While she was recuperating, she happened to read a pamphlet written by the Rev. Arthur Ross, the transcript of a message he had preached in which he attacked women's rights to preach. The message was directed against Mrs. Palmer, an American evangelist who was touring England at the time. Mrs. Palmer toured with her husband, but she was by far the more prominent minister of the two. It was her preaching during a series of revival meetings in nearby Sunderland that attracted Rev. Ross's criticism. Catherine was outraged.

The incident caused such a stir that Rev. Ross spoke of publishing a second pamphlet on the subject. Writing to her mother, Catherine declared,

> I hope he will wait a bit till I am stronger. If he does bring out any more in the same style, I rather think of going to Sunderland and delivering an address in answer to him. William says I should get a crowded house. I really think I shall try. . . . William is always pestering me to begin giving lectures and certainly this would be a good subject to start with. I am determined it shall not go unanswered.[21]

Despite William's support and encouragement, Catherine decided against responding with a public address. She determined instead to publish her own pamphlet. She also began visiting another area of the circuit while William was away. When he returned and read what she had written, he encouraged her to continue and to make it a thorough teaching on the issue of women in ministry.

Catherine poured her heart into the pamphlet, dealing honestly with every Scripture reference Rev. Ross had raised as evidence against a woman's right to teach in the church. She then brought out the many Scriptures he had conveniently left to one side, and she concluded with example after example of women anointed by God for public ministry. Her case was thorough and convincing. When she finally concluded her case, the manuscript was sent off to be printed.

With her heart unburdened, Catherine's focus quickly changed from women's rights to childbirth when, on January 8, 1860, Emma Moss was born. The birth of her fourth baby enabled Catherine to take time out from her responsibilities and enjoy a short season of much-needed rest. She began to reflect on their work at Gateshead, the new converts, her booklet, and of course, the future. As she pondered the possibility of ever returning to the revival work they had conducted when they were first married, an over-whelming compassion for the state of the lost rose in her heart once more. Speaking later of the time after Emma was born, she said, "I could not sleep at night with thinking of the state of those who die unsaved."[22]

During this time, Catherine began to feel convicted of her refusal to do more for the Lord in public ministry. A few months earlier, she had received an invitation from church leaders to speak at a special prayer meeting. Her response was loud and clear: "Of course I declined," she said to her mother. "I don't know what they can be thinking of!"

The very thought of preaching still terrified Catherine. Now, in light of the scorching rebuke she had written against Rev. Ross's objection to women preachers, she began to feel uncomfortable with her response to their request. She believed passionately in all she had written, and yet she had refused to obey God's promptings to preach.

With the conviction of the Holy Spirit on her life, Catherine recognized how time after time God had prompted her with a word to speak, and each time she had stubbornly refused. Oh, how she wished she could be free of the timidity that was such a curse! She recalled the boldness she had experienced in the weeks after her conversion and saw for the first time how her spiritual growth had been stunted by her disobedience. As this revelation came, Catherine lay on her face before the Lord and solemnly vowed, "Lord, if Thou wilt return unto me, as in the days of old and revisit me with those urgings of Thy

Spirit which I used to have, I will obey, if I die in the attempt. I care not: I will obey!"[23]

William saw incredible potential in Catherine as a speaker, and he continued to be her greatest encourager, asking her to help him by speaking at different meetings. Each time she refused, feeling no prompting of the Spirit within. When the moment of breakthrough finally came, it caught them both by surprise.

William had planned to hold a mass outdoor meeting in Gateshead on Sunday, May 27, 1860. When the day dawned, stormy weather forced him to cancel these plans. Over a thousand people gathered in the chapel instead for the morning service. As Catherine sat with young Bramwell, listening to William's challenging message, the Spirit of God fell upon her. She was suddenly filled with a compelling urge to speak to the congregation. The unction of the Holy Spirit interrupted her own thoughts and prompted her to speak, saying, *Now, if you were to go and testify, you know I would bless it to your own soul as well as to the souls of the people.*

In her mind she replied: *Yes, Lord, I believe Thou wouldst, but I cannot do it.* The vow she had made a few months earlier was all but forgotten in her moment of testing. Suddenly there came into her mind a familiar mocking voice: *Besides, you are not prepared to speak. You will look like a fool and have nothing to say.* Recognizing its source immediately, Catherine was riled. *Ah! That is just the point,* she responded. *I have never yet been willing to be a fool for Christ. Now I will be one.*

At that moment, as William brought the meeting to a conclusion, Catherine leaped to her feet and strode down the aisle, painfully aware of the murmur that quickly arose from the people. Her husband, thinking she was unwell, quickly rushed to her side. "What is the matter, my dear?" he asked.

"I want to say a word," Catherine replied, now feeling quite nervous. Caught completely by surprise, William turned to the people and announced, "My dear wife wishes to speak." Stunned, he found a seat, anxious to hear what had finally caused her to do what she had so often refused to do before.

Catherine turned to face the congregation. As her eyes glanced cautiously over the puzzled crowd, she opened her heart to them and began to speak.

> I daresay many of you have been looking upon me as a very devoted woman, and one who has been living faithfully to God, but I have come to know that I have been living in disobedience, and to that extent I have brought darkness and leanness into my soul; but I promised the Lord three

or four months ago, and I dare not disobey. I have come to tell you this and to promise the Lord that I will be obedient to the Heavenly vision.[24]

With all humility, she confessed her sin of refusing the public podium despite God's prompting otherwise and encouraged all to obey any stirrings of God in their own hearts. William looked on, admiration and joy rising in his heart, as many in the congregation began to weep. The Spirit of God moved powerfully as she spoke, drawing sin-hardened hearts to repentance. When Catherine concluded her brief message, William rushed to her side and spoke quickly with her. Having gained her consent, he eagerly exclaimed, "Tonight, my wife will be the preacher!"[25]

The news traveled fast. Just thirty minutes later, Ballington and Kate, too young to attend the morning meeting, were found dancing around the scullery table, chasing the maid who had arrived home with the news. Squeals of delight echoed from the kitchen as they sang triumphantly, "The mistress has spoken! The mistress has spoken!"[26]

That evening the chapel was packed to the doors—every available space filled. People stood in the aisles while young children squashed together on the floor and window ledges. No one wanted to miss this first address of the woman they had come to know and respect.

They were not disappointed; Catherine spoke with captivating passion and sincerity. Forthright, fervent, and with an incredible ability to cut to the heart of an issue in moments, she wasted no words as she arrested the attention of her listeners. Her text, appropriate for such an incredible day, was taken from Ephesians 5:18: "Be filled with the Spirit."

Within weeks Catherine became renowned as "The Woman Preacher," a title that stayed with her until she preached her last message twenty-eight years later. Together with William, she forged the path for the recognition, respect, and release of women in ministry. In this regard, the Booths, and later The Salvation Army, led society, challenging and reforming the accepted standards of a culture that thwarted the purposes of God to reach every creature with His grace and gospel. Their actions were founded on the principle of freedom in Christ Jesus—freedom for men and women to be all that God created them to be.

News of Catherine's debut in the pulpit also caused a great stir across the churches. Invitations to preach began to reach her, and she soon became recognized as a preacher outside the Gateshead circuit. Her already busy life picked up in pace as she juggled the responsibilities of wife, mother, and minister of the gospel. With so many demands on her time, Catherine learned quickly to rely entirely upon the Holy Spirit for His empowering of her ministry. She later recalled this season of her life, saying,

> Whenever I spoke the chapel used to be crowded, and numbers were converted. . . . It was not I that did this but the Holy Spirit of God . . . with four little children, the eldest then four years and three months old. It looked an inopportune time, did it not, to begin to preach? . . . While I was nursing my baby, many a time I was thinking of what I was going to say next Sunday; and between times noted down with a pencil the thoughts as they struck me. But oh, how little did I realize how much was involved! I never imagined the life of publicity and trial it would lead me to. . . . All I did was take the first step.[27]

All her life, God had been preparing Catherine for the work of a preacher. Now, as she yielded her will to His, He empowered her for the task. She continued to battle against her own timidity, but having taken that first step, she never turned back. In a letter to her parents, she describes the difficulties she faced:

> William has been confined to the house for a fortnight with a bad throat attack. I have consequently had extra care and work. . . . I went to Bethesda last night to supply for William, the bottom of the chapel was crowded, forms round the communion rail and aisles; I spoke for an hour and five minutes. I got on very well and had three sweet cases and from all accounts today the people were very much pleased. I cannot tell you how I felt all day about it; I never felt in such a state in my life. I could neither eat nor sleep. I was pressed into it against my will and when I saw the congregation I felt almost like melting away. . . . William is of course very pleased. . . . If I had only time to study and write I should not fear now, but I must be content to do what I can consistently with my home duties and leave the future to the Lord.[28]

William's "bad throat" was the first symptom of an illness that lasted over three months. William was laid out by the sickness and on the advice of his doctors was soon packed off to a hydropath clinic, a mode of treatment in vogue at the time. The leadership of the Gateshead circuit approached Catherine and requested she take on William's preaching schedule while he was away. She initially refused, knowing that she could not possibly do this and manage her household alone. However, when they approached her again she agreed to preach Sunday nights. This was on top of her usual duties within the church and other preaching engagements she had already accepted. William was away for a total of nine weeks, and by the time he returned in October Catherine was utterly exhausted. As the year came to a close, the routine of family life was gradually reestablished, and William and Catherine began to think once more of the future.

They had both become quite settled in their home environment. The fruitfulness of their ministry at Gateshead was satisfying. With the needs of their growing family foremost on their minds, the thought of remaining in circuit work had become a comfortable one. William could not, however, escape the call upon his life. He knew without doubt that he was called as an evangelist. As his thoughts turned to their future, he began to wonder again about resuming revival campaigns. The cost to William and Catherine was now much greater, and so they committed it to prayer, seeking God for His direction.

Their thoughts of the future came during a season when God was dealing with them in the area of holiness. They had both grown up under the Wesleyan teaching on holiness. Wesley taught that it was not enough that a person's sins be covered over by the righteousness of Christ. He argued that a Christian should "be inwardly transformed so that his life is not one of continuing sinning and forgiveness, but one of obedience to the will of God as he knows it."[29] Wesley firmly believed the blood of Christ was able not just to cleanse from sin but also to break the power of sin in a believer's life. His own experience led him to believe and teach that such holiness was available to every believer and that it was an instantaneous experience received by faith and lived out every moment. It was this "second blessing," this experience of holiness, that now became a focus of the Booths' lives and ministry. William later described holiness in the following way:

> In conversion the chains that bind men to sin are broken but the tendency to evil still lingers behind. In Holiness the bondage is not only entirely destroyed, and the soul completely delivered from these evil tendencies, but is free to do the will of God, so far as it is known, as really as it is done in Heaven.[30]

Like other holiness preachers of their day, Catherine and William understood that while it is possible for believers to be partially holy, holiness in its entirety is a state that is experienced at a specific moment in time. Explaining this concept many years later, William said:

The line which separates a state of entire from a state of partial Holiness may be approached very gradually, but there is a moment when it is crossed. The approach of death is often all but imperceptible, but there is a moment when the last breath is drawn. Just so there is a moment when the body of sin is destroyed, however gradual the process may have been by which that state has been reached. There is a moment when the soul becomes entirely holy—entirely God's.[31]

Intricately entwined in their understanding of the holiness God longed to impart to every believer was the renouncing of all sin and the total consecration of their lives to God. When William had knelt in prayer at seventeen, he had wholeheartedly determined to give all of his life to God. At every opportunity throughout his life, he renewed this commitment to God in prayer.

For Catherine, however, there was one thing she now struggled to release to God—William. In a letter to her parents, she describes her dilemma.

> I spoke a fortnight since at Bethesda on holiness, and a precious time we had. William has preached on it twice, and there is a glorious quickening amongst the people. I am to speak again next Friday night and on Sunday afternoon. Pray for me. I only want perfect consecration and Christ as my all. . . . I have much to be thankful for in my dear husband. The Lord has been dealing graciously with him for some time past. . . . He is now on full stretch for holiness. You would be amazed at the change in him. . . . As has always been the case with every quickening we have experienced in our own souls, there has been a renewal of the evangelistic question, especially in my mind. I felt as though that was the point of controversy between me and God. Indeed I knew it was. . . . I determined to bring it to a point before the Lord, trusting in Him for strength to suffer, as well as to do His will, if he should call me to do it.[32]

After wrestling with God in prayer, Catherine chose to yield all of her life to Him, come what may.

Soon after she laid William and their future on the altar before God, revelation broke through into her spirit. As she knelt with William to pray one evening, her heart was suddenly filled anew with faith in her all-sufficient Savior, and she received assurance from God of His purifying work in her soul. An overwhelming sense of peace flooded her being, and she knew she had been made holy. Catherine later reflected on this experience, declaring, "From that moment I have dared to reckon myself dead indeed unto sin, and alive to God through Christ Jesus my Lord."[33]

Both Catherine and William had come to a place of total surrender before God. As much as they knew how, they gave up everything to Him. They chose to align their own will with His, regardless of cost and consequence. Speaking later of the lessons she learned, Catherine said,

> We must place everything at his service—our children, business, homes, and everything. If I understand it, that is nonconformity to the world. . . . Now, will you give up conformity to the world? If so, you may, every one of you, be transformed. . . . You may advance . . . on to the glorious vantage ground . . . of . . . a triumphant saint of God.[34]

And again,

> You see what consecration means. It means *don't care*. "I don't care for the consequences. I don't care what all the world thinks of me or says of me. . . . I don't care what happens. I will have this salvation if it is to be had." When you come to that you will get it. . . . That is consecration.[35]

After receiving revelation from God, every believer enters a time of trial during which he or she is tested in obedience to the revelation. It is obedience that causes revelation to become reality in the believer's life. In this way, the Word becomes flesh. Catherine and William, having received revelation of the power of God released through obedience, were soon to face the biggest test of their lives.

CHAPTER 5

Obedience at Any Price

YEARS AS AN INDEPENDENT EVANGELIST (1861–1865)

This is the kind of totally committed response the Lord Jesus called for: a desire for Him at any cost. Absolute surrender. A full exchange of self for the Savior. It is the only response that will open the gates of the kingdom. Seen through the eyes of this world, it is as high a price as anyone can pay. But from a kingdom perspective, it is really no sacrifice at all.

—JOHN MACARTHUR

William pressed the stamp into the hot wax, resolutely sealing the letter that was destined to seal his fate with the Methodist New Connexion. Leaning back in his chair, he pondered again the words he had written. In the letter to Mr. Stacey, president of the 1861 conference, William shared the burden of his heart to fulfill the call of a traveling evangelist: "My soul has lately been brought into a higher walk of Christian experience,"[1] he had written as he requested them to reconsider his involvement in revival work.

He offered a couple of suggestions as to how he could fulfill this role within the New Connexion. His preference was to be reappointed to the position of itinerant evangelist, working under the president and receiving the same salary as other ministers. Alternatively, he had suggested, he could be a regular minister, provided he was free to accept invitations from around the country to preach. As William took hold of the letter in his hand, he knew one thing was certain: to continue in circuit work would be to disobey God. Kneeling with Catherine a short time later, William once more committed their way to the Lord before posting the letter.

Conference was due to meet in Liverpool in May. Meanwhile, William and Catherine had accepted an invitation to conduct a series of meetings in Hartlepool over Easter. They shared the preaching during the weekend. On Monday William returned to Gateshead while Catherine stayed on by request to hold an extra meeting. This soon turned into a whole week of extra meetings. "You will be surprised to find I am still here," Catherine scribbled in a quick note to her parents.

> I told you I had to stay Monday evening. Well the Lord came down amongst the people so gloriously, that I dare not leave, so the friends telegraphed to William and I stayed. . . . I preached again on Tuesday evening. I gave an invitation and the communion rail was filled with penitents again and again during the evening. . . . I preached again on the Wednesday and Friday nights, and also gave two addresses in the morning and afternoon on holiness. Above a hundred names were taken during the week. . . . If you could know how I have labored, talking to penitents as hard as I could talk for two hours every night after preaching, you would not believe that it could be me. I scarcely can believe it myself.[2]

All this from a petite and physically frail young woman who only a year ago had refused to preach!

In May William insisted that Catherine attend Conference with him. They both knew the significance of the decision that would be made concerning their future. Although Catherine was not permitted to take part in the proceedings, she was free to join others in the public gallery during the discussions.

Finally, during the second week, William was invited to read his letter to the members. The debate that followed was long and heated. Some argued that it was an insult to the minister to introduce an outside agent. Others, while admitting to William's exceptional evangelistic gifting, declared he could be of greatest use in a regular circuit. Many who had in private assured William and Catherine of their utmost support spoke hesitantly or kept silent altogether! As the debate drew to a close, Dr. Cooke stepped in and proposed, as a compromise, that William be appointed to a circuit and given the liberty to take some time to do revival work elsewhere.

William immediately refused to accept the idea, stating that, practically speaking, it would be impossible. The circuit that the conference had in mind for William was Newcastle-on-Tyne. There was no way, permission granted or not, that William would be able to leave such a large and difficult circuit to conduct revival meetings elsewhere. Their concession was no more than a token gesture. Despite his protests, the motion was put to a vote. William's heart sank as he heard the proposal carried.

Far above, in the doorway of the public gallery, Catherine strained to hear the result of the ballot. As the decision was announced, she could contain her anger and disappointment no longer. "No—never!" she exclaimed emphatically as she locked eyes with William. Without hesitating, William picked up his hat, stood to his feet, and strode defiantly out of the chapel. He met Catherine at the base of the gallery stairs, where they embraced and walked out.

The proposal made by the Conference stood unchanged by the Booths' dramatic response. William was called back a few days later to explain his objections, but as he sat waiting to speak, he heard his appointment to the Newcastle circuit announced again. It was clear that no matter what he said, the decision had been made.

William and Catherine did not know what to do. They had to leave their home in Gateshead to make room for the incoming minister, so they requested leave from the Newcastle circuit. Leave without pay was granted, and they were given permission to move into the preacher's house in Newcastle for up to six weeks. Catherine expressed in a letter to her parents the confusion they felt:

> We don't know what to do. We only want to do *right*. If I thought it was right to stop here in the ordinary work I would be glad to do it. But I cannot believe it would be right for my husband to spend another year in . . . circuit preaching. . . . [William] thinks of me and the children, and I appreciate his love and care, but I tell him God will provide if he will only go straight on in the path of duty. . . . Whatever be the result I shall make up my mind to endure it patiently, looking to the Lord for grace and strength. . . . We have nothing coming in now from any quarter.[3]

As they examined their options, Catherine and William came face-to-face with the cold, hard facts. They had a family of four children to care for. Without the surety of the income supplied by the New Connexion they would be homeless, without any steady support. They struggled in their minds to reconcile their responsibility as parents with their responsibility before God. Finally they put aside their fears and took hold of faith, choosing to obey God and to trust Him with the consequences of their step of obedience.

Catherine wrote once more to her parents, trying to help them understand their decision.

> I hope neither you nor my dear father think that I want to run precipitately into the position we contemplate. . . . I have no hope that God will ever assure us that we shall lose nothing in seeking to do His will. I don't think this is God's plan. I think he sets before us our duty, and then demands its performance, trusting solely in Him for consequences. . . . If we could always *see* our way, we should not have to walk by faith, but by sight. . . . The Lord help me to be found faithful. I don't believe in any religion apart from doing the will of God. Faith is the uniting link between it and the soul but if we don't do the will of our Father it will then be broken. If my dear husband can find a sphere where he can preach the Gospel to the masses I shall want no further evidence as to the will of God concerning him. If he cannot find a sphere I will conclude that we are mistaken and be willing to wait until one opens up. But I cannot believe that we ought to wait until God guarantees us as much salary as we now receive. I think we ought to do His will and trust Him to send us the supply of our need.[4]

When a letter arrived from the Conference president, objecting to William's ongoing leave from his appointed circuit, a decision had to be made. William and Catherine had approached everyone they could think of, searching for an avenue of work, but no door had opened for them. After a day of fervent prayer, with Catherine's full support, William handed in his resignation. Their formal connection with any of the Methodist groups was over.

Both at the age of thirty-two, with four young children to raise, William and Catherine gave up their home, their income, their security, and every supportive friend they had, apart from family, and stepped out into the unknown. With little other than their unshakable faith in God, they moved back to London to stay with Catherine's parents.

God quickly proved himself faithful to His obedient servants. Shortly after their arrival in London, they received an invitation from Cornwall. The letter came from a young New Connexion minister who had been converted during one of William's earlier revival campaigns. The minister, sympathetic toward the Booths' predicament, begged them both to visit Hayle to conduct revival meetings. He didn't have much to offer: the chapel was small, and the circuit could not afford to pay their speakers.

Catherine's parents tried hard to persuade William to wait and see what other doors may open, but he was keen to get started. It was finally decided that the Mumfords would take care of the children while William and Catherine headed for Hayle to conduct six weeks of meetings.

As they stepped out in obedience, God stepped in. The result was a mighty revival lasting eighteen months and seeing seven thousand people added to the kingdom. Catherine eventually organized for their children to join them as the work spread from Hayle to its surrounding districts and towns.

Fishermen rowed ten miles across dark, stormy seas to attend. Others walked through the night to be present at one service in the morning before returning for work the following day. The entire Cornwall area was shaken to its core as men, women, and children were touched and transformed by the Lord. The spiritual atmosphere in many towns and villages was dramatically improved. "Business is no longer carried out," one local noted. "The shopkeepers and their customers are all busily engaged in the Booth meetings."[5]

The Spirit of God moved powerfully on people during the meet-

Catherine in the 1860s

ings and even on the streets. One young boy met Catherine as she was walking home alone after a service one day. They strolled together for a while. Catherine spoke simply and honestly with the child, telling him what it meant to give himself to God. Before they parted, they knelt together on the side of the road to pray. The young boy would later become a Salvationist, and he looked back on that day as the beginning of his spiritual life.

Writing home to her parents, Catherine described the meetings: "I never saw people cry and shout as they do here. I can do nothing in the way of invitation in the prayer meetings; the noise is so great. I occupy myself with going to the people in the pews."[6] And again, "On Wednesday night William preached in the largest Wesleyan chapel about half a mile from the other. It was crammed out into the street. I should think there were 1,800 people inside, and I never witnessed such a scene in my life."[7]

William and Catherine shared the preaching, often speaking simultaneously in different venues. In April of 1862 Catherine began to hold afternoon meetings for women only. The attendance at the first of these women's meetings was estimated to be twenty-five hundred. One lady spoke of these services, declaring, "There never was such a sight seen in St. Just before. Mrs. Booth talked with such divine power that it seemed to me as if every person in the chapel who was not right with God must at once consecrate themselves to His service."[8] Such was the power of God at work through William and Catherine during the eighteen-month revival.

"All Britain is now open to you,"[9] another evangelist proclaimed excitedly to William as they rejoiced together over the new souls added to the kingdom. Nothing, however, was further from the truth. The movement that had once so openly embraced William now firmly closed its doors. Despite the wonderful results reported by the New Connexion ministers in Cornwall, an instruction was issued by the 1862 conference banning the Booths from holding any further meetings in their churches. Wesleyan and Primitive Methodists across Great Britain soon followed suit, also forbidding the Booths the use of their chapels. Meetings planned in Penzance were cancelled, and the mighty move of God in Cornwall came to a sudden stop.

The Booths were forced by their convictions to tread the path of so many pioneers of old. As God poured out His new wine through their lives and their ministry, it became more and more obvious that a new wineskin was required to contain it.

Catherine and William were once more forced to move on. Their family continued to grow, with Herbert Howard, their fifth child, born in July of 1862. They ministered in Cornwall until the end of the year, before heading for Wales in early 1863. The Booths had been invited to hold meetings in Cardiff, where they were faced with the difficulty of finding a venue. Most churches had vetoed them and their revival meetings. After much searching and deliberation, William and Catherine took on a circus tent! This was the first time they used a secular building, a practice that would later become an invaluable tool for drawing in the unchurched masses. Despite the unusual location, the meetings were wonderful, with hundreds giving their lives to Christ. In one of her weekly letters to her parents, Catherine said, "The Circus answers much better than we expected. William had a good attendance in the morning. I had it full in the afternoon. . . . William had it crowded again at night—a mighty service, and fifty-six names taken in the prayer meeting."[10]

Around the same time, Catherine wrote, "My time now is never my own. I am subject to so many callers and if I had the strength for it, and no other claims upon me, I might almost be engaged in dealing with the anxious."[11] Despite the great numbers who flocked to the front during the altar calls, Catherine and William were filled with concern for each individual who sought their help in finding God. Although they were drawn to the great masses that did not know Jesus, they were able to focus with sincere love and compassion on each person they ministered to.

For the next two years, the Booths continued their traveling ministry. Campaigns were held in Newport, Walsall, and throughout northern England, using first Birmingham and then Leeds as their base. The strain of continual meetings and travel affected them both. William was often away from home five days out of each week, and the constant battle to find venues for their meetings took its toll. Finances were always tight, and this added extra pressure to their lives.

Soon after the birth of Marian, their sixth child, on May 4, 1864, Catherine began to conduct her own revival campaigns. She encountered very little opposition as a woman preacher, and her first series of meetings resulted in more than five hundred conversions. The success of their revival meetings did not, however, make the time they spent apart any easier. William and Catherine missed each other desperately. They longed for a place in which they could settle more permanently, a place they could call home. It was at Catherine's suggestion that in 1865 they moved to London and set up home in Hammersmith.

"The Woman Preacher" was quite a curiosity in London society. Catherine received many invitations to preach. It was here that she held her first campaign among the "upper classes."

The circumstances in London could not have been more different or difficult for William. Most of the chapels remained closed to him. Only a few smaller churches invited him to preach. As a family, the Booths now leaned almost entirely on money raised through Catherine's meetings in London's prominent churches to survive. While God opened the way for Catherine's ministry among the wealthy, it seemed every door remained firmly closed to William. He determined in his heart to travel to the country, conducting revival campaigns as before. God, however, had a different plan. As William made arrangements to hold a series of meetings in Derby, he was surprised by the growing attraction in his heart to the poor working-class masses that called the city "home."

The teeming crowds on the streets of East London were to William the most spiritually and morally destitute people he had ever seen. As he walked through the slums, he was almost overcome by the stench of open sewers, rotting refuse, and stale ale wafting from the crowded public-houses. His eyes rested on one lifeless face after another, and in an instant he was back in the pawnshop, confronted by the soul-destroying effects of poverty. His heart ached for the masses: men, women, and children who would never cross the threshold of a chapel to hear the only message that could ever lift them out of the hell they experienced daily and save them from the hell they faced for eternity. Where could he go to find a people more needy than these?

A powerful sense of destiny rested upon William as he strode through the busy Bethnal Green and Whitechapel slums on his way home one summer evening in June of 1865. He had just finished preaching in a nearby chapel, filling in for a minister who was unwell. The congregation was quickly forgotten as the stinking depravity of the East London streets bombarded his senses. He approached a small crowd that had gathered outside the Blind Beggar pub on the Mile End Waste, just in time to hear the leader of an open-air gospel meeting ask if anyone else would like to speak. Always ready to seize an opportunity to preach, Booth did not hesitate long enough to be asked twice.

With fiery zeal and an authority known only to those who fear the Lord, he scuttled the complacent hearts of his listeners with a directness and compassion few could withstand. Booth finished his appeal and continued on to the warmth and comfort of his Hammersmith home, but the sights and sounds of reality would not leave him.

Within days, the leadership of the East London Special Services Committee, the organization responsible for the street meeting, approached William and asked if he would take temporary charge of their work. They had planned to hold a series of services in a dilapidated tent on the site of an old Quaker burial ground in East London, a stone's throw from the slums of Whitechapel Road.

At first, he hesitated. Speaking later of his initial reluctance, he said,

Here was the open door for which I had longed for years, and yet I knew it not, and moreover was unwilling to enter it. The main reason for this was that I feared my ability to deal with people of this class; I had made several efforts, but apparently failed, and the thought saddened and oppressed me beyond measure. I would have given worlds had they been mine to have been qualified to attract and interest and lead to salvation the masses I saw around me, as completely outside the Christian circle as the untaught heathen of foreign lands, but I despaired of accomplishing it. This I thought was not my vocation. I had forgotten Nottingham Meadow Platts and the work in it when a boy of sixteen, twenty years before. However, as was my usage, no squeamish difficulties were allowed to interfere with duty. I accepted the invitation, and the hour and the day found me at my post. On the Mile End Waste the first open-air meeting was held, from whence we processioned to the tent.[12]

The date of this first meeting was July 2, 1865.

For six weeks, William preached night after night to the rowdy ruffians gathered from the streets. Each evening up to three hundred people would crowd into the old canvas tent, which provided seating on rough wooden benches. The smell of sweat and stale beer mingled with the fumes from the naphtha[13] lamps to create an oppressive pungent atmosphere. Every evening, William passionately preached of the One who could save their souls. Drunken men did their best to break up the meetings, mocking and laughing at William while he spoke. He carried on regardless, his booming voice more than a match for the disruption they caused. In spite of the rough surrounds, every night the Spirit of God moved on the hardened hearts, drawing desolate souls to repentance and salvation.

For William, the meetings were different from any other revival services he had conducted. He ached with compassion as night after night the lost souls of East London found their way into his heart. In prayer, he cried out to God for direction. He knew the tent mission was only temporary, but he found within a growing desire to reach the thousands who seemed so far beyond every other Christian work. Like his Savior, William was drawn to the helpless crowds who were truly like sheep without a shepherd. Reflecting later on this time, he said,

> From the first the meetings were fairly good; we had souls at almost every service, and before the fortnight had passed I felt at home; and more than this, I found my heart being strongly and strangely drawn out. . . . I was continually haunted with a desire to offer myself to Jesus Christ as an

apostle for the heathen of East London.[14]

One morning a few weeks after he had started the tent meetings, William found himself on the Mile End Waste wandering among the shabby stalls of shopkeepers displaying their wares. The degradation and hopelessness of the people engulfed his heart until it broke. As he slowly wound his way along the busy street, his eyes wandered over the teeming mass of lonely people swarming all around him. William was something of a novelty on the slummy East London streets. His white choker and tall hat gave him away instantly as a minister and drew many stares from those who rarely saw a "man of the cloth" in their part of town.

All of a sudden William's gaze connected with the wild, dark eyes of a rough young man walking toward him. It was as though the look exchanged between them conveyed something of William's heart. Both men stopped in their tracks, their eyes still locked.

Finally William spoke. "I'm looking for work," he said, his voice filled with sadness. "I've got no place to put my head in." William seemed oblivious of the young man's intention to find him some loose change from his pocket. Pointing to the crowd of men milling outside the Blind Beggar public house, he continued, "Look at those men, look at them! Forgotten by God and man. Why should I be looking for work? There's my work, over there, looking for me." The sadness returned to his voice as he repeated, "But I've got no place where I can put my head in."

"You're right, sir," replied the young man respectfully through his thick Irish accent. "Those men are forgotten by God and man, and if you can do anything for them t'would be a great work."[15]

William looked into the face of the Irishman. "Listen," he went on, "I'll be preaching later over on the Mile End Road. Will you come by to hear me? Will you bring some of the lads along with you?" he asked, pointing again to the young men outside the public house.

"I will, sir," he replied seriously, "I will." As William turned away and walked toward his Hammersmith home, he had taken another step in his heart, a step that carried him closer to his destiny.

The following evening, when he stood in the tent to preach, the unruly crowd made such a noise he had to shout to be heard. He decided instead to drown them out with a hymn. The volume of singing rose, overpowering the shouts and laughter of the drunken men. Suddenly, partway through the hymn, the revelers stopped their noisy racket. William watched curiously as they settled down, their gaze fixed on a lone man who began pacing up and down the aisles of the tent, glaring at anyone who stepped out of line. William recognized him immediately as the Irishman he had met on the street the day before. The meeting continued without interruption.

After the service William discovered the man was Peter Monk, a prize-fighter. He thanked him for his help and then looked again into his eyes. "You're not happy; you know you're not happy," he said.

The Irishman shrugged his shoulders as he asked, "What reason is that?"

William's answer was direct. "You'll perish like a dog," he said. "You're living for the devil, and the devil will have you."

"Who made a prophet of you?" the Irishman answered.

"My Father in Heaven," came the quick reply. As the Irishman lowered his eyes to the floor he felt a caring arm around his shoulders. "I'll make a man out of you yet," said William. A few nights later the Irishman, kneeling on the dirt floor at the end of a service, found William's arm around him once more. "You're not happy," he heard whispered in his ear as the Spirit of God brought repentance to his heart. After many tears and much prayer, the Irishman stood to his feet. He was a new man: a man ready to die for the one through whom he'd found his Savior.[16]

William's mind was all but made up. He hurried home late after an evening service some nights later, feeling weary but thrilled by the wonderful conversions that had taken place. Catherine had already arrived home from her own service, and she waited by the fire for his return.

When the front door opened, she looked up to greet her love. William strode into the room where she sat, his face filled with excitement. "Darling," he announced, "I have found my destiny."[17] Sinking his tired body into a chair, he began to share his heart. "Oh, Kate!" he exclaimed passionately,

As I passed by the doors of the flaming gin-palaces tonight, I seemed to hear a voice sounding in my ears, "Where can you go and find such heathen as these, and where is there so great a need for your labors?" And I felt as though I ought at every cost to stop and preach to those East End multitudes.[18]

Catherine sat quietly, gazing into the fire, her heart disturbed by William's outburst. Her thoughts turned immediately to their six children asleep upstairs, and to their seventh due in just five months. The supply of money required to feed, clothe, and house this large family was scant. Times were hard and Catherine was somewhat of a realist. The way of an evangelist in

1865 was a difficult one. The only way they survived was through the collections taken up from their more well-to-do audiences. She didn't dare imagine how they would manage with William working among the poverty-stricken masses of East London.

In this moment of decision, Catherine returned to the principle she had learned years earlier in Gateshead. She chose the path of obedience and left the consequences to the Lord. After a moment of silence and prayer she answered, "Well, if you felt you ought to stay, stay. We have trusted the Lord once for our support, and we can trust him again."[19] Together they chose to forge ahead, with little except a strong conviction from God to sustain them.

Torn apart by the poverty, drunkenness, prostitution, and disease that characterized the slums of England, but convinced of the power of God to change even the hardest man, William laid down his life to win the East-Enders to Christ. As his eldest son later reflected,

> It was the spectacle of sin and suffering that moved him to give himself to East London. He went out and looked upon the woes of the people both by day and by night. And he could not walk a yard in those dreadful streets without suffering in heart and in mind. He heard in all that misery a heartbreaking cry for help. And he had no rest until he gave himself to the work of rescue. The true way of relief for any who is conscious of misery of any sort is to take a hand at fighting it.[20]

His mind made up, William threw himself into his work in East London. He had indeed found his destiny.

The way ahead was not easy. After six weeks of meeting in the old tent, it was clear they needed to find an alternate venue. The gaping holes in the canvas did little to protect them from the icy cold wind. The East London Special Services Committee appealed to William to continue the work, and they searched for alternative venues for the evening meetings. A dance hall was found for the Sunday services, while other locations included a wool store, stables, and a loft. The tent was used for afternoon meetings until it was torn apart by the fury of a fierce autumn storm. Meetings were held every day from July 2 until August 20, when William fell ill. He resumed the services one week later.

William sent an account of his work in East London to the *Revival* on August 17, 1865. In this report he outlined his proposals for the mission.

> We have no very definite plans. We shall be guided by the Holy Spirit. At present we desire to be able to hold consecutive services for the pur-

pose of bringing souls to Christ in different localities of the East of London every night all the year round. We propose holding these meetings in halls, theatres, chapels, tents, the open-air and elsewhere as the way may be opened or we seem likely to attain the end we have in view. We purpose to watch over and visit personally those brought to Christ, either guiding them to communion with adjacent and sympathetic churches or ourselves nursing them and training them to active labor. In order to carry on this work we propose to establish a Christian Revival Association. . . . We shall also require some central building in which to hold our more private meetings, and in which to preach the Gospel when not engaged in special work elsewhere.[21]

He finished his report with an appeal for funds.

Once again God proved faithful. As William and Catherine sought first the purpose of the kingdom, He provided for their needs. A few days after they had taken their step of faith, William was invited to visit Samuel Morley to discuss his work among the poor. Mr. Morley listened intently as William shared his dream to see the East-Enders saved. Afterward, questioning him about his family and their means of support, the wealthy manufacturer pulled out his pen and wrote William a check for one hundred pounds. This was the first of the annual contributions he made to the family.

William and Catherine had seen firsthand the faithfulness of God as they stepped out in obedience to His call. They had learned by revelation and then by experience to obey the Lord and to trust Him with the consequences. This foundation of total consecration was crucial for the accomplishment of the work God had set for their lives. From its outset, William preached, by word and example, that to follow God is to obey Him.

The Booths' message of total surrender and radical obedience to God attracted great criticism, especially in the early days. To many in the established churches, the call for no compromise, no holding anything back, no denying God in the small things, was too serious and too difficult to obtain. William and Catherine disregarded their comments, choosing instead to live and preach according to the standard of obedience set out in the Word of God.

The very same issues stood in the way of the nineteenth-century Christians as stand in our own way today. When preaching his message of total obedience, William encountered those who cried, "The cost is too high, the sacrifice is too great!" Writing on this issue some time later, he stated:

> They say plainly that husband and wife, father and mother, brother and
> sister, houses and lands, friendly circles and business and money and poli-

tics and health and big idols and little idols bar the way, and they cannot suffer what it would cost them to come and stand forth before the heavens, having dared to leave and offer all up for the sake of Him who left and offered all for the sake of them.[22]

Challenging his readers, he turned their attention to the martyrs of days past, writing:

> O friends, what about these heroic spirits? What about those faces that look at you today through that blinding smoke and those devouring flames? Are there then two standards of service, one high and Christ-like for them, and one much lower, made to meet the case of little, lean and cowardly souls? Nay, are there three ways for the feet of those who travel toward eternity? One wide and broad for the wicked, another straight and narrow for martyrs and martyr spirits, and the other a middle middling, sort of silver-slipper path, for those who would have the pearl without the price, the crown without the cross.
>
> No! No! No! Look again at those martyr-men. They stood up there before heaven and earth, and said in the loudest language that can be spoken in this or in any other world, that they gladly gave up, not only friends and kindred, lands and money, and every other earthly treasure, but life itself, which to them, as to everybody else, is far dearer than all else put together, for the truth and love and cause of Jesus Christ.[23]

William was convinced the one thing holding back the full blessing of God was the reluctance of people to surrender all to Jesus: "Men and women who will die at their post are the very sort in demand just now in The Salvation Army and elsewhere. They are what the world needs, what we are praying for and what God wants."[24]

In his address to Salvationists for the New Year in 1906, William answered the question "What I should do with my life were I called upon to live it over." He penned: "I should offer my life up, without a moment's hesitation, on the altar of redeeming love. I should place myself—body, soul, and spirit—at the feet of Jesus Christ, ready and willing literally to live, suffer, fight and die for Him."[25] This passion-filled warrior of the nineteenth century knew the power of the dedicated life, the power that comes as a disciple decides to be entirely committed, thoroughly devoted, and totally obedient to the Lord. He lived his days knowing that "a crucified life is an awesome weapon in the hands of a holy God."[26]

William and Catherine's consecration—their unreserved obedience, their total surrender, and their intimate devotion to God—was undoubtedly the source and secret of their strength. They knew that "no amount of money, genius, or culture could move the hand of God. Holiness alone energizes the soul, the whole man aflame with love, with desire for more faith, more prayer, more zeal, more consecration—this is the secret of power."[27]

Some years later, Bramwell questioned his father, curious to know how he could keep on without tiring despite all the setbacks and difficulties they had faced. In answering, William described how he had knelt in the chapel in Nottingham at the age of fifteen and vowed that "God should have all there was of William Booth."[28] This yielding of his life to God was the secret of his strength.

As his daughter Eva was later to add, "That wasn't really his secret—his secret was that he never took it back."[29]

With the conviction that God had called him to bring light into this darkness, William began his work in the derelict East End slums. His work was to become the foundation of an organization expanding in his lifetime to reach to the ends of the earth. Although this motivator of men possessed remarkable vision, it is not likely he or Catherine envisaged the future scope of the work they began in 1865.

CHAPTER 6

Prayer, Faith, and
the Power of the Holy Spirit

THE MISSION BECOMES AN ARMY (1865–1878)

Go back to the upper room; back to your knees; back to searching of the heart and habit, thought and life, back to pleading, praying, waiting, till the Spirit of the Lord floods the soul with light, and you are endued with power from on high. Then go forth in the power of Pentecost, and the Christ life shall be lived, and the works of Christ shall be done. You shall open blind eyes, cleanse foul hearts, break men's fetters, and save men's souls. In the power of the Spirit, miracles become the commonplace of daily living.

—SAMUEL CHADWICK

There is a Heaven in East London for everyone," William cried passionately, "for everyone who will stop and think and look to Christ as a personal Savior." A few curious people paused to listen as they walked along the dirty street. They were fascinated by the tall, bearded preacher dressed in a black frock coat, waving his umbrella wildly at the small crowd gathered before him.

William concluded his message with an invitation for his listeners to attend a meeting in the dance hall on New Road. Together with the handful of missioners who stood with him, he struck up the chorus of a well-known hymn. The sound of the music brought two drunken men stumbling from the door of the Blind Beggar, accompanied by the boisterous laughter and coarse encouragement of the pub patrons. As the men lurched toward the singers, mocking and blaspheming, they found themselves swept along the street amid the growing crowd heading for the dance hall where their meeting was to be held. Other drunkards staggered out of the pubs they passed by, sneering and shouting abuse at the small band. The people of Whitechapel looked on with wonder at the singing parade, some following the procession to New Road.

Open-air preaching and processions were used from the outset of the Booths' work in East London. William was painfully aware that although the working class they were trying to reach would not enter a chapel or cathedral, they would stand out day or night, in any weather, to listen to a speaker who set up on a street corner. Every open-air meeting would culminate with an indoor service, allowing interested people to hear the gospel in full and have an opportunity to respond, without the distractions that so often accompanied the outdoor gatherings. William encouraged his co-workers,

> In this actual closing with Christ consists the only or chief ground of hope we have for sinners; without it, all mere resolutions and head knowledge will avail but little; therefore we attach but little importance to instructing men's minds or arousing their feelings, unless they can be led to that belief in Christ which results in the new creation.[1]

William and his helpers soon got used to the disruptions caused by drunken roughs during their open-air meetings. With quick thinking and good humor, they would dispel any aggression that arose and carry on with their singing and preaching. Resistance came from the owners of the public houses, too, as they saw some of their best customers converted. When they complained to the police about the processions, claiming they stole their customers away, an instruction was issued forbidding the missioners to march on the sidewalks. This did not deter William—instead of using the sidewalks, they held their processions on the road!

They did not always come away from their open-air work unharmed. Anything opponents could find was thrown their way, and often they hit the mark. On many evenings, William would trudge the eight miles to his Hammersmith home, arriving weary and battle-scarred, his clothes stained with blood or rotten fruit and his body bruised. This was the price they had to pay as they sought to save the worst of sinners—a price they never considered too high.

The purpose of this new work in East London was to bring the message of salvation to those the church had failed. They aimed to reach men and women like the drunken miner who once sought out the assistance of a parson. "Read your Bible," was the parson's reply. The man had to confess he could not read. The parson then suggested he should come to church. When the man explained he had only working clothes, the parson ran out of solutions. Such was the attitude of many image-conscious clergy of the day. The heart of God longed to help the drunken miner, but his spiritual adviser was powerless to do so.[2]

The limitations and spiritual poverty of the church had alarmed William since his rebuke as a teenager for bringing the poor into Nottingham's Broad Street Chapel. His years of revival preaching had convinced him that the gospel message was indeed the power of God for the salvation of all humankind. God had laid on his heart the plight of those the church had written off as not worth reaching. "To me," he declared, "men, especially the worst, possess the attraction of gold mines."[3]

The drunkards, prostitutes, and criminals of East London were the ones William strove to reach with the gospel of Christ. His passion for the very worst sinners was passed on to all who worked with him and to his children.

Bramwell Booth never forgot the first time that, as a teenager, his father led him into an East End pub: the illumination from gas lamps playing eerily on men's inflamed faces, drunken, disheveled women openly suckling tiny children, the reek of gin and shag tobacco and acrid bodies. After a moment, seeing the appalled look on his son's face, William Booth said quietly: "These are our people. These are the people I want you to live for and bring to Christ."[4]

William's early years in East London were a tough, uphill struggle. There were many obstacles to overcome and great difficulties to weigh him down. Meetings were held every day, with up to four services on Sunday, all of them preceded by open-air preaching. "The bulk of the preaching in all these services fell on me," William later recalled, "but the power and happiness of the work carried me along."[5]

Financially, the work relied heavily upon offerings and donations by members. The hire of the dance hall alone cost over a pound every week. It seemed an impossible thing to raise finance for the work when most of the converts joining the mission were among the poorest of the poor; however, God remained faithful, and the necessary funds always arrived. As one early convert reported,

> No-one in the audience seemed worth sixpence, but we had a box at
> the door that people might give what they could when they were going

out—and almost every Sunday we found in it a golden sovereign! [Twenty shillings, or one pound. See Appendix A for a chart of the relationship between pounds, shillings, and pence and other common coins of the period.] We never discovered how it got there! We used to say that the Lord Himself put it in![6]

During the first twelve months, many of those who had originally supported William's work left. Some had only intended to serve during the original tent crusade, but others departed because of William and his methods. A few objected to the holiness doctrine adopted and preached by the Booths, while others felt William laid too much emphasis on repentance. Still others were offended by the nature of the prayer meetings held after the service for those who came forward to the penitent-form.

William heard their complaints, but he refused to budge. His uncompromising stand on a definite conversion experience and total consecration to God's service meant that only those who held the same views could remain. God sifted the fainthearted from among the ranks very quickly. William did not despair when co-workers left. Instead, he only became more determined to build up those who remained with him.

By July of 1866, twelve months after commencing the work in East London, a core group of sixty members had formed around William. Many of these were new converts, simple people with little or no education, yet when touched by the transforming power of God, they became valuable agents in the war for souls.

No one could dispute the miraculous power of God that was radically changing the lives of the new believers. Under the influence of empowered preaching, the Spirit of God brought desperate men and women to their knees. In the prayer meeting after the service they would confess their sin, crying aloud for mercy and resolving to live the remainder of their lives in the service of God. Christians would gather round to intercede for their salvation while one counseled them. William refused to allow the Bible to be used with seekers in a way that led them to understand that if they only believed in the words of some text, they would be saved. When finally they rose from their knees, those who had met their Savior knew in their hearts beyond a doubt that they were saved. They were thoroughly converted and determined to live life completely surrendered and totally committed to the One who had rescued their soul. Those who were not yet ready to give up their life of sin received prayer and were encouraged to continue to seek God. Much prayer and counsel often preceded a person's conversion, but when it happened, it was immediate and absolute in its nature.

Despite his uncompromising stance on such issues, William's willingness to consider even the most unorthodox ideas (if they might further his one purpose of saving souls) quickly became a key to the success of the mission. He was a man of great vision and innovation, one who was not limited by current thinking or methods. As a result, the organization that now grew around him bore little resemblance to the established churches and missions of the day. The innovation affected every aspect of their lives. For the first few years, it seemed everything was in a state of flux, and change occurred rapidly.

With no chapels of their own, the mission constantly hunted for suitable buildings for meetings. At first the dance hall was used. Later they hired theatres and even rented an old ale house. Their weekday assemblies were held in odd places, including a stable and a room at the back of a pigeon shop. Since their campaign in the circus tent in Wales, both William and Catherine had realized the value of holding meetings in secular buildings. The poor would happily endure the most cramped and uncomfortable places if they felt welcome and at home.

Although the poor had found their way into William's heart as a young boy, his years of training within the Methodist church had done little to equip him to communicate with them effectively. At times it seemed as though a barrier separated him from those he sought so desperately to reach. One evening, while preaching in Whitechapel to a restless, inattentive crowd of about twelve hundred, out of desperation he called on an old gypsy hawker, who had been converted a few weeks earlier, to testify to what God had done for him. As the old man unfolded his story in a simple yet awkward manner, a strange stillness fell upon the people. William watched in amazement as the new convert captured their hearts and minds. In that moment, he realized an important truth: a simple street hawker could command the attention of this sort of audience in a way that he could not.

As a result of this observation, William took what was recognized to be a radical step. Many years before, he had declared to Catherine, "I am for the world's salvation; I will quarrel with no means that promises help,"[7] this in response to her comments about women in the ministry. True to this resolve, he began to involve his converts, both men and women, in giving testimonies during the meetings. Army stories say that Booth preached some of his best sermons through the lips of other men—often through illiterate men. "He never monopolized the meetings. He made others help him—they were as much theirs, as his. This helped to make them attractive as well as effective."[8] He soon discovered that although the new converts lacked education and finesse, the crowds responded enthusiastically to their raw humor and unpolished style. The power and truth of their stories had tremendous impact.

The involvement of new converts in the work of the gospel encouraged both them and the mission to grow. Every convert was urged to testify to the work of God and immediately involved in the task of spreading the gospel. The Booths organized their people and provided a place for each of them; they were determined that even the newest recruit would feel he or she was making a meaningful contribution to the advancement of the gospel. "I want you all in the thick of the battle; remember victory or defeat depends on your own particular bayonet point," was repeatedly William's strong encouragement.

Although William had originally regarded his work in East London as a link between the unchurched masses and the churches, he quickly discovered that his idea of getting people saved and sending them to the established churches was not practical. For a start, the new converts refused to go when sent; second, they were neither welcomed nor wanted; and finally, William himself wanted at least some of them to work with him in his mission to save others in East London.

He soon faced the challenge of how to care for the new converts, how to help them become established in their faith, and how to keep them from falling away. To William, there was no point in seeing so many come to salvation if they were not nurtured in their new life and put to work in the kingdom. In 1865 he wrote,

> They need to be brought to see that they are not only called to the adoption of sons, but to the work of servants—not only to feel the privileges of the Kingdom but to be actual co-workers for God in bringing others to share these blessings. Even when Christians are brought to discern this duty they require to be taught how to discharge it.[9]

Convinced of this need, William began to hold meetings on Friday evenings to encourage and equip the new converts to carry out the work of dealing one-on-one with sinners.

William continued the technique he had adopted as a traveling evangelist. The name and address of everyone who came forward during the meetings was taken, and each convert was visited on a weekly basis by one of the missioners in order to help them in their new life. Classes were held on Sundays and during the week to disciple the new believers.

New converts were put to work immediately. They participated in the open-air assemblies and gave their testimonies during public meetings. The mission adopted the visitation ministry pioneered by Catherine many years before: converts were sent out two-by-two to distribute tracts, pray for people, and invite them to the meetings. They also visited the sick and provided clothing and food for desperate families, and all were pledged to share their new-found faith with their friends and neighbors. "Every man saved . . . and every man at work, always at work, to save other people"[10] quickly became the aim of the mission.

The length to which these fresh recruits went to see the gospel preached is an indication of the degree of their commitment, passion, and faith. They would do anything to draw a crowd. Some dressed up as prisoners; others as John the Baptist. One man placed a violin case on the pavement, shouting, "Stand back! It might go off!"[11] As the curious crowd backed away, the man took up his violin and began the open-air meeting with a lively jig! Another man lay silently in the snow every evening for a week. When, by the end of the week, a large and inquisitive crowd had gathered in the marketplace, the man leaped to his feet and preached his heart out, much to the surprise of his captive and stunned onlookers. No matter what method was used, once a crowd had formed, the gospel was preached with power and passion.

William and his followers were always as practical as they were spiritual—they could not ignore the physical needs of the people they sought to reach. "When you give a gospel tract to a hungry man, wrap it up in a sandwich!" he instructed his workers.

As we have seen, the seed of the welfare work of The Salvation Army had been sown in William's life at a very young age; his own childhood experience of poverty had prepared him for his work among the poor. As a teenager, he and Will Sansom collected money from their friends to help an old beggar woman who lived on the streets of Nottingham. They rented a small cottage and furnished it as a home for this dear lost soul. William's compassionate heart would often challenge his hands to action: "Love spoken can be easily turned away, but love demonstrated will last for a lifetime," he reminded himself.

To Catherine as much as William, the value of every human life was very real; neither could dismiss as worthless any person for whom Christ had died. Catherine had first encountered the intense hardship endured by the poor when she began to visit them during their time with the New Connexion in

Gateshead. Her heart was broken over their poverty of life, both spiritually and naturally. She recalled,

> I remember in one case finding a poor woman lying on a heap of rags. She had just given birth to twins, and there was nobody of any sort to look after her. I can never forget the desolation of that room. . . . I was soon busy trying to make her a little more comfortable. The babies I washed in a broken pie dish.[12]

Such memories never fade.

Catherine, like her husband, was crushed by the state of poverty experienced by so many families across England. "The state of the masses in our own country is to me a cause of daily, hourly grief and apprehension," she said.

> Since coming more in contact with them, I have found their condition to be so much worse than anything I had previously conceived, that I have often felt confounded, disheartened, and almost paralyzed. I have seen many hundreds of thousands of the lower classes gathered together during the last two or three years, and have often said to myself, "Is it possible that these are our fellow-countrymen in this end of the nineteenth century, in this so-called Christian country?"[13]

Acutely aware of the suffering the poor endured, the Booths were compelled to care not just for people's spiritual well-being but also for their physical needs. This was William's firm challenge to his followers:

> You can't expect people whose chief concern is the source of their next meal, or somewhere warm to stay during the icy London winter, to hear and respond to the Gospel message. No-one gets a blessing if they have cold feet, and nobody ever got saved while they had toothache![14]

The physical needs of the masses were overwhelming. Four years of civil war in the United States had upset trade across the Atlantic, resulting in rising unemployment and poverty in England. Unemployment forced greater numbers of working-class families into the slums of East London each year. Children as young as five were compelled to work for up to fourteen hours a day in factories, earning no more than a pittance. People frequently starved to death, their lifeless bodies discovered among the refuse and waste in the dirty alleyways. Sickness and disease were rampant among the deprived of Victorian England. The open sewers and poor water supply further enhanced the spread of disease. In 1866 a cholera epidemic swept through East London, fueled by the contamination of the main water supply. During that summer more than eight thousand East-Enders died from cholera and other diseases.

It was in these conditions that the Booths initiated their work in East London. Although the provision of food and clothes for the poor was a costly venture for the struggling mission, it was even more impossible to ignore their needs. At first these efforts were little more than an ambulance waiting at the foot of a cliff to pick up those who had plunged into the depths of poverty.

Early initiatives included tea and breakfast meetings, which provided the poor with a little food prior to a gospel service. Meal tickets were handed out among the East-Enders, with up to 240 people receiving free bread and meat each week. William was always careful to ensure that at no time did attendance at a meeting become a condition for receiving practical help. To William's evangelistic heart, the thought of trying to secure converts by providing them with practical assistance was abhorrent. Even though this was never their aim, in the face of extreme poverty it was a very real risk. Speaking of these early attempts at welfare work, William later said,

> Free teas, petticoats, and blankets made many hypocrites; no money was ever given—not even to those who had just been saved . . . though the Soldiers seemed to love and help each other, and God most surely helped the converted who relied on His help.[15]

As the bitterly cold winter months approached, the Booths opened a soup kitchen. Initially run for the duration of winter, the soup kitchen provided hot soup with bread for the starving masses of East London. Over twenty-five gallons of soup were distributed on a daily basis.

While William toiled tirelessly among the poor, Catherine continued her meetings in other parts of London. The family had moved in November from Hammersmith to Hackney, and on Christmas Day their seventh child, Evangeline Cory, was born. In February of 1866, six weeks after baby Eva's birth, Catherine began a series of services in Peckham. She preached twice on Sundays and several times during the week for a total of ten weeks without a break. She always spoke of William's work among the poor and invited people to partner with them in East London in any way they could. As a result of her meetings, donations were received to help with their mission.

After this grueling schedule, Catherine fell ill with symptoms of dysentery. She lost much weight and was advised by doctors to spend some time recuperating in the country. While visiting Catherine in Tunbridge Wells, William was invited to preach at Dunorlan, a large home in the area. He could not accept the invitation due to his commitments in Whitechapel, so it was agreed that Catherine would take the meeting instead. Mr. and Mrs. Reed, Dunorlan's owners, invited Catherine to spend the weekend with them.

The following Sunday, as Catherine walked with her hosts across the grounds to the meeting hall, Mr. Reed asked her to be sure to be finished speaking before four. Catherine smiled as she said, "You must be my time-keeper, for when once I am started I am apt to forget myself."

As Catherine stood to speak, she looked across the little hall, full for the occasion. She began to preach and immediately the presence of God came into the room. They all lost track of time as the Lord ministered mightily through Catherine's message. When she suddenly remembered her instructions, she stopped mid-flight and turned to Mr. Reed. "Ought I to stop now?" she asked. Her host raised his hand, tears falling from his eyes as he replied, "Go on, go on. Never mind the time."[16]

Catherine concluded her message and then knelt with those who responded, praying and talking with them as they sought God. Mr. and Mrs. Reed became great friends and supporters of the Booths from that time on, and their home was often used as a place of rest and recuperation for William and Catherine.

Although Mr. Reed was impressed with William's work among the poor, he disagreed with their use of secular buildings for meetings. Reed had made a fortune as a grazier in the Tasmanian colony, and he made an offer that at first seemed heaven-sent. He proposed to provide ten or twelve thousand pounds for the building of a hall as a center for the mission in East London. Further support was also proposed for the Booth family themselves. With seven children to care for and a growing work to fund, this proposal would have lifted the burden of financial worry from their shoulders.

Although tempted to accept the offer immediately, William and Catherine felt a hesitation in their spirits. The caution came over the conditions that accompanied Mr. Reed's generous proposal. The stipulations gave Mr. Reed the right to withdraw the use of the hall if at any time he did not approve of the methods adopted by the mission. Furthermore, to accept the offer, William had to agree to confine himself to work in the East End.

Neither William nor Catherine could have imagined at the time the incredible growth and expansion the work would undergo in years to come. Foremost on their minds was the urgent need for a base for the mission. The temptation to accept the offer and receive immediate financial relief was strong. In the depths of their hearts, however, came the caution of the Spirit of God, and they rejected the offer rather than allow its restrictions to dictate their future. Mr. Reed was astounded but refused to alter the conditions of his support. They remained close friends, and he later provided unconditional personal financial support for the Booth family.

Catherine's recovery from her illness was very slow, and it was months before she was able to resume preaching. To add to the physical stress upon her body, she became pregnant again. While out walking one day with the children, she came across a large house on Gore Road between Bethnal Green and Hackney, overlooking a beautiful park. Although the rent was high, it was perfectly suited to their large family and closer to their mission field. After discussion and prayer, the family moved into their new home. It was here that their eighth child, Lucy Milward, was born on April 28, 1867.

The mission grew very quickly, much faster than William ever anticipated. In early 1867 they gave up the dance hall and began to meet in Effingham Theatre and the Oriental Hall. By March they were conducting seventy services a week in nine different preaching stations in East London.

In September of 1867 William issued the first report on the two-year-old mission, now named The East London Christian Mission. They had taken on the Eastern Star, a former beer house, as their headquarters. Meetings were held every evening at the base, and it also provided a shop for the sale of Bibles and tracts, a reading room with cheap refreshments, Bible classes, believers' meetings, mothers' meetings, a soup kitchen, and accommodation for some of the full-time mission workers.

As the work expanded, so did the need for funds. By this time, a total of forty pounds was required every week to finance the work. A few wealthy businessmen were willing to support the mission, impressed by the results they were achieving. Others, however, were very skeptical. Mr. F. A. Bevan, head of a large banking firm, gave a donation of ten pounds, but he accompanied it with a cautious letter: "As I don't want to encourage you in keeping up the extensive machinery you have set afloat, I must decline to help the work."[17] Other support was obtained in the form of grants from established mission societies.

All finances were accounted for with the utmost diligence. From the outset of the mission, William and Catherine determined never to draw on mission funds for their own support. William stated,

> Having some years ago given up a stated income in the ordinary ministry for evangelistic work, I am wholly dependent on God for the support

of myself and family. Hitherto I have not been necessitated to appropriate a penny of the general funds to my own support, the Lord having sent it specifically for that purpose through a few devoted servants in different parts of the country.[18]

The money received by the mission was set aside into one of four different funds. The fund for General Spiritual Work provided support for the evangelists and full-time mission workers as well as rental and general expenses. The General Poor Fund supplied money for their relief work. The Destitute Saints Fund provided financial assistance to members of the mission, while the Building Fund contained money set aside for the purchase or construction of their own facilities.

Although Catherine was not directly involved at first in the evangelistic work of the mission, she was, as always, William's greatest supporter. The long, tiring hours and the constant demands and pressures of the growing organization took their toll on him. Catherine was the only one with whom he could really share his burden and the only one who could inspire his heart to press on. "Kate," he would say as he took hold of her hand, "let me pray with you." Together they would kneel, consecrating their lives to God and leaning on Him for all their needs. God sustained them through the hard times as their fledgling ministry among the poor took root.

However, Catherine was concerned about some of the reports she heard. Everything seemed to be expanding so fast. She cautioned William, saying, "My dear, don't go too fast; don't go ahead of the teaching of the Holy Ghost."[19] It was not until October of 1867 that she saw for herself the wonderful work of God in the lives of the East-Enders. Talking later of this meeting she said,

> I went and saw the marvelous results. I saw twenty-thirty-fifty of the biggest blackguards in London broken all to pieces on a single Sunday night—just as much broken down as the Jews were under Peter's sermon. I spoke to them and applied the test of the Gospel, and I was bound to say, "This is the finger of God!"[20]

The Booths were accustomed to fervent, prevailing, believing prayer, and they instilled this passion into the hearts of everyone who worked with them. They knew what it was to intercede for the lost and to labor on their knees until the breakthrough came. William constantly exhorted his volunteers,

> Bring more faith into your praying. . . . Do not be content with merely

telling God about your wants, or expressing your desires, or even in reminding yourself of His ability and willingness to supply your needs, but take hold of His word, and believe that He does, there and then, if it be His blessed will, give you the things for which you ask.[21]

William and Catherine had learned through the years that great strength could be gained from times of personal prayer and from praying with others. Every opportunity was taken as a chance to invite God to intervene in the affairs of humans through prayer. William prayed with his people every day. He prayed with all who sought a meeting with him, be they believers or not. After talking business he would inquire after each one's soul and then spend time with them in prayer. In private and public, in open-air meetings and indoor services, dynamic, powerful petitions were made on behalf of the lost. Every new advance, every forward step was made on a strong foundation of prayer. Any under the leadership of the Booths soon learned to seek hard after God, to pray in faith, and to persevere in prayer. As they followed William and Catherine's examples, their own lives became a testimony of the miraculous.

Convinced of the unequalled value and importance of faith-filled prayer, William constantly urged his followers to give themselves unreservedly to seeking God. "You must pray with your might," he once wrote.

> That does not mean saying your prayers, or sitting gazing about in church or chapel, with eyes wide open, while someone else says them for you. It means fervent, effectual, untiring wrestling with God. It means that grappling with Omnipotence, that clinging to Him, following Him about, so to speak, day and night, as the widow did to the unjust judge, with agonizing pleadings and arguments and entreaties, until the answer comes and the end is gained. This kind of prayer be sure the devil and the world and your own indolent, unbelieving nature will oppose. They will pour water on this flame. They will ply you with suggestions and difficulties. They will ask you how you can expect that the plans and purposes and feelings of God can be altered by your prayers. They will talk about impossibilities and predict failures; but, if you mean to succeed, you must shut your ears and eyes to all but what God has said, and hold Him to His own word: and you cannot do this in any sleepy mood; you cannot be a prevailing Israel unless you wrestle as Jacob wrestled, regardless of time aught else, save obtaining the blessing sought—that is, you must pray with your might.[22]

Prayer undergirded every activity of the mission, and it, too, was subject to William's innovative planning. In 1868 he called the first all-night prayer meeting. Said an early convert,

> An eight hour prayer meeting was a new idea, but it seemed only natural that people ablaze with love for God and sinners should pray all night when their work and duties forbade them doing so all day. Besides, Christ set them the example Himself. Anyway, at this first "all night" so desperate, so unceasing, and so tremendous was the uproar that towards dawn the Irish living around finding sleep impossible, gathered round the door. "Sure they're killing themselves," they whispered with awestruck looks![23]

The work continued to grow at an extraordinary rate. New stations were opened, and by 1868 William had twenty full-time workers and dozens of committed helpers. Approximately 120 meetings were held every week, enabling them to preach on average to fourteen thousand people. Services were held every night and also during the day. "The gin-palaces are always open," William argued. "The emissaries of evil are always at work; why should the ambassadors of Christ wait for the evening?"[24]

With the numbers of converts increasing steadily, a more systematic approach had to be taken to ensure all received adequate counseling and care. After their names and addresses were recorded, they were given a ticket admitting them to a private meeting the following night. At this meeting they were met by experienced Christians who spoke with them to determine the depth of their convictions and the grounds on which their faith was based. They received further counsel and prayer before being introduced to a reliable convert who became their mentor, watching over them and helping them in their new life.

William was a keen observer of people and trends, and this, together with his insatiable appetite for change, enabled him to capitalize on new ideas as they sprang to his attention. Among these innovations was the "Free and Easy"—the mission's spiritual alternative to the public-house sing-along. "Free and Easy" meetings were held on Sunday afternoons and lasted an hour and a half, with singing, prayer, and as many as forty new converts giving their testimonies.

The unusual methods adopted by the Booths began to attract more criticism from some in the established churches of the day. While the rapid growth of their work had gained William acknowledgment in London, his appeal for funds brought at least one stinging public rebuke.

I beg to call your attention to the disorderly mob which nightly parade the

Mile End Road and its vicinity singing some rude doggerel verses which doubtless they please to style hymns. There must be, surely, someone in authority who has power to put a stop to such profanity and vulgarity.[25]

With the backing of the highest authority in heaven, however, the work in East London continued its forward march.

In October of 1868 the first edition of *The East London Evangelist* was published. William dedicated the magazine to

> all those who, obedient to the Master's command, are simply, lovingly, and strenuously seeking to rescue souls from everlasting burnings, through His own precious blood, who, believing in the promise of the Father, are seeking with strong cries and tears for a mighty outpouring of the Holy Ghost to stem the rising tide of error and superstition, break up the slumbers of the professing church, arrest the attention of a dying world, and clothe the religion of Jesus with its primitive simplicity, fervor, and energy.[26]

The magazine was published monthly and sold for a penny. It communicated the progress of the mission and contained teaching, direction, and encouragement from both William and Catherine.

The motto on the cover of *The East London Evangelist* was Acts 11:21: "And the hand of the Lord was with them: and a great number believed, and turned unto the Lord." Typical of the dramatic conversions taking place in the meetings was the story of John Allen. Jack, as he was known, was a drunken coal porter whose foreman had been converted a few weeks earlier. He refused to listen as his boss told him about Jesus and wouldn't go near a meeting until dared to do so. A mission worker told his story:

> When Jack came in with trousers-knee patched, coat elbows torn, the top buttons of his trousers undone, and a belt round his waist, his face and hands all black with coal dust, he looked indeed an outcast.
>
> At the close of the meeting, knowing how deeply he was convinced of sin, but finding him still unwilling to come out to the penitent-form, they "mobbed him," as one who was present eloquently described the process. That is to say, twenty or thirty men and women of God knelt all around him where he sat near the door, and began to plead with God for his salvation. How thoroughly natural for a gang of converted roughs to mob anybody they wanted to see converted!
>
> After a long time spent in prayer, he began to groan and bellow like a bullock for mercy himself, and this continued for about twenty minutes.

He then sprang to his feet, and stretching out his long arms he cried, with glaring eyes, "I do believe! I do believe! The blood of Jesus cleanses me from all sin!"[27]

Jack became an anointed evangelist for the mission, personally leading over two hundred sailors to Jesus. "For him," wrote William some time later, "to stand and say 'Look at me!' was an argument neither skeptics nor devils could answer."[28]

Christmas Day of 1868 was another turning point for the Booths and their ministry. Their work among the East-Enders was into its third year. Things were progressing well, many souls were being touched and saved, but neither William nor Catherine could have imagined the army of followers that would later march under their banner, taking England and the world by storm. All they knew was the desperation of the thousands of men and women living in poverty—poverty of body and soul.

The children woke early, and the house was filled with all the excitement of Christmas. Catherine stayed home with her young family while William walked the eight miles from Hammersmith to Whitechapel to conduct the morning service. He had become well accustomed to the sights and sounds of the slums, but as he made his way home after the meeting, the hopelessness and degradation of the East-End streets pierced his heart with renewed power.

The stench of the slums penetrated his nostrils as his eyes took in the magnitude of human suffering and depravity that threatened to overwhelm him. Men and women, already reeling from the effects of alcohol, staggered along the dirty streets. Children clothed in rags shuffled through the garbage that spilled out from the alleys, hoping to find a discarded morsel of food. Some as young as five wandered about in a drunken stupor and appeared to be near starvation. William tried desperately to rid himself of the hellish sounds, sights, and smells as he reached the warm sanctuary of his Gore Road home. But his heart was broken.

Although they struggled financially, the family Christmas celebrations were memorable, with a special feast, joyful singing, and much laughter. This year, however, was different. As he joined in with the children's games, William's mind was haunted by the images of the streets. Finally he could bear it no longer and, pacing the floor, he exclaimed, "I'll never spend another Christmas Day like this again. The poor have nothing but the public house, nothing but the public house!"[29]

The compassion in his heart for the poor in London's East End compelled him to action. They could no more turn away from the practical needs of the people than they could sit on the bank of a river and watch a drowning child gasp for breath. True to his word, the following Christmas the Booths and others prepared three hundred Christmas dinners, which they distributed to starving families, warming the hearts of many.

These compassion ministries that developed naturally alongside William's evangelistic work were extremely costly and at times had to be scaled down for lack of funds. This was always the last resort. "I am almost worn out," William wrote in one appeal. "People are starving in Poplar. It is impossible to visit them without the means of relieving them. . . . I had thought of giving up the soup kitchen, but . . . the soup and bread are all that many poor creatures have to eat the day through."[30]

Rather than close down the soup kitchen, however, William started up a Food-for-the-Million shop, one of five that he established in the East London slums by 1872. The aim of the shops was to provide the poor with hot soup, day and night, and a three-course dinner for sixpence. The management of these shops was given into young Bramwell's hands. Rising as early as three o'clock in the morning, the dedicated teenager would traipse the four miles to Covent Gardens Market with a barrow to beg for discarded vegetables and to buy a few sacks of bones. The administration of the shops kept him busy, but they never paid their way. The food was too cheap, and some of the managers were dishonest. William was unable to spare any time to help Bramwell, and the shops were eventually closed down. The original soup kitchen was sold. For a time the lack of funds was so severe that people needing help had to be referred to the Charity Organization Society.

While welfare work had proved to be costly and difficult to administer, the Booths and their workers could not escape the burden in their hearts to provide practical assistance for the poor. They could not separate body from soul as they ministered salvation to the lost. William and Catherine did not set out to build an organization that provided welfare services. Each work of welfare began as they came face-to-face with situations of overwhelming need. As William stated, "All the social activity of the Army is the outcome of the spiritual life of its members. All social service must be based on the spiritual, or it will amount to little in the end."[31]

Reflecting on their early attempts at social work, William later said,

Our social operations are the natural outcome of Salvationism, or, I might say, of Christianity as instituted, described, proclaimed and exemplified in the life, teaching and sacrifice of Jesus Christ. Social work, in the spirit and practice which it has assumed with us, has harmonized with my own personal ideas of true religion from the hour I promised obedience to the commands of God. . . . All this time, nevertheless, I felt, and often keenly felt, that there surely must be some way by which, without any evil consequences, I could legitimately fulfil the cravings of my own heart, as well as comply with the commands of my Lord, who had expressly told me that I was to feed the hungry, clothe the naked, care for the sick, and visit the prisoners. For a long time, however, I failed to see how this work could be done in any organized or extensive manner.

Gradually, however, the way opened, and opened largely as a result of our determination to make the godless crowds hear the message of salvation. In the very earliest days of the Army, therefore, in order to reach the people whom we could not reach by any other means, we gave the hungry wretches a meal, and then talked to them about God and eternity. Then came the gradual unfolding of our social methods.[32]

Each new venture unfolded as a result of a simple step of obedience to God.

The Booths' earlier decision to refuse to allow their work to be limited to East London was soon justified as the mission pushed beyond its geographical boundaries. When stations were opened by request in Croyden in July of 1869 and in Edinborough a month later, the East London Christian Mission became simply The Christian Mission. Evangelists were sent to conduct meetings in the new stations. As Catherine traveled the country conducting meetings and campaigns, the opportunities for expansion grew even more. By the end of 1869 three more stations had opened in Bow Common, Old Ford, and Canning Town.

With the Sunday congregations in East London alone now reaching eight thousand people, a central hall was needed. In 1870 the mission purchased a large market building on Whitechapel Road and fitted it out for their purposes. It contained a spacious meeting hall, classrooms, a soup kitchen, and a bookshop. The building, called The People's Mission Hall, was opened on April 10, 1870 (William's forty-first birthday), with a packed congregation and 150 seekers responding to the gospel. Catherine preached on the opening day, as William had been taken ill with what was later discovered to be typhoid fever.

The organizational structure of the mission had developed by necessity as the work grew. At first The Christian Mission was centralized, with each individual station coming under the central administration in East London.

While laid out with typhoid fever for three months in 1870, William established the mission's first constitution, setting out their beliefs and doctrines. In essence he formulated the constitution along the lines of the only church structure he had known. He was named general superintendent of the mission, and he had authority over all decisions apart from those made at the annual conference, the first of which was held in November of 1870. Of the thirty-four members of conference, six were women. The constitution clearly stated that, equally with men, women would be involved in both the work and government of the mission.

While William recovered from the fever, Catherine took charge. As she visited and preached in the different stations, her heart went out to the people—men, women, and children whom God entrusted to her care. She took them on as if they were her own flesh and blood and, in a very real sense, became to them a mother. As W. T. Stead, a close family friend and one of her biographers, said,

> These converts, whom, until they had come within range of her voice, she had never seen, were straightaway adopted into her family. As members of that family they were entitled to carry to her—their mother—all their troubles, difficulties, doubts, and temptations.[33]

The pressure on Catherine was enormous as she endeavored to lead the mission, visit and preach at various stations, and conduct her own campaigns. William returned to work after three months, but it was far too soon. He suffered bouts of illness throughout 1871, and by Easter of 1872 had to pull back again. Doctors diagnosed a nervous breakdown; the cause was severe stress from being overworked. One proposed a year's complete rest, while another suggested he might never recover enough to return to his work. As Catherine stood before the Easter Sunday congregation gathered in The People's Hall, she declared that even if William were to die, the mission must continue.

With eight children of her own, a sick husband, and a busy ministry to oversee, it would seem Catherine had time for little else. Yet, as Bramwell later recalled, when an opportunity to care for yet another individual came her way, she did not refuse.

> Near my father's house on the corner of Victoria Park there was a little street of workmen's houses. . . . In the course of my early work in the Mission I frequently visited in this street, especially the sick, which as a lad I

was rather fond of doing. In one of these houses I came across the wife of one of our own people, belonging to the Society in Bethnal Green. The man was a foreman in a cardboard box factory in the City. They had numerous family, and the wife who had lately given birth to another child, was very ill. It was soon evident that she was sick unto death. . . . Her last request to me was that I would take charge of her baby—the latest of her family. Perhaps not altogether realizing what I was undertaking, I promised that I would.

Naturally I turned to my mother for assistance, and after a certain amount of negotiation the little boy—Harry, we called him—was brought into our home and placed under the care of my sister Emma . . . who was at the time in delicate health, and who found in the training of this baby delightful occupation. The child grew and prospered and gave early evidence of being a child of God. While still in his teens he developed a singular gift for caring for the sick.[34]

Thus in 1873 the Booths' ninth child came into their home, and Harry, who it appears may also have gone by the nickname of "Georgie Booth," grew up as one of their own.

With the reigns of leadership once more in Catherine's hands, the unity of heart and purpose that Catherine and William had labored to attain during their engagement came into play, more so than ever. Although William was struck down by sickness, the uncertainty of his recovery did not threaten the future of the mission. With help and support from sixteen-year-old Bramwell, Catherine was able to lead their people, courageously continuing the forward movement of the work.

The huge workload meant she was no longer able to conduct her own meetings, and this added to the financial burden they carried as a family. The difficulties she faced were most often carried alone, but they are portrayed a little in a letter in *The Christian Mission Magazine*:

I have found my position trying and arduous in the extreme since my dear husband was compelled to leave us; but the Lord has wonderfully strengthened me. . . . It would be too much to say that the work has not suffered; but . . . all our workers have been kept in unity and love and the usual services have been sustained without diminution. It is our one absorbing desire the work should grow, whatever instrument should be laid aside. We want more of the Holy Ghost. Our difficulties in this East London you cannot possibly estimate unless you were in the fight. It seems sometimes so hopeless a task to make any great inroads on this mass of wickedness that we are tempted to despond.[35]

Yet even in the most difficult of circumstances, the Booths' faith in God did not waver. In a letter to Bramwell at this time, William wrote,

> Bless you for all your thoughtfulness for me and all the burden you have borne. . . . Now is the time for us to trust. We will do our duty and leave events calmly to God. . . . I have confidence in God. Look up. Rest and hope in infinite Love.[36]

To William and Catherine, faith and obedience always went hand in hand.

In October of 1872, when William resumed leadership of the mission, he was aware that all was not well among his people. By this stage the mission had decentralized, with stations and districts coming under the command of their own superintendents. No new stations had opened during 1871 and 1872; furthermore, some stations were experiencing difficult times. The work at Bow Common was struggling, division among leadership was evident in Croyden, stations at Tunbridge Wells and Brighton had closed when their evangelists left, and the progress in some other stations was far from healthy.

William knew from experience the demands upon the leaders of the mission stations. He encouraged them to persevere and, where necessary, he brought in new leaders. He knew only too well that not all his people were ready for the responsibilities of leadership. He wrote,

> It is one thing to attract hundreds of people to witness some strange and unusual religious service; it is another and a very different thing to drag men and women out from among all their associates and associations to commence a new life, and to maintain that life steadfastly. . . . Who can wonder if hearts grow weary and hands hang down—if even desertions take place in the midst of such a conflict?[37]

With all this in mind, William made an honest assessment of the mission and had to admit that the once vibrant work was now in danger of stagnation.

Although they pressed on and some advances were made, by 1875 it was clear to William that his workers' enthusiasm and passion for souls were being slowly suffocated by the form of government adopted under their constitution. Men and women who had committed their lives to this endeavor were being weighed down and held back by endless meetings and discussions. Meeting after meeting filled page after page with resolution after resolution. People began to get bogged down with detail at the expense of important tasks at hand. Mission leaders became committee members instead of active workers. Committees had been established for every conceivable issue, from distributing tracts to sharing testimonies in public meetings.

George Railton, a dynamic twenty-four-year-old evangelist who had begun working as William's private secretary in 1873, described rather cynically the situation that now existed within the mission.

> The poor convert who had been brought to the penitent-form two months since must appear trembling before an elders' meeting. If he ventured to aspire to public speaking he must pass another examination before the exhorters' meeting. Did he wish to distribute tracts, he must see the tract committee. . . . If the tract distributor came across cases of extreme need, then he must apply to another committee for the help to the extent of a shilling or two which he might be allowed to give. By-and-by would come round the solemn day for the local preachers' and quarterly meetings. . . . O those elders' meetings . . . prolonged till midnight many a time![38]

In 1876, William reviewed the year and came to this conclusion:

> In many of the old stations we appear, from the returns, to have had something like stagnation during the year. We have only got a net increase of two hundred members. . . . I should conclude I was out of my place if I spent twelve months at a place and did not leave it tangibly, unmistakably, visibly better than I found it.[39]

Clear and direct leadership was required from William at this critical time of growth and change. The slow, tedious process of government by conference was not only restricting the growth and expansion of the mission, it was threatening to destroy its life altogether.

One by one, William's most fervent evangelists and workers voiced their protests. "We gave up our lives to work under you and those you should appoint, rather than under one another,"[40] Railton declared. "You tell us what to do and we will do it," said another. "I can't see the good of a lot of talk, with one wanting one thing and one another."[41]

William did not know what to do. He sensed God had greater plans for the mission, but at this stage he had no clear direction. Together with Catherine, he faced the difficulty of pioneering a new work of God, having no pattern or model to follow. It was clear that a new wineskin was required for their labors among the poor, but as to its nature they were still uncertain. One thing was clear: Unless William had direct leadership of the mission, it would never keep up with the opportunities for expansion.

During 1876, to add to the difficulties they faced as a mission, both William and Catherine were laid out again with sickness. Catherine was diagnosed with angina pectoris[42] and William suffered a relapsing stomach fever. Smallpox struck the Booth household, with thirteen-year-old Lucy, George Railton,

An early Army family

and the maid, Mary Kirton, all being infected. The dreaded disease had five years earlier left Marian with permanently impaired sight and considerable disfigurement. Now it claimed the life of the Booths' beloved maid. Mary, the first to contract the dreaded disease, had insisted on being treated in the hospital and eventually passed away. In the midst of this personal suffering and hardship, William was forced to rest. Now he further sought the Lord for direction for the mission.

Finally, after great consideration and prayer, William decided to act. In January of 1877 he called a meeting for all mission leaders and evangelists to discuss the constitution and future of the organization. The time was ripe for change. It was agreed unanimously that the mission had outgrown the committee style of government and that it should come under the direct authority of General Superintendent William Booth. They concluded that theirs was a war and as such, the annual conference should be a council of war, not a legislative assembly.

Although it did not yet officially carry the title of The Salvation Army, the mission naturally adopted a military style of government under William's direct leadership and the officers appointed by him. With the restraint of endless meetings suddenly lifted and the vision and purpose of the mission clearly in the hands of its leader, the stagnating organization came to life. Renewed passion pulsed through the stations as evangelists and workers found new liberty to give their all for the salvation of souls.

In June of 1877 at the annual conference, William freely acknowledged his blame in allowing the mission to drift in the wrong direction. The conference committee was abandoned, and William accepted responsibility for the appointment of leaders.

> There is a question of confidence as between you and me, and if you can't trust me it is of no use for us to attempt to work together. Confidence in God and in me are absolutely indispensable both now and ever afterwards.[43]

He explained his desire for their annual conference to become a council of war, saying,

> The Commander in chief calls the principal officers around him to receive information and counsel from all. Each brings his facts and expresses his judgment as to what is necessary and important to do, and then in view of all this he resolves upon a program of operation. This is our council of war. We are here to consider practical questions and how we can best deal with them. To receive reinforcements and station our army, and above all we are here to help each other's souls, to cry together to the Living God for the rebaptism of the Holy Ghost.[44]

The changes, though radical, were accepted with little serious opposition. A few evangelists who were not happy with the new form of government were encouraged to leave, and they were helped to find a place of service elsewhere.

Finally, at the War Congress in August of 1878, the changes were legalized when the new deed of constitution was adopted. The general, as William had become known, stood to address his leaders:

> We are sent to war. We are not sent to minister to a congregation and be content if we keep things going. We are sent to make war . . . and to stop short of nothing but the subjugation of the world to the sway of the Lord Jesus. We must bear that in mind in all our plans . . . our aim is to put down the kingdom of the devil. . . . This mission is going to be what its officers make it.[45]

With its leadership clearly established, its vision and strategy defined, and the war for souls ever in its sights, The Christian Mission had become an army of Salvationists. A change of name was the natural completion of this God-ordained process.

Early in May of 1878 William had been adding his final touches to the annual report. The title page was headed: "The Christian Mission under the superintendence of the Rev. William Booth is a Volunteer Army recruited from amongst the multitudes who are without God and without hope in the world."[46] He called Railton and Bramwell to his room and asked Railton to read the document aloud. When Bramwell protested over the term "Volunteer Army," William rose to his feet, strode across the room, and took the pen from Railton's hand. Decisively, he crossed out "volunteer" and replaced it with "salvation." As he did, both Bramwell and Railton leaped to their feet and declared simultaneously, "Thank God for that!"[47] Over the next few months The Christian Mission gradually adopted the title The Salvation Army.

Neither William nor Catherine had set out to build an army; they simply followed the call of God on their lives, obeying Him with every step. William summed up this process when he said,

> We tried many plans. . . . Gradually the Movement took more of the military form, and finding, as we looked upon it . . . that God in His good providence had led us unwittingly, so to speak, to make an army, we called it an army, and seeing that it was an army organized for the deliverance of mankind from sin, and the power of the devil, we called it an army of deliverance, an army of salvation—The Salvation Army.[48]

The organization that had begun thirteen years earlier had come of age. The name was new, the governmental structure was revolutionary, and the methods were considered outlandish, but as William wrote in 1879, their primary purpose remained the same.

> We are a salvation people—this is our specialty—getting people saved and keeping them saved, and then getting somebody else saved. . . . Look at this. Clear your vision. Halt, stand still and afresh and more fully apprehend and comprehend your calling. You are to be a worker together with God for the salvation of your fellow men. What is the business of your life? Not merely to save your soul and make yourself meet for Paradise? . . . No, you are to be a redeemer, a savior, a copy of Jesus Christ Himself. So consecrate every awakened power to the great end of saving them.

> Rescue the perishing. There they are all around you everywhere,

crowds upon crowds, multitudes. Be skillful. Improve yourself. Study your business.

Be self-sacrificing. Remember the Master. What you lose for His sake, and for the sake of the poor souls for whom He died, you shall find again. Stick to it. Having put your hand to the salvation plough, don't look behind you.[49]

CHAPTER 7

To Gain, Train

PREPARING A SOLID FOUNDATION IN
THEIR CHILDREN AND RECRUITS (1878–1886)

A profound dislike for merely absorbing knowledge and a strong compulsion to learn by doing is one of the most reliable signs of genius.

—SYLVIA NASAR, *A Beautiful Mind*

Make your will, pack your box, kiss your girl, be ready in a week."[1] The general's orders were clear. The level of commitment required of his workers was unmistakable—radical obedience was essential. Nothing more and certainly nothing less. Only godly go-ahead daredevils were equal to the call.

With the restraints of bureaucracy lifted from their lives, William's fiery followers were free to wage war—the war of salvation. The Army swept across England, setting the nation ablaze. The results were incredible: In the last six months of 1878 alone, the number of stations increased from 50 to 81, and the number of evangelists working for the Army rose from 88 to 127! Speaking to his followers at the end of this year of transition, William said,

> The quality of the work has improved as much as the quantity during the year. We have never had to rejoice over such single-eyed, simple-hearted devotion on the part of the workers and never over such mighty conquests of the very choicest servants of the wicked one.[2]

Typical of these evangelists was "God's chimney sweep," Elijah Cadman. His working life had begun when, as a six-year-old, he answered a "Wanted—

Small Boys for Narrow Flues" advertisement and was immediately put to work. The last child in a family of five, unusually small and with no education, Elijah was well suited to such a task.

Life for young Elijah had been extremely tough. As a boy, he was rarely sober, often found in a drunken state, crumpled in the corner of a rat-infested alley. By the time he reached the age of seventeen, he was proud to declare, "I can fight like a devil and drink like a fish." God, however, had a different road for Elijah to travel.

One December day he was watching a public hanging at Warwick. As the execution was carried out, Elijah's friend pointed to the dangling bodies and quipped, "That's what you'll come to, 'Lijah, one day!" The sudden realization of his own guilt was so shocking that he immediately gave up drinking and fighting. He began going from village to village, ringing a town crier's bell in front of each inn until a crowd gathered. "This is to give notice, sixty thousand people are lost," he would bawl. "Lost! Lost! Lost! Lost every year through the cursed drink. Mr. Cadman, the 'Sober Sweep from Rugby,' will give an account of his drinking experiences! Come and hear him! Come and hear him!"[3]

Some years later, at the age of twenty-one, Cadman surrendered his life to Christ as he listened to a street-preacher. In 1876 his life was revolutionized when he heard William Booth powerfully preach the message of the gospel. He immediately laid down his life, took up his cross, and joined the growing army of volunteers. William was quick to recognize the potential preacher and evangelist in Cadman. He looked beyond his past into his future as a child of God. It wasn't long before Cadman and his wife sold their chimney-sweep business, their home, and other possessions and moved to Hackney in the east of the city to take charge of the work there. Later that year he reported, "We are making a powerful attack on the devil's kingdom. . . . King Jesus is our great Commander. . . . We have an army here that will face the world, the flesh, and the devil."[4]

In 1877 Cadman was sent to "open fire" on Whitby, a small fishing village in Yorkshire. William was determined to prevent any of the stations from becoming a community of settled, contented Christians enjoying their favorite preacher. Evangelists were sent out to these new areas for a maximum period of six months to begin the work and to see the new converts established in the faith. Whitby's people were spiritually dead, and Cadman declared as he departed, "By the help of God, I'm going to wake them up."[5]

Soon after, monster posters began appearing in the Whitby streets, declaring war and calling for two thousand men and women to join the Army in the fight against the devil's kingdom. When the general, as Cadman had dubbed William, visited the station one month later, some three thousand followers had been won in the salvation war!

The results from the other workers were just as impressive. In March of 1878, two young girls, one hardly able to write, the other barely nineteen years old, were sent to begin

Two Invercargill Army ladies

the work in the Tyne district. They advertised their arrival as "Two Hallelujah Lasses" and held open-air meetings inviting people to hear them preach. They had virtually no money, no contacts within the towns they visited, and no introduction. Yet within twelve months they had planted twenty-two stations, with forty-seven officers and over three thousand members. In one area, their impact among the drunkards was so great that the pub owners tried to bribe them with three hundred pounds to move elsewhere. The crime rate in the same town dropped by half.

When they left one area, the Darlington and Richmond *Herald* reported,

> It was incredible that two girls without friends, without learning, without great gifts of eloquence, without any of the elaborate machinery which the church regards as almost indispensable for its operations . . . should raise out of the gutter and dram shop[6] a vigorous working church. . . . The Bishop of Durham could not do it! All the ministers of the town could not do it! . . . It is cheering beyond expression to see demonstrated once more the power of a sublime thought to transform the hearts and revolutionize the minds of men, that what reason, self-interest, prudence, patriotism, the exhortation of the benevolent, and the entreaties of friends utterly failed to effect has been effected before our eyes again and again by the simple proclamation of the simple Gospel.[7]

Such was the fire and passion of the Army's seasoned soldiers. They were warriors of whom it could be said, "They can suffer, they can die, but they cannot flinch; they will not yield." They would dare anything and risk everything to reach the lost.

The uncompromising nature of the Booths' personal obedience and commitment was foundational to the style and structure of the organization that formed around them. Although they did not initially set out to build an army, its militant style developed naturally under their leadership and in the climate of the day.

The nineteenth century was a militant era itself, impacted by the American Civil War and the Russo-Turkish Crimean War. The well-known hymn "Onward Christian Soldiers" was released to the world in 1865, the year that marked the beginning of the Booths' work in East London. These were the glorious days of the great British Empire, and the rank structure of Queen Victoria's soldiers was easily adopted by The Salvation Army.

The militant style developed rapidly, and by 1878, when the mission was declared to be The Salvation Army, the name had already woven itself into the fabric of the organization. As Catherine once stated:

> We are an army. We grew into one, and then we found it out, and called ourselves one. Every soldier of this Army is pledged to carry the standard of the Cross into every part of the world, as far as he has opportunity. Our motto is "The World for Jesus."[8]

The disciplined structure of the military soon permeated every aspect of this holy army. Service titles such as general, commanding officer, captain, soldier, and cadet were adopted. Salvationists began to speak of prayer as "knee-drill," of offering envelopes as "cartridges" that must be "fired" regularly, and of their local mission base as the "corps," each of which had its own "citadel" or "fort."[9]

No army could be complete without a banner, and these were soon fashioned to reinforce the identity of each outreach. Catherine presented the very first Army flag to the Coventry Corps in 1878. The flag was red, referring to the saving blood of Christ, bordered in blue as a symbol of purity and a holy life. It was inscribed with the words "Blood and Fire" on a central yellow sun to denote the power of the blood of Christ and the fire of the Holy Spirit— the two vital elements of the life and work of Salvationists.

As she presented the flag to each new corps across England, Catherine declared,

The flag is a symbol, first of our devotion to our great Captain in heaven and to the great purpose for which He came down and shed His blood, that He might redeem men and women from sin and death and hell! Secondly, this flag is emblematical of our faithfulness to our great trust. Jesus only wants faithful soldiers in order to win the heathen for his inheritance and the uttermost parts of the earth for His possession. May God help us to be faithful . . . faithful to conscience, to principles, to man and to God. This flag is also an emblem of victory! In this war of ours victory is sure. . . . But by what power is this victory going to be achieved? By fire! The Holy Ghost![10]

And further, "Let all go that occupies the room which the Holy Ghost might fill in your souls. . . . Charge on the hosts of hell and see whether they will not turn and flee!"[11]

An early Salvation Army uniform.

With the growing military structure came the suggestion of a uniform. From delivery boys to postmen, many people of the Victorian era wore their own distinctive uniforms. It was not long before the Salvation soldiers began to create a uniform of their own. The first Salvationists wore a brass "S" on their lapels. Others adopted blue-and-red armlets inscribed with "The Salvation Army." Eventually the uniform evolved into the red Guernsey with a yellow "Salvation Army" on it. Badges, hats, bonnets, and handkerchiefs were also adopted as part of the dress code. The uniforms made a visual statement of commitment and courage and were proudly worn by all.

The Army grew so rapidly that it soon became impossible for the oversight of the work to occur effectively from headquarters. In 1880 the work across England was divided into seven divisions, and "majors" were appointed to share the responsibility of oversight. This change was made amid some doubt and fear of creating a system of rank. William continually emphasized that unity of direction and submission to leadership were essential to the growth and expansion of the Army.

In January of 1881 headquarters was departmentalized, with Bramwell assigned chief of staff. Later that year, Army headquarters moved to a larger, more central building on Queen Victoria Street in London.

In 1882 the first Articles of War were introduced. This document included a brief statement of Christian doctrine as well as a pledge to maintain Christian conduct and further the work of the Army. It had to be signed by all recruits before enrollment. Abstinence from alcohol also became a condition, and those who could not fully agree to this or other stipulations withdrew.

With the adoption of these military practices came the all-too-familiar criticism that has been leveled so lavishly at those who choose to forsake all to serve and follow Christ. William was touted as being legalistic and exerting too much control over his people. To such critics he had only one answer: He could not lead the rapidly growing Salvation Army without such a system, and they had experienced firsthand the stifling effects of committee-style leadership. He emphatically declared, "Had the children of Israel been managed by a committee they would never have crossed the Red Sea."[12]

Both William and Catherine knew that the secret of the successful expansion of the movement was at least partly due to the strict structure and management of the troops. Though the rules seemed hard, they ensured that those

Dunedin's inaugural Salvation Army congress, Christmas, 1883

who stayed were aware of the cost, committed to the cause, and prepared to do battle in order to triumph over every obstacle and opposition to their passion of spreading the gospel. The Army's volunteer workers were just that—volunteers. They were under no misapprehension of the level of commitment required of them. People were never forced to join the Army and comply with the disciplined lifestyle—those who chose to follow God in this way were committed because of their devotion to God and their desire to obey Him, not because of the pressure or persuasion of man. Neither were they ever forced to stay; many of those who chose to leave to work in different fields remained good friends with the Army.

William was always prepared to adopt any measure that advanced their cause of the salvation of humankind. As the Army took ground across England, a new sound accompanied them. Their general was well before his time when he led his people to adopt popular music into worship services. However, the instigation of the first Salvation Army band was completely unplanned.

Enthusiasm was the hallmark of young and old in the early Salvation Bands.

It happened in 1878 when William was offered the service of William Fry and his three sons to act as bodyguards during open-air work in Salisbury. Almost as an afterthought they took their brass instruments along with them to the marketplace. Fry was the choir and orchestra leader of the local Methodist church. William agreed to their offer to play, much to the horror of the local evangelist, who fumed his way through the first two songs—until he noticed the enthusiastic participation of the crowd that gathered. The little group accompanied the singing, and the Army's first brass band was born.

What a way to draw a crowd! Tambourines, "dustman's bells" (dustbin lids), hunting horns, and banjos soon accompanied the rowdy "music" produced by the primitive brass instruments. The lack of musical finesse and the crude instruments were more than compensated for by the contagious enthusiasm and energy of the musicians.

The Invercargill Salvation Army Band

A controversial step was taken in 1882 when the general consented to the adaptation of hit tunes into the Salvation Army repertoire. Although doubtful at first, he began to realize the ease with which the unchurched would sing the words of songs that went with a familiar popular tune. The way ahead was sealed one evening as he heard a converted sailor leading the singing in a Worcester theatre. The catchy tune seemed familiar to William, who loved to sing, and he caught hold of a passing officer, inquiring, "That's a fine song. What tune is that?"

The officer shook his head disapprovingly. "General, that's a dreadful tune. Don't you know what it is? That's 'Champagne Charlie Is My Name.' " William stood silently for a moment, listening as the congregation finished the song with great gusto. Finally he turned to Bramwell and concluded emphatically, "That's settled it. Why should the devil have all the best tunes?"[13] From that moment, William encouraged the use of secular sounds to reach the unchurched masses. "Soul saving music is music for me,"[14] he declared as he explained his decision to the troops.

The Army embraced their new weapon with great enthusiasm. Within a year of the commencement of the musical department, there were four hundred Salvation Army bands pumping out a myriad of hit songs.

For all its innovation and initiative, the Booths and their holy Army knew that only Jesus could change the hearts of people. While they encouraged their troops to adapt the modes and means by which they related the gospel, they were unyielding when it came to the content of the gospel message. The message of the Cross was never to be compromised. Catherine explained their stand in a lecture given to a packed audience in 1880.

> When my dear husband resigned his position as an ordinary minister, and gave himself to evangelistic work, he saw that the churches had gone above the heads of the common people. . . . Years after this when he took his stand in the East of London, it flashed upon him, as an inspiration from heaven, that if they were to be reached it must be by people of their own class, who would go after them in their own resorts, who would speak to them in a language they understood, and reach them by measures suited to their tastes. . . . I speak of adaptation . . . with respect to modes and measures of bringing the Gospel to bear on the people. . . . I teach no adaptation of the Gospel. I will keep the blessed Gospel whole, as it is.[15]

While the majority of the growing numbers of volunteers and evangelists had been converted at Army meetings, others came from outside the organization. Stirred by Booth's passion for the souls of men, they, too, had chosen to sacrifice all in order to bring salvation to those who struggled hopelessly under the oppressive conditions of nineteenth-century England. Perhaps the attitude that drew them is best summed up in something William published in *The War Cry* in early 1885:

> What are you living for? What is the deep secret purpose that controls

and fashions your existence? What do you eat and drink for? What is the end of your marrying and giving in marriage—your money-making and toilings and plannings? Is it the salvation of souls, the overthrow of the kingdom of evil, and the setting up of the Kingdom of God? Have you the assurance that the ruling passion of your life is the same as that which brought Christ to the manger, led Him to fight the foul fiend of Hell in the wilderness, bore Him onward on the back of suffering and tears and ignominy and shame, sustained Him in drinking the cup of anguish and enduring the baptism of blood, bore Him through Gethsemane, nailed Him to the Cross of Calvary, and enabled Him in triumph to open the gate of the Kingdom? Is this what you are living for? If not, you may be religious—a very proper person amongst religionists—but I don't see how you can be a Christian.[16]

This was the measure the new recruits to the Army used to determine their "Christian" responsibilities and actions—and by relying entirely on the grace of God and the empowerment of the Holy Spirit, they seemed miraculously to measure up. Many of the officers were as young as seventeen and eighteen years of age, yet they commanded corps of hundreds of soldiers and successfully ministered to crowds of hostile and unruly people.

As the Booths forged ahead, leading the Army in its quest to evangelize the nations, the importance of training became more and more evident. Both

The Invercargill Corps gather for a picnic celebration, New Years Day, 1884

William and Catherine were convinced that the equipping of their workers was essential for the Army's ongoing success.

Training was already a hallmark of their own lives. Catherine, of course, had always loved studying, and although William had never been a good scholar in the intellectual sense, he had diligently applied himself when it came to learning things he felt would help him win the lost. As a young man, William had taken a keen interest in the lives and works of the men and women of God who had achieved any measure of success in the fight against evil. He learned all he could from those who forged ahead in the work of the Lord. Recognizing early God's evangelistic call on his life, he had hunted the world over to find those who were successful in winning souls. He studied their journeys and the messages they preached, striving to discover the principles and methods that had led to their success.

The Booths' strategy and thinking was greatly influenced by revivalists, including Wesley, Caughey, Finney, Marsden, and others. Intrigued by their faith and persistence, William and Catherine closely examined their methods and their messages, their achievements and their shortcomings. Reminiscing at the age of eighty, William was able to say,

> From the day of my conversion to God I have never read a biography, heard an address, or attended a meeting, without asking myself the question: "Is there anything here from which I can learn how better to fulfill my own mission in enforcing the claims of my Lord; and saving the souls of men?"[17]

For the Booths, life was for training and training was for life. As William led The Salvation Army into battle, he endeavored always to "learn how best to fight the enemies of God and man, bring them to submission, transform them into good soldiers of Jesus Christ, unite them for most effective actions, and lead them forth to combat with the foe."[18]

As parents, William and Catherine were fully aware of the importance of training their young family. When Catherine was still a teenager, she had recognized the awesome responsibility of the God-given influence of parents over their children. During their engagement she made parenthood a topic of discussion with William, and before they married they had agreed upon the importance of the training of children. Even when Catherine began her ministry of teaching and preaching, she did not neglect her responsibilities as a mother. She was convinced that the training of her young ones was of equal importance in the eyes of God to the work of the ministry.

Catherine always made sure that their commitment to the call did not in any way detract from their commitment to their family. She took it upon herself to make sure their home was one of love. She wisely understood that the primary element for a secure and happy home is complete harmony and love between husband and wife. Again, according to the principles they set out early in their marriage, William and Catherine never argued a matter in front of the children. They were open in the expression of their love and affection for each other, and their children were always secure in the atmosphere of their parents' love for each other and for God.

Financially the Booths were never well off, but this did not prevent Catherine from transforming the houses they occupied into warm and comfortable homes. In the early years, when they were involved in the traveling ministry, she carried with them a nursery carpet, which created for her young children an atmosphere of familiarity and home, regardless of where they were. She encouraged creativity and a fun-loving nature in each of her children. She made sure they always had plenty of toys and encouraged them to play together, enjoying all manner of games and activities. Their home, no matter how temporary or how humble, was always a haven of love, laughter, and joy.

The Booths' lives were totally dedicated to God and to the work to which they were called. It is easy to imagine their children feeling second in importance at times to the work of salvation. William and Catherine worked hard to prevent this. No matter how busy life became, Catherine always had time to talk with her children, and these times of sharing their hearts were treasured moments. Both Catherine and William endeavored to involve each child in the work of the kingdom; their home constantly bustled with life and activity and the children grew up in an atmosphere of genuine faith, sharing both the struggles and the rewards of that faith. On a daily basis they experienced God through the lives of their parents. Family prayer times were lively and passionate as the children learned to talk with God during times of need and moments of celebration.

The Booths' policy of never receiving financial support from Salvation Army funds meant they always lived very simply. As a result, the children had a great appreciation and awareness of the struggles faced by many poor families, but they also understood and experienced the wonderful provisions received through prayer. They rejoiced as a family when they saw firsthand how God supplied finances and resources, including dedicated and valued workers.

Great care was taken to incorporate the children into each aspect of the

Army's work. Their participation allowed them to grow personally in knowledge and experience of God from a very young age. As Evangeline once remarked, "My parents did not have to say a word to me about Christianity. I saw it in action."[19]

Catherine took upon herself most of the responsibility for the training of her children. Her views on the matter were very clear, no doubt shaped somewhat by her own mother's influence. When she taught Salvationists on the subject of training children, she opened her address with the solemn reminder, "Settle it in your minds that your child belongs absolutely to God, and not to you—that you are only stewards for God, holding your children to nurse them and train them for Him."[20] She herself had dedicated each of their children, and even their children's children, to God long before any of them were born. Catherine firmly believed this devotion of her children to God was essential if they were to follow after Him with their lives. From the moment of birth, each child became a recipient of her ceaseless prayers.

Portrait of Evangeline Booth, commonly known as Little Eva

In the Victorian era, education consisted almost entirely in the rote learning of factual information. Religious instruction was no different, with children encouraged to learn Bible passages and hymns by heart. Catherine despised such attempts at educating children about God. "This mere teaching," she said, "informing the head without interesting or influencing the heart, frequently drives children off from God and goodness, and makes them hate, instead of love, everything connected with religion."[21] She believed that this method of instruction, together with the hypocritical example of parents who said one thing in public and behaved the opposite in the home, caused many young people to harden their hearts toward God at an early age. Catherine was a firm believer in consistency in training children. "Mother," she once wrote in an instructional pamphlet, "if you want to train your child you must practice what you teach, and you must show him how to practice it also, and you must at all costs of trouble and care, see that he does it!"[22]

In training her children, Catherine recognized the importance of not only imparting knowledge but also training the heart. For this reason, she insisted on keeping her children at home and hired a governess to help with their studies. She had seen the negative effects of providing young people with a "good education" at the expense of good heart training. Apart from a few brief periods of time during which some of the children attended schools, all of their education was received under the watchful eye of their mother. She openly opposed the concept of sending children to school before their characters had been shaped and their principles formed. To do so, she believed, was to ask for trouble.

Her beliefs were confirmed by Bramwell's brief experience of preparatory school. He had won a place at the City of London School and was the youngest boy in his class. The ten-year-old bore the brunt of the boys' taunting comments and was immediately nicknamed "Holy Willie." Not content with their verbal abuse, his bullies took hold of him one day and bashed him repeatedly against a tree in an attempt to "bang religion out of him."[23] Bramwell staggered home, bruised and spitting blood. The lively young boy was stricken with pleurisy and rheumatic fever after his ordeal and took many months to recover. Catherine was furious with the educational system that allowed such behavior. "All the mischief comes from upsetting God's order," she declared, "cultivating the intellect at the expense of the heart; being at more pains to make our youth *clever* than to make them good!"[24]

Catherine believed in starting early, in molding children to be Christians from babyhood. She began to teach them about God while they were still toddlers. She recalled,

> I used to take my eldest boy on my knee from the time when he was about two years old and tell him the stories of the Old Testament in baby language, and adapted to baby comprehension, one at a time, so that he thoroughly drank them in, and also the moral lessons they were calculated to convey. When between three and four years old, I remember once going into the nursery, and finding him mounted on his rocking horse, in a high state of excitement, finishing the story of Joseph to his nurse and baby brother, showing them how Joseph galloped on his live "gee-gee," when he went to fetch his father to show him to Pharaoh.[25]

As her young family increased in number, she began to hold Sunday meetings for them at home. She believed Sunday should be a happy day, a day to take pleasure in God's goodness. Her meetings always began with a simple song and then a prayer that they all repeated aloud, sentence by sentence. She gave them a short lesson, always making sure it was interesting and fun for the children to hear. After the message they prayed together and sang some more. The children did not attend public services until they were old enough to take some interest in them.

"One of the worst signs of our times," Catherine believed, "is the little respect which children seem to have for their parents. There are numbers of boys and girls from twelve to seventeen years of age, over whom their parents have little or no control."[26] Catherine believed it was the responsibility of parents to nurture and develop the natural tendency toward obedience that exists within a young child. She was a firm believer in shaping the will of the child by enforcing obedience from a very young age.

"Begin soon enough," she encouraged other mothers. "That is the secret of success. There is a way of speaking to and handling an infant, compatible with the utmost love and tenderness, which teaches it that mother is not to be trifled with; that, although she loves and caresses, she is to be obeyed."[27] And again,

> Oh, mothers, if you love your children, begin early to exact obedience. Do not be afraid to use your authority. One would think to hear some parents talk of their relations with their children that they did not possess an iota of power over them. All they dare to do, seems to be to reason, to persuade, to coax. . . . What has God given you authority for, if He did not intend you to use it—if your child can do as well without it?[28]

The foundation of the obedience Catherine exacted from her children was never fear but love—love for God and love for their parents. Evangeline later shared her memories of her mother's discipline:

> She would never overlook disobedience, inconsideration of others—no matter who the others were—and never leave wrongdoing uncorrected. My mother believed that children should be convinced at an early age that most unpleasant consequences follow misbehavior. But our correction came to us always with expressions of her own sorrow and always of her love.[29]

Catherine encouraged parents to persevere in requiring obedience from their children, especially in the first battle of wills that occurs between a child and his parents. Of this moment she said,

> You must persevere. You must on no account give up. . . . If he con-
> quers you this time he will try harder next, and it will get more and more
> difficult. Almost all mothers mistake here; they give up because they will
> not inflict on themselves the pain of a struggle, forgetting that defeat now
> only ensures endless battles in the future.[30]

Catherine worked hard to shape and train each of her children, dealing with
each one on an individual basis.

Catherine had a deep love for all young people. Even before she was married, when she met a young girl or boy, she was compelled to wonder what
they would become, what they would achieve in life. She believed in encouraging children to follow after God from the time they were very young. She
knew from her own childhood experiences not to underestimate the dealings
of God in the hearts of her children while they were just toddlers.

Catherine's greatest concern was for her children's souls, and she set out
purposefully to win each of them to Christ. She once said,

> The great end of Christian training is to lead children to realize the fact
> that they belong to God, and are under a solemn obligation to do every-
> thing in a way which they think will please Him. Parents cannot begin too
> early, nor labor too continuously, to keep this fact before the minds of their
> children. . . . I am convinced that the Spirit of God works mightily on little
> children long before grown people think they are able to understand.[31]

The way in which Catherine believed she could best help God's work in
her children's hearts was determined long before any of them were born. During their engagement she had written to William on this subject, saying,

> It seems to me . . . error of a very serious nature is almost universally
> prevalent in Methodist teaching. It seems to be the first and most impor-
> tant and eternal duty to drill into the mind an idea of estrangement from
> God, a conviction of moral degeneracy and actual alienation. Now I con-
> ceive that in direct opposition to this mode, the first idea, the very foun-
> dation of religious training, should be to impress the young heart with a
> sense of God's fatherhood, His tenderness and love towards mankind gen-
> erally. The young soul should be drawn towards God, not repulsed from
> Him. . . . Let these two ideas, first God's fatherhood and love; second, the
> obligation arising out of this relationship to keep His commands, take pos-
> session of the mind of a child and they will produce a sense of moral

degeneracy far deeper and more influential than could be produced by any other means.[32]

Catherine believed, with the apostle Paul, that it is the kindness of God that leads a person to repentance.

The Booths' eldest son was only seven when he first sensed the conviction of God on his life. At the time Catherine and William were holding meetings in the circus tent in Cardiff, and after one of these meetings Catherine approached Bramwell as he sat in the congregation. "You are very unhappy," she said tenderly. "You know the reason?"

It was clear that God had been dealing with the young boy's heart. He was unhappy, and he knew the reason why. Yet when Catherine asked if he was ready to make a public decision to serve God, the answer was an immediate "No!" Bramwell described his mother's response. "She put her hands suddenly to her face and I can never forget my feelings on seeing the tears fall through them on to the sawdust beneath our feet. I knew what those tears represented. But I still said 'No!' "[33]

Bramwell, Booth's oldest son, was destined to follow in his father's footsteps.

Some months later, after a meeting in Walsall conducted specifically for children, Catherine was delighted when she discovered her eldest son kneeling among the crowd of penitents. A young man knelt by his side to counsel him. "He made me confess my wickedness," Bramwell recalled, "made me realize what a fearful thing it was to want my own way—it was going against the One who died for me."[34] Bramwell wept aloud as the Spirit wrought repentance in his tender heart. When his mother came to his side and prayed with him, he experienced the forgiveness of God and knew he had been saved.

Catherine believed strongly in child conversion, and she saw each of their nine children give their lives to God during childhood. She was also aware that such a step was the first of many that must be taken as the children grew to maturity. As a loving mother and a wise counselor, she continued to do all she could to encourage them to give themselves entirely to God.

Catherine's training of her children brought great reward. As all matured, they, like their parents, regarded the salvation of the world as their primary object in life. Each one took on a prominent role in the work of The Salvation Army. Bramwell began as a teenager to handle the administration and served faithfully, first as chief of staff and then as general after his father's death. Ballington and Herbert were involved in fieldwork and the training of cadets. Kate and Emma were also involved in cadet training and fieldwork in England, France, Switzerland, India, and the United States. Evangeline led the work in the United States for some time and later served as the Army's first female general. Lucy and Marian were intricately involved with the Army in England. The Booths' adopted son, Harry, went with Emma to India at the age of fifteen and became the first Salvation Army doctor there. He served there for thirty years and was posthumously awarded the Victoria Cross after he heroically died in 1919 as a medical officer attached to the Indian Army.[35] In each of their children, William and Catherine strove to reproduce those qualities necessary for service in The Salvation Army—character traits such as perseverance, sacrifice, hard work, and a compassion for the underprivileged.

William and Catherine, although good parents, were by no means perfect. William's schedule was constantly busy, and he did not always take time for his growing family. He sometimes allowed himself to become so absorbed in his work for God and so distracted by the pressures of ministry that he did not give his children the time and love of a father. In his weakness, he favored those of his children who worked the hardest and accomplished the most. Results impressed him. His children recalled him being most loving and encouraging toward them during their younger childhood years.

As leaders of their dedicated army of volunteers, the Booths realized early their responsibility to nurture and train others aside from their own natural children. Their Methodist upbringing had instilled in their hearts an acute awareness of the need to disciple new converts in a way that would see them grow to reach full maturity. They passed this concern on to their followers, and it became the duty of every officer to devote three hours each day to visiting converts.

Like their general, many of the Salvationists had made a simple start in life. They had little or no education and often no knowledge of the practical principles of health and hygiene. The Booths quickly discerned the need to instruct and train the new converts in these and other fundamentals of living. Education in the ways of raising a family, nutrition, hygiene, relationships, and being a good employee were deemed to be of great importance. Meetings were held every week for the purpose of teaching new believers on the issues of everyday living.

Catherine looked upon this area as her specialty; it was through her loving instruction of their converts that she was dubbed "The Army Mother," a title that remains to this day. As biographer Laura Petrie declared, "To decide whether William or Catherine Booth was the Founder of The Salvation Army is to venture on the speculation whether child derives its being from father or from mother. The Army was started, not on one motor, but on two."[36]

Catherine's greatest influence was made as she taught converts how to live as children of God. Her messages were always firmly grounded in Scripture and they came from a heart full of empathy and love. She once said,

> If anybody were to ask me the one most powerful quality for dealing with souls—that on which success in dealing depends more than on any other quality of the human heart and mind, I should say sympathy. That is the capacity to enter into the circumstances and difficulties and feelings of the individual with whom you are dealing. . . . Don't you think sinners feel? At the penitent-form, in the barracks, in the street? Don't they know when they have got a fellow-heart, a brother or sister, who really enters into their circumstances . . . who suffers with them? That is what sinners want.[37]

In Catherine, all people found such a heart.

Although both William and Catherine were compassionate toward the people they ministered to, neither could ever be accused of watering down the gospel message. Catherine once declared,

> You must preach God's justice and vengeance against sin as well as his love for the sinner. You must preach hell as well as heaven. You must let your Gospel match the intuitions of humanity or you may as well throw it into the sea, and thus save both trouble and money. A Gospel of love never matched anybody's soul. The great want in this day is truth that cuts—

convicting truth—truth that convicts and convinces the sinner, and pulls off the bandages from his eyes.[38]

In addition to the practical aspects of daily life, Catherine was committed to teaching their followers to live holy lives. Through her inspired instruction, Salvationists learned that "Jesus Christ Himself established in . . . the Bible, a standard, not only to be aimed at, but to be attained unto—a standard of victory over sin, the world, the flesh and the devil: real, living, reigning, triumphing Christianity!"[39] Explaining her teaching further, she said,

> We teach the old-fashioned Gospel of repentance, faith, and holiness, not daring to separate what God has joined together. . . . We teach that a man cannot be right with God while he is doing wrong to men—in short, that holiness means being saved from sin . . . and filled with love to God and man.[40]

Catherine was, of course, a gifted speaker, yet she knew that teaching alone could not change a heart; no one could ever be reformed through the education of the mind. As they ministered to sinners and new converts alike, William and Catherine always emphasized the work of the Holy Spirit. "There must be extraneous power brought into the soul," they believed. "God must come to man."[41] They witnessed time and again the remarkable transformation of the most sin-stained souls as the Spirit of God brought conviction of sin and repentance. "Everyone who deals with souls," Catherine once said, "should have a clear and definite understanding of the conditions on which alone God pardons and receives repenting sinners. These conditions always have been and ever must remain the same. . . . God's unalterable condition of pardon is the forsaking of evil."[42]

As the Army grew, it became impossible to communicate with the troops through meetings alone. The monthly publication *The East London Evangelist*, which had become *The Salvationist* soon after the mission reached beyond the borders of London, began to be distributed weekly as *The War Cry* and was a vital means of disseminating information to Salvationists across the world. Despite the numerous name changes along the way, these publications always held to the original intent set out for them in their first issue: to "clothe the religion of Jesus with its primitive simplicity, fervor, and energy."[43] *The War Cry* became a powerful tool for discipleship and for informing the troops of developments in The Salvation Army.

One of the most remarkable things about William and Catherine was the

"Joe the Turk" (See page 178.)

incredible volume of writing and documentation of their work that they did in an age when the only way to record a sermon was by hand. They produced manuals and guidelines on many practical aspects of life in addition to their newsletters, sermons, and correspondence. Though new outposts were often started with little financial support or manpower, those pioneering new stations did not lack for the experience of others who had done similar work—if they could only read!

As parents, William and Catherine had learned the vital lesson that effective training needed to be more than instruction. From the moment of their conversion, believers were therefore encouraged "to hear" and "to do." Opportunities were immediately provided for them to testify and serve in the Army. A sense of responsibility for the work of the gospel rested heavily on every believer.

Until 1880 no facilities existed for the formal training of cadets for leadership in The Salvation Army. The need for intensive leadership training became more and more apparent as the Army grew. When William and Catherine moved to a sixteen-room home in Clapton Common, their old family home in Hackney was turned into a training school for thirty women cadets under the leadership of daughter Emma. A year later a training home for men was opened, with son Ballington taking charge. In these early facilities the new cadets underwent a seven-week course, which was highly practical and extremely grueling. The prerequisites for those desiring to undergo officer training were "great stamina" and "faith."

Life in training was lived at a rapid pace, and by 1886, when the course was increased to six months, it was not uncommon for cadets to completely wear out a pair of boots before graduation. Their training was always hands-on. Preaching before abusive crowds, visiting and caring for the sick, preparing their own meager meals, and keeping the "barracks" in pristine condition were all part of the daily routine for the future officers.

The training focused initially on matters of the heart. When questioned about how they trained their officers, Catherine responded in the following way:

> We begin with the heart. . . . True, we receive no candidates but such as we have good reason, after careful enquiry, to believe are truly converted. Nevertheless, we find many of them are not sanctified; that is, not having fully renounced the flesh or the world, and not thoroughly given up to God . . . which we regard as indispensable to the fullness of the Holy Spirit and success in winning souls. . . .
>
> Not only is the daily lecture devoted to the most heart-searching truths . . . every cadet is seen privately, talked and prayed with, and counseled according to his or her individual necessities. . . . We take it to be a fundamental principle that if the soul is not right, the service cannot be right, and therefore we make the soul first and chief care. . . .
>
> The next point is to instruct the candidates in principles, discipline, and methods of The Army, through which they are to act upon the people. Not only is this done in theory in the lecture room, but they are led into actual contact with the ignorance, sins, and woes of the people.[44]

While studying the Bible and devouring Booth's manuals of orders and regulations and Salvation Army doctrines, the cadets' most powerful lessons were learned by experience. The second three months of training required future graduates to personally campaign in towns and villages around England. They were never shielded from the hard realities of leadership in the Army during these campaigns. Firsthand experience was gained of the nature and hardships of a field officer's life. They faced the fierce persecution of angry crowds, the tiring schedule of daily meetings and visitation, and the ceaseless financial burden of Army life.

Through the arduous cadetship, all were prepared for the hard work that lay ahead of them as officers. "I sentence you all to hard labor," William joked grimly to one passing-out parade, "for the rest of your natural lives."[45] The difficulties and persecution were so much a part of life for the Booths and their officers that they knew only those called and impelled by God would be able to go the distance.

All who came to William and Catherine to inquire about entering cadet training were left with no doubt as to the totality of the call. Catherine once spoke to a young woman seeking to become a recruit, asking,

> Have you thought what it means to cast in your lot with us? As time goes on you will probably see those you love much better than yourself or your own life pushed about or stoned or sent to prison. You will have to see them spoken evil of and written against in the newspapers. You must make up your mind to it all—to it all.[46]

Those who heard the call of God and answered by laying down their lives were thoroughly equipped for the task through the Army cadetship. Their leaders' passion for souls and total consecration to God were powerfully imparted to their spirits. As they prayed, served, studied, and sought after God, they were empowered from on high to fight in the battle for souls. Catherine once said,

> Christ's soldiers must be imbued with the spirit of war. Love to the King and concern of His interests must be the master passion of the soul. . . . If the hearts of the Christians of this generation were inspired with this spirit and set on winning the world for God, we should soon see the nations shaken to their center, and millions of souls translated into the Kingdom.[47]

By the time the first International Congress was held in London in June of 1886, twenty-six hundred men and women had passed through the training homes and been commissioned to serve in The Salvation Army among nineteen nations of the world.

It has been said that "the world knows little about its heroes." The Booths, however, were ones who recognized the hero potential in their converts. These were the men and women they poured their lives into and focused their training upon. Realizing their own limitations, they set about reproducing in these officers the character qualities, vision, values, and principles necessary for the expansion of the Army's work. In this respect, The Salvation Army was unique among Christian organizations. The Army worked tirelessly to produce hardened, seasoned veterans of the Cross—leaders who were equipped and prepared to train hard, work hard, and wage war to bring God's salvation message to the world.

The Booths' long-sighted vision for the Army extended far beyond their own lifetimes. With the future in mind, they sought to instill in their people the principles and values of the Word of God and The Salvation Army. One day the general would die, but the Army's purpose must continue in the hearts of those that would follow. Wisely, William lived by the motto, "Don't do the work of a thousand men; get a thousand men to do the work."

CHAPTER 8

High Cost

ENDURING PERSECUTION AND THE STRUGGLES OF A
GROWING WORLD MOVEMENT (1878–1885)

Are you worried because it is so hard to believe? No one should be surprised at the difficulty of faith, if there is some part of his life where he is consciously resisting or disobeying the commandment of Jesus. Do not say you have not got faith. You will not have it so long as you persist in disobedience. Your orders are to perform the act of obedience on the spot. Then you will find yourself in the situation where faith becomes possible.

—DIETRICH BONHOEFFER

How wide is the girth of the world?" Booth challenged the huge crowd of Salvationists gathered at a London rally in 1885. "Twenty-five thousand miles," came the rousing response.

Booth feigned thoughtfulness. His hand stroked his flowing beard, the furrows on his brow deepening as his gaze moved steadily across the breadth of the crowd. "Then," he roared, thrusting wide his arms, "We must grow till our arms get right round about it."[1]

By 1884 the movement had grown astronomically to over nine hundred corps, with more than 260 of these being overseas. Immigration to places as far flung as America, Canada, and Australia had excited the hearts of soldiers seeking a new start in these developing countries. Once settled in their new homelands, they would hold meetings—"Army style," of course. Immediately, as people responded to the gospel, word was sent back to headquarters in

London that the work had been established and reinforcements were required. Officers were hurriedly dispatched with teams of soldiers to support and oversee the extension of the work in these lands. "Hold the standard high, let us tell the world of the blood and fire,"[2] encouraged the general as Salvationists departed for distant shores.

The Salvation Army holiness meetings were often the medium through which men and women received the call to leave all and follow Christ. Time and again, converts would attend these assemblies with nothing in mind beyond their own spiritual growth, only to find themselves seized by conviction to lay their lives down in service to God.

An early Salvationist family in Invercargill

With no reputation to lose, Salvationists strove to see the kingdom of God advance in villages and towns across the length and breadth of the land. Morale soared. Divine intervention was commonplace. Anonymous financial gifts would regularly arrive with uncanny timing. A "barrel full" of these miraculous tales could be purchased from any street storyteller for a farthing. Unswerving, unalterable, unquestionable trust in the power of the living God catapulted them forward with unequalled momentum. Their detractors stood by bewildered as week after week this dedicated, determined band advanced the cause of the gospel with unparalleled haste.

Their meetings were unconventional by any measure. While other Christians in England relied on tradition and decorum, The Salvation Army's reliance on the flowing of the Holy Spirit was unnerving to most. This drew attention from all corners, which had its mixed blessings, but the Booths were unmoved by any criticism or praise—they would do things God's way, no matter what the rest of the world thought.

On Wednesday, May 21, 1879, the *Newcastle Daily Chronicle* printed the following "objective" account of one of their meetings:

> The people present, taken as a whole, were the roughest lot I have seen at any of these meetings. . . . Taking a policeman into my confidence, I asked him if he knew any of these young men. "Know any of them?" he said. "Why, I know them all. This one is from Newcastle; the other sitting near him is one of the worst roughs we have"; and so he went on, with a description almost as long as the catalogue of ships in Homer. There was a fair sprinkling of women amongst the audience, too; and most of these were young ones, who did not appear to have been much troubled, previously, with thoughts about religion. I went to the meeting at about two o'clock A.M.. It had then been going on for some two or three hours; but so far it was very orderly and cool. There was a long, low platform in the middle of the room, round which the "Hallelujah Lasses," the "Converted Sweep," the "Hallelujah Giant," and other notabilities concerned with the movement were seated. . . .
>
> Singing was followed by what is called "Witnessing," various officers of the Salvation Army narrating their experience of "what the Lord had done for them." About half an hour was occupied in this wise; and, but for the ordinary interjections of enthusiasm, the time passed quietly enough. It would have been impossible to guess at what followed. . . .
>
> The General requested his audience to sit still and sing when the "witnessing" was concluded. He gave out these lines:
>
> I need Thee every hour, Most gracious Lord!
> No tender voice like Thine can peace afford.
> I need Thee, oh I need Thee: Every hour I need Thee,
> Oh, bless me now, my Savior! I come to Thee.
>
> The words were taken up by the whole audience; the chorus was rolled out to a rattling tune, and was no sooner finished than it was commenced again with additional vigor. This chorus might have been sung perhaps a dozen times when there was a shrill scream, a bustle round the platform, and a general rise of the audience. Seats were mounted; hands were raised in the air; the singing was mingled with loud "Hallelujahs," burst of vociferous prayer, shouting, and hysterical laughter.
>
> To add to the confusion four of the forms fell backwards, and threw their occupants into a common heap on the floor. . . . Sinners were creeping to the penitent-form; the Salvation Army was rejoicing; fully one third of those present acted as if they were more or less insane. . . .
>
> Several figures are bent double near the platform, groaning and wringing their hands. The "Hallelujah Lasses" have surrounded them; the tall figure of the proprietor of the "Hallelujah Fiddle" gyrates around them;

the sweep is dancing and shouting "Glory be to God"; and the "General" is smiling placidly and twiddling his thumbs. . . .

As may be seen from what I have written, until penitents "throw themselves at the feet of Jesus," as it is called, a meeting of The Salvation Army is a tolerably sane affair. The fat is at once in the fire, however, when penitents come forward. . . . Half a-dozen crop-headed youths—boys they are, indeed—are praying vociferously, with their faces towards me. Did I say praying? I only suppose they were. It was vociferous shouting, with closed eyes. Their bodies sway to and fro; their hands are lifted, and brought down again with a thump on the form; they contort themselves as if they were in acute agony. The hymn resounds high above their prayers; . . . everybody is carrying on a separate service on his own account.

Meanwhile the "lasses" are busy with the work of conversion. It proceeds by stages, with a separate hymn for each. The final stage is reached with the singing of "I do believe, I will believe, that Jesus died for me." The process being thus rendered complete, the converts retire to their seats with red faces. Let us follow one of them. He is a broad-faced, shock-headed youth, of about twenty. A few minutes since, he was foaming out of a well-developed mouth. Now he is dancing about the floor, shouting "hallelujah" and wringing the hands of all those who will yield their arm to him. . . . He has in fact been converted. . . .

Here . . . was an extraordinary effect produced without anything that can be called preaching. It was the singing that appeared to be most powerful. . . . After more singing, there was another rush to the penitent-form, another repetition of the same hymns, of the same gesticulations, of the same frantic prayers. But a quite new interest was added. I watched the proceedings for some time from my point of vantage on a back form; and then struggled through the crowd to get a look at the penitents. They had fainted away. Here lay a woman in a dead swoon, with six "Hallelujah lasses" singing round her, and not one of them trying to bring her round even by so much as sprinkling water on her face. On the other side of the platform was a man lying at full length, his limbs twitching, his lips foaming, totally unregarded. . . .

I appealed to the "Hallelujah Giant." The General had stated on Monday that he was not a quack doctor, but a real doctor. It struck me as peculiar that he should sit there singing under such circumstances, and I said, "Really, cannot you do something to bring these people round?" "My good man," he replied, "won't you sit down? They will come round all right." They may have done so—both their recovery and their conversion may have been complete—but it was hard to stay there and witness so much of what looked like gross inhumanity. When I came away people were swooning all over the place. I had to step over a man in a fit in order to get to the door.

When I reached the street and the pure air it was a fresh, gray morning. . . . "Is this a common sort of thing here?" I asked of the policeman outside. "Very," he said, "but it has reduced our charge sheet, and I haven't had a case for two months." I didn't ask him if it was as good for the persons who took part in such "services" as it was for the charge sheet. Neither he nor I could properly answer that question.[3]

While it cannot be said that these sorts of manifestations occurred in all their meetings, it is easy to see from this account how a milder English conscience could have been offended by such proceedings. Many today, in fact, have described similar meetings as having little to do with godliness. Yet even the reporter of this meeting seemed unable to fully dismiss the change that was wrought in the lives of young men and women who had otherwise been scoundrels and criminals, whom the churches of the day would have been unlikely to welcome to their public gatherings. It cannot be denied that the Holy Spirit was at work in The Salvation Army at the time, and it seems just as difficult to say that such conversions could have happened without His miraculous power. Though operating in such a way did at times cost them greatly in public opinion, this was of little concern to those who experienced the touch of God as the Booths let His Spirit have free reign in their gatherings.

Just as they were willing to weather the storms of unfavorable public opinion, the early Salvationists were prepared to bear any cost to see salvation come to ordinary men and women like themselves. However, as the work of the Army expanded, the disruptions and attacks against them began to take on a more serious and sinister form. Their willingness to pay the price was regularly tested to the limit. The reality of the battle was plain to these unsung heroes of the Cross. It was suddenly becoming clear that they did indeed risk life and limb to proclaim the timeless message of righteousness, truth, and grace.

Preaching on the streets was at times like preaching in hell. Teams of Salvationists faced ridicule, scorn, and hatred as they openly proclaimed the gospel in the degraded slums. Many of the poor and destitute were strongly atheistic, hating the name of God and fiercely opposing those who spoke of any form of religion.

By 1880 this holy Army was attracting severe opposition. Those who stood to lose most from their success became their greatest enemies. Hotel

Tireless campaigner John Nashan Garabedian, arrested 57 times, also known as "Joe the Turk"

and brothel owners faced falling profits as their previously thriving businesses began to suffer. The escalating conversion rate of many of their most loyal customers was plainly evident. They were conspicuous by their absence.

In 1881 pub owners from the village of Basingstoke incited a crowd of young hooligans into attacking the local Salvation Army Corps as they marched in the streets prior to their meetings. The level and frequency of the violence of this angry mob against the Salvationists prompted the detachment of a special force to police the streets in the village. While Basingstoke soon settled down, many other villages across England erupted as violent hordes went on a rampage against the Army.

In Salisbury a public notice was posted announcing the formation of a society for the express purpose of bringing an end to the Army's public work:

> The sole object will be to stop the parading of the streets by the Salvation Army. They will employ various ways and means with which to accomplish this end. They will cause to be forcibly broken the ranks of The Salvation Army when in procession through the streets, and they will use every means in their power to stop and resist those processions from doing so.[4]

This society went on to declare that although they would instruct their supporters to have due respect for those of the "weaker sex," they would not take responsibility should any women be assaulted.

The Salvationists refused to strike back, but at times their survival depended on quick thinking and defensive action. They knew their fight was not against the flesh and blood of those who opposed them but against the evil forces inciting these people to violence. They understood that the chief weapon of their warfare was prayer—prayer for their greatest persecutors. At times, however, the patience of even the most enduring soldier wore thin. One officer in Manchester grew so tired of the man who constantly taunted her with "Here's a woman that can work miracles" that she took hold of him by his neck-scarf and replied, "I can't—but I can cast out devils."[5] With that she hurled him out of the meeting place.

William and Catherine never hesitated to lead their Army from the front, often finding themselves in the thick of the action. In 1882 they joined Sheffield Salvationists in a procession prior to their meeting in the town hall. The Booths rode out front in a small carriage as the Army band led dozens of uniformed Salvationists in the parade. A thousand-strong mob of local hoods called "The Sheffield Blades" lined the pavements, shouting abuse as the Army passed by. Suddenly a roar went up and the mob erupted onto the

A group of early women officers, known for their dedication.

street. Armed with an imaginative array of weapons—from rotting food, dead animals, and great clumps of clay to rocks and heavy clubs—the angry thugs attacked the procession.

The general rose to his feet, missiles flying in all directions. With eyes ablaze he commanded his followers, "Stay near the carriage, stay near the carriage." They did. Pushing on together the battered troop finally found refuge in the safety of their meeting place, but not without injury. One lieutenant was struck between the eyes by a stone and then hit in the base of the skull by a cudgel. Fellow officers held him to his horse until they reached the hall. "I hope they'll get saved,"[6] the soldier whispered as he slipped from his mount and lapsed into a coma.

When they finally entered the hall, a great cry went up from the audience at the sight of the Salvationists' blood-stained uniforms and the buckled brass instruments. "Now's the time to get your photo taken,"[7] Booth half jokingly quipped to his assistants as they stood beside him on the platform.

Early Army band members had to be tough as nails (The Fry Family of Salisbury, England)

Although their sense of humor helped to make light of their struggles, William and Catherine were deeply concerned by the attacks against their people. They were troubled not only as leaders but also as parents. They had raised their children to serve God in The Salvation Army, but it was not always easy to release them to His service, especially during times of growing persecution. A year earlier, in 1881, as the opposition in England began to increase, they had commissioned twenty-three-year-old Kate to lead a small team to establish their work in France.

Kate was a gifted preacher. She began preaching in open-air meetings at the age of sixteen and could hold the attention of unruly crowds of fifteen hundred men and women, reaching into their hearts with words she spoke. While Catherine encouraged Kate to press on in obedience to God, yielding her life to Him, she also struggled with the knowledge that her daughter's obedience could prove to be costly.

It had been difficult for Catherine to release Kate to the work in France, and she shared some of her struggle with those who gathered to farewell the team.

> All our confidence is in the Holy Spirit. We should not be so foolish as to send so frail an instrumentality if we believed it depended on human might or strength and we do so because we know that it depends on divine

strength and because we believe that our dear child is thoroughly and fully given up to God. . . . I have offered her to France, and I believe the Lord will take care of her; though I shall feel very much the parting because I shall feel that she has gone from me for ever.

Calling on Kate and the two young women who made up her team, she handed them the Army flag, saying, "Carry it into the slums and alleys everywhere where there are lost and perishing souls, and preach under its shadow the everlasting Gospel of Jesus Christ."[8]

Kate's preaching gift and feisty militant spirit stood her in good stead for the difficulties she faced in this hard and hostile territory. France proved a difficult country to break into. Together with her fellow Salvationists, she preached night after night to rowdy, drunken audiences with little response. Kate and her team were threatened, mocked, and spat upon, receiving nothing but heckling and criticism for six long, wearisome months.

Finally the breakthrough came. This particular evening meeting was disrupted from the first moment by the torments of a woman known locally as "the devil's wife." Of immense size, she would stand in the meeting hall, her hands on her hips and sleeves rolled up above the elbows, and with one wink she would set everybody screaming and yelling. On this evening, everything Kate and her lieutenants did or said was ridiculed by "the devil's wife." The tone of the assembly grew more and more unruly, and soon some of the audience began to dance. The meeting seemed lost until, in a master stroke, Kate turned defeat into victory.

Through the riotous din she shouted, "*Mes amis!* I will give you twenty minutes to dance if you will give me twenty minutes to speak!" The crowd agreed, and after twenty minutes of dancing the busker's music was silenced by the interruption of an outspoken Frenchman who called for Kate to begin.

For an hour and twenty minutes she preached with passion and great authority under the anointing of the Holy Spirit, calling her listeners to genuine repentance and faith in Jesus Christ. A strange silence rested on the people as she spoke. The tide had turned. Hundreds of men and women were saved in the two years that followed. Kate had learned for herself that salvation was indeed "for all men," and like her parents, she committed her life to the work of God with renewed vigor, first in France and then in Switzerland.[9]

Kate's victories, however, were not without cost. As William and Catherine led their people through mounting persecution in England, Kate faced great opposition and even imprisonment while in Switzerland. In 1882, as word of her imprisonment reached her parents, she showed what being raised in the Booth household had done for her faith. In reply to concerns from England, she simply telegraphed, "No need for anxiety about me; Jesus here."[10]

For Catherine, the persecution of her children seemed harder to bear than her own battles. In a letter to Kate during her time in prison, she wrote,

> My precious Child,
>
> Words cannot convey what I have suffered about you during the last twenty-four hours. . . . This is a test of one's consecration certainly; still I can say my soul does not draw back, and I know yours does not. . . . Take care you insist on your right, and don't suffer unnecessarily, because of your health. . . . There are times when it is as needful to claim our rights as it is at others to sacrifice them. The Lord wants you to fight another day . . . so take all the care you can. . . . Saviors must be sufferers, and sufferers just to the extent in which they are given up to be saviors. . . . It is hard work to flesh and blood, especially when our bodies are so weak; but dearest girl, His grace is sufficient, and it shall be sufficient both for you in prison and for me lying awake in the night imagining what you are passing through. . . . Be sure we are all praying for you, and doing all we can.[11]

Kate and her co-workers were eventually acquitted and released, but the persecution against them continued.

Back in England, the opposition was also increasing, with escalating violence threatening the work of the Army. There was little the local police could do. Protection, on the rare occasion it was provided, was definitely a luxury for these soldiers. On one occasion, fifteen hundred extra officers were placed on duty to shield the Army during its scheduled Sunday parades. However, even this was not enough. The angry mobs continued their violent and unprovoked rampages. The Booths' concern for their people deepened, but they always remained stalwart to their sense of purpose and maintained their sense of humor in encouraging their troops. "We must have gotten hold of something good," William once stated, "because Hell is so evidently excited about it." Later he exclaimed, "We must be right! Who can question it when this is the sort of opposition we meet with?"

The attacks were not confined to the streets and laneways or open-air parades. The rioters stormed the Army citadels, causing many indoor meetings to close due to uncontrollable chaos. In 1882 alone, sixty buildings used for Salvation Army purposes were all but destroyed by rioting crowds, and 669 soldiers were assaulted. It seems no one was exempt from attack, regardless of age or gender. Of these 669 soldiers, 251 were women, and 23 were under the age of fifteen.

Tragically, greater injuries were also inflicted. In Guildford that same year, the wife of the corps officer was kicked to death. A fellow woman soldier was so severely beaten during the same parade that she also died some days later from the wounds she sustained. It is difficult to imagine this degree of persecution of Christians occurring in a "Christian" nation such as Britain in the nineteenth century.

In Whitechapel, East London, Salvation Army lasses were tied together with rope and pelted with live coals. It was not uncommon for parades heading for the evening meetings to be showered with tar and burning sulfur. "Blood and Fire" had become a reality for this army of God, unfortunately not only in the way originally foreseen.

While English law permitted the Army to hold open-air meetings and parades, when they supposedly incited violence among local louts and caused a disruption of the peace, local magistrates were instructed to do all in their power to prevent their public work.

The first Salvation Army lassies' band, 1888

Often the magistrates and local police officers were completely unsympathetic toward the Salvationists, many of whom were wrongly fined for petty charges such as "praying in a public place." When they refused to pay the fines for unjust charges, the Salvationists were sentenced to jail. However, this only strengthened their resolve and inflamed their courageous spirits with a heightened fire and passion to see their communities saturated with the gospel.

As the law continued to turn a blind eye to the injustice and violence, the wild mobs grew even more daring. Hooligans in Oldham banded together and formed the first of many groups across England and the world under the ominous title of "The Skeleton Army." With skull and crossbones emblazoned on their banners, and armed with weapons of flour, red ochre, and deadly jagged brickbats, Skeleton Army units attacked Salvationists with renewed vigor.

While William and Catherine faced the task of holding the Army together under intense persecution, attack came from other directions as well. William was hated by many influential leaders, especially those who held positions of authority in England's churches. He bore the brunt of great criticism and slander, being labeled an "indecent charlatan" and even the "Antichrist"!

At this point in their ministry, the Booths were either loved or despised; no one could ignore the nationwide impact of the Army's work. Some religious leaders were very supportive. For instance, to his surprise, William was asked to address the 1880 Wesleyan Church Conference. The movement that had earlier expelled him now invited him to speak! Other mainline denominations, recognizing the effectiveness of the Salvation Army, adopted their approach to evangelism and attempted to begin similar works. There was even a proposal by the Church of England hierarchy to unite the Army with the established church.

While their supporters encouraged them, many other leaders took offense at their methods of public preaching and especially at their decision not to include baptism and the sacraments of Holy Communion as essential practices of The Salvation Army. In spite of persecution, the Booths stood firm, refusing to be swayed by public opinion. They were confident the steps they took were divinely directed, radical though they were.

At first they had adopted baptism and communion, but after prayerful consideration they abandoned these practices, believing there was no scriptural warrant for them as essential to salvation or to be perpetuated throughout the ages as a "sacrament." William and Catherine were well aware of the tendency for new converts to become dependent on religious forms and rely on such things as baptism and communion for their spiritual well-being. They knew that if Salvationists were to achieve their purpose, they would need to find strength for their service through the Word of God and the empowerment of the Holy Spirit. They would not do anything that might encourage their members to rely on an outward form rather than seek the grace of God personally by faith. Furthermore, as many in their ranks were reformed alcoholics, there was little wisdom in suggesting they take the wine of Holy Communion. "Neither water, sacraments, church services, nor Salvation Army methods will save you without a living, inward change of heart and a living active faith and communion with God,"[12] William explained.

The Booths were also criticized and deeply resented for their insistence of the equality of men and women in the work of God. The Salvation Army welcomed and encouraged women preachers—a radical move for the Victorian age when a woman's place was clearly defined as being in the home. William, encouraged by Catherine's belief that their movement would benefit greatly if women were involved to the same degree as men, firmly planted the equality of genders before God into the growing structure. "The best men in my Army are the women,"[13] he often stated. For much of the Army's history, the women officers outnumbered their male counterparts five-to-one. Their courage was legendary, and stories were published of their remarkable love and sacrifice, even for those who taunted them. One such story was entitled "The Lass From the Army."

> She was a Salvation Army lass, and her lot was a hard one. Working from seven in the morning till six o'clock at night, weaving hair-cloth, was dull and poorly paid work, but in addition she had to bear the constant and thoughtless gibes of her fellow-workers. One Autumn morning a spark from a bonfire on some adjoining allotment gardens entered an open window, alighted on a heap of loose hair, and the next minute the place was ablaze. A rush for safety of the work-girls followed.
>
> "Is everybody down?" asked the foreman. His question was answered by one of the weavers, who holding up a key, shrieked, "My God! I locked Lizzie Summers in the 'piece shed' for a joke not a minute ago!" The "piece shed" was a room to be reached only through the burning building, through which it seemed impossible to make way. Girls and men were standing aghast and helpless, when two figures stumbled through the smoke, which poured from the weaving-room. One was seen to be Lizzie Summers; the other was, for the time, unrecognizable. It was The Salvation Army lass. She had stayed behind, burnt, blistered, and half-suffocated, to batter down the door in order to liberate and save the life of her coarsest-tongued tormentor.[14]

Perhaps the one thing that drew most criticism from some leaders of the Christian churches was the nature of the Army's meetings. Many respectable people would never have entered such a meeting, but they were able to read about them in the press. The *Saturday Review* was one of many papers that described their meetings in detail. "Those must have been very dull or unsympathetic persons who could resist the pious jollity of the meeting," stated the article. The opening song

> was sung, or rather roared, again and again. . . . Those . . . who blame the apathy and cold-bloodedness of the English character can never have attended a Hallelujah meeting. . . . The sight of many hundred pairs of radiant eyes and waving arms . . . the manifest affection of all these rough people for one another, the absence of anything like hypocrisy or self-seeking in the whole affair, were not to be overlooked by any candid spectator. That the nature of the prayers and speeches was oddly boisterous, and that shouts of laughter pervaded what was intended to be a serious divine service, interfered not in the least with the sincerity of the worshippers.[15]

The freedom of expression and emotion that characterized the Army meetings was slammed by some as being both disrespectful and irreligious. The criticism "cut us to the heart," Catherine declared, "but they do not and shall not move us from our purpose."[16] Catherine received many invitations to speak at various public meetings in defense of the Army's work among the poor, invitations she gladly accepted. A great deal of support still came from wealthy Christians, and some of these had found themselves caught in controversy over the Army. Catherine's desire through her lectures was not to retaliate but to help the churches understand their work.

While Catherine fiercely defended the Army, William largely ignored his critics and refused to waste precious time and energy on the accusations and slander hurled their way. He was able to focus instead on resolving the more important issue facing his troops: the attack against their right to preach and parade in public.

William contacted Home Secretary Sir William Harcourt, providing evidence of magistrates in Worthing refusing to summons those who had assaulted his officers. The attacks in Worthing in 1884 had been so violent and constant that the general had commanded his officers to cease their open-air meetings for a time. When Harcourt chose not to get involved, asserting that the state had no power over the local authorities, Booth refused to give in. Not to be denied, he gathered more evidence describing how the Skeleton

Army in Worthing was supported and funded by prominent community members. Once again, Harcourt turned a blind eye.

Furious but realizing he was fighting a lost cause in demanding the assistance of the home secretary, Booth finally consented to allow the troops in Worthing, under the leadership of Captain Ada, to recommence their Sunday parades. Concerned for his people, he again appealed to Harcourt, informing him of the Army's decision to march.

What followed was one of the most violent and bloody clashes ever made against The Salvation Army. Many of the Skeletons received a court summons for assault and disturbing the peace, but this did not stop them. Over the days that followed, they continued their violent rioting, assaulting police officers, disrupting indoor Army meetings, and looting a shop owned by a Salvationist. The mob was further inflamed when its ringleaders were sentenced to a month's hard labor for their involvement.

A special squadron of forty guards was eventually called into the village to disperse the rioters and clear the streets. Further clashes occurred over the weeks that followed. However, at long last the police were now clearly in defense of the Salvationists. Victory was declared as police notices went up decreeing all Skeleton Army subscribers to be criminals, with the immediate penalty of three months' hard labor. The Army had won a decisive battle. To the amusement and delight of Captain Ada and her battle-weary troops, some citizens who had previously condoned the attacks against them now rallied together to form a voluntary bodyguard at all open-air meetings. Their persistence and the persecution they endured had somehow elevated The Army as champions of free speech in Britain.

The victory in Worthing signaled the beginning of the end of the intense persecution in England. As the months went by, other villages adopted a hardline attitude against the Skeleton Army and reaffirmed the Salvationists' rights to hold public meetings. The Army emerged from the five-year period of extreme persecution battle-weary but stronger than ever before.

There was still much work to be done. In 1881 a new outreach of the Army had been born when a young prostitute knelt at the mercy seat toward the conclusion of an Army meeting. She was counseled and ministered to by Mrs. Cottrill, one of Booth's officers. "How can I be a Christian—in the life I'm living?" the girl asked.

"You must give up the life," Officer Cottrill replied. As she talked with the young girl, she was faced with an immediate dilemma. What was she to do

Florence (Bramwell) Booth fought violently against teenage prostitution traffic.

with this new convert now under her care? One thing was for sure—if she genuinely wanted to begin her Christian life, she could not return to the brothel that was all she knew as "home." Although it was nearly eleven at night, Officer Cottrill took her new charge to a home where they had taken girls before, but the manager was far from welcoming. "I can't have anyone in at this hour; we don't keep open all night," came the terse response. They tried a coffee house but didn't have enough money between them to cover the cost of the shelter. Finally, with their options disappearing, they tried another lodging place, only to be told, "We don't take females."[17]

It was nearly midnight when the weary Salvationist decided there was no other option but to take the young girl into the shelter of her own home. They crept quietly into the dark house, endeavoring not to wake Mr. Cottrill and their six children. After providing the girl with supper and a makeshift bed on the kitchen chairs, Officer Cottrill crawled wearily into bed. The plight of the young girl weighed heavily on her mind, especially as she realized how many others were trapped in the same desperate cycle of poverty and prostitution.

Prostitution permeated every level of Victorian society. The authorities largely turned a blind eye to the practice, preferring to ignore its existence rather than uncover and deal with the problems it caused. To their horror, the Salvationists knew for a fact that many girls, some as young as ten years of age, were working the streets as prostitutes. While one young girl was sleeping safely tonight, there were hundreds more like her on the streets and in brothels all across London.

Although Officer Cottrill eventually helped return the young girl to her parents' home in Brighton, her house soon became a refuge for others. The work grew, with Salvationists beginning midnight marches and meetings especially to attract young girls trapped in prostitution. As more came to Christ,

Mrs. Cottrill set aside her basement rooms to house them. It was hard work, and they encountered a great deal of opposition. Officer Cottrill and her helpers were often abused and physically assaulted by men as they rescued the young girls from the streets. Mr. Cottrill was not a Salvationist, and although sympathetic and supportive of his wife's rescue work, he began to resent the girls' invasion of their home. In 1884 a refuge house was finally opened in Whitechapel to care for the growing number of girls snatched from a life of prostitution. The work was put in the charge of Florence Booth, Bramwell's young wife.

The Army's work with the girls was founded on love. Those taking refuge in the home were free to come and go; they were never forced to stay. The Salvationists caring for the young prostitutes relied purely on spiritual influence to lead them to a new life. Their one aim was salvation, and their only confidence was in the power of God to renew even the most broken, sinful heart. It was no life of luxury for the girls—funds were very short and they were all required to help pay their way by making Army uniforms. But the results were worth it: In the first year alone, eighty-six girls passed through the home, all but twelve of whom were successfully rescued from their life on the streets. By the end of three years, over eight hundred girls had been rescued through the home.

Meanwhile, on the opposite side of the globe, an Australian Salvationist pioneered another form of rescue home. Major James Barker had been visiting prisoners in the Melbourne jail and was so successful among them that a great proportion of his converts were ex-criminals. These men and women begged him to let them help him in the work of his corps.

Guests in a Wellington girls home

In Auckland, New Zealand, 1931, mobile soup kitchen for poor families

"Give me a chance," one sixty-year-old pleaded on his release from prison. "I don't want to die in jail." Barker consented, and his chief of staff took the old man home, fed him, and found him work. One month later, the dying man's final faltering words were, "The Army was like home."[18] When Barker heard this, it suddenly occurred to him that a home was exactly what these ex-criminals needed.

The first Salvation Army Prison Gate Home was opened close to the jail in December of 1883, and a vital ministry was born. At first Army officers were placed on guard at the prison gate to invite men to come to the home as they were released. Also waiting at the gate, however, were old acquaintances of the prisoners. These men would do their best to lure the prisoner back to his former way of life, and tussles often broke out between them and the Salvationists. A change of strategy was needed. The Salvationists placed a notice on the walls of the prison declaring, "Any prisoner who is desirous of leading a new life is at liberty to communicate with the officer in charge of the Prison

Gate Brigade who will be permitted to see him with a view to this end a day before discharge."[19] The Army's work with ex-criminals was so successful the Australian government provided them with funding and the freedom to do whatever they could to help solve the problem of rising unemployment.

William was so impressed by the work of the Australian Salvationists in the prisons that he immediately began a similar work in London. The Prisoners' Rescue Brigade began in London in 1884. Upon release, the prisoners were brought into the home of a Salvationist who helped them to find God and to begin their new life. The first home for prisoners was opened in July. Writing about this new venture in *The War Cry*, William said,

> Like each onward step of the Army our work for the salvation of ex-convicts has been begun with no cut-and-dried plan, but just as we have seen our way to reply to the cry of our hearts for the deliverance of these poor captives from the tyranny of the devil, without waiting to know how to do it.[20]

During the 1880s the Booths recognized that, although they were working among the poor all over England, they were not reaching those caught in the greatest depths of poverty. The training cadets were the first to take up the challenge to reach the slum dwellers. In 1884 spring flowers sent to the women's training home were distributed as a gift of love to the poor. Tracts were attached to the flowers with simple messages like "Sin is horrid, chuck it up!" and "Give the devil the slip!"

A more focused strategy to the poor was born out of a night of prayer. Emma put the proposal to her staff at the training home the next day: "Why not take a room in one of the worst districts and send a few cadets to live there? Let them dress as the people do (only be clean), visit, sympathise, and put before them the example of a good life!"[21] The plan was quickly put into action, and four cadets took up residence with a supervising captain. Their practical training was focused on taking Jesus into the dirty, disease-ridden homes of the slum dwellers.

In 1886 the cadets' work in the slums was incorporated into the London division when the first slum post was opened by a Salvationist couple in South London. Their purpose was to live among the poor and to make the slums their mission field. They lived simply, dressed modestly, and began visiting their neighbors. The public houses, lodging places, and food outlets became their favorite haunts for meeting people and distributing *The War Cry*. Their work in the slums was very effective, so the Army opened more slum posts in

London, Glasgow, Liverpool, Manchester, and Newcastle.

As they visited the public houses, the plight of the infants and children touched their hearts more than anything else. Many spent their daylight hours in the public houses or in factories where their mothers worked. They were neglected, undernourished, dirty, and often very sick. In an effort to improve the children's health and well-being, the slum officers began a crèche,[22] taking young children into their care for twelve hours each day. The children were fed and bathed at the crèche and occupied with songs and stories. The work, although tiring and heartbreaking, was extremely rewarding. In one year alone, as many as six thousand children received care from the Salvationists.

As the Army pressed on, reaching out to people with the message of the gospel, the welfare work also continued to grow. To those who saw it all as a carefully planned crusade, Booth responded, "We saw the need. We saw the people starving, we saw people going about half-naked, people doing sweated labor; and we set about bringing a remedy for these things. We were obliged—there was a compulsion. How could you do anything else?"[23]

While William focused his efforts among the poor, Catherine was able to take their cause to the wider Christian church. In the 1880s she was invited to conduct meetings in London's fashionable West End; the meetings were held in public halls and were packed to the door with many wealthy and middle-class people eager to hear "The Woman Preacher." The majority of those in her West End audiences were Christians, by name at least. Catherine used the meetings as opportunities to stir them from their comfortable complacency. Messages entitled "Aggressive Christianity," "Holiness," and "Practical Christianity" powerfully challenged the hearts of her hearers.

To Catherine, class did not matter. She looked upon each person as a soul desperately in need of God, whether aware of the fact or not. She did not pander to the upper classes; instead, she passionately exposed their arrogant attitudes toward the poor. Not all were happy to hear her remarks. One gentleman insisted there was still a great amount of love for the Savior in the churches. Catherine's reply cut straight to the heart. "Yes," she said, "for their idealistic Savior. But suppose Jesus was to come to your chapel as He went about Palestine, with a carpenter's coat on, or as He sat upon the well, all over perspiration and dust with travel, where would your chapel steward put him to sit?"[24] The man's face fell immediately as her point hit home.

To Catherine, sin was sin, regardless of who committed it. She abhorred the hypocrisy that marked many of the established churches. "Alas! Alas!" she declared in one meeting,

Is it not too patent for intelligent contradiction that the most detestable thing in the judgment of popular Christianity is not brutality, cruelty, or injustice, but poverty and vulgarity. With plenty of money you can pile up your life with iniquities and yet be blamed, if blamed at all, only in the mildest terms; whereas one flagrant act of sin in a poor and illiterate person is enough to stamp him, with the majority of professing Christians, as a creature from whom they would rather keep at a distance.[25]

As she preached under the anointing of the Spirit of God, men and women flocked to the penitent-form, ready to repent of their hypocrisy and to consecrate their lives to Jesus Christ. Through her ministry, a number of wealthy professionals and high-society people gave up their lives of luxury and ease to join the ranks of The Salvation Army. All thought of future security was pushed aside as these men and women chose to stand and fight side by side with the poor and uneducated in the war for souls.

The foundation of the Booths' ministry was love—their hearts were full of compassion toward those they met who did not know Jesus Christ. The love that rose in their hearts for people carried with it a sense of responsibility; they could not ignore their Savior's command to "love one another, as I have loved you" (John 13:34; 15:12). The Spirit of God filled their lives with Christ's love for people, and in obedience they gave expression to that love.

By 1885, as they celebrated twenty years of mission, the Army was operating a total of 802 corps in England and 520 corps in ten overseas nations. The number of officers already serving full time in the Army was close to three thousand, and there was no evidence that its growth was slowing down. William had been unprepared for the rapid expansion, and the burden of responsibility weighed heavily upon him and his family. The cost of spreading the gospel and equipping and caring for the multitudes that had pledged their lives to the Army's cause stretched funds beyond their limit. Checks were often written in faith, with the knowledge that until God provided, the payments couldn't be made. Yet God was faithful and the money always came in, often from unknown and unexpected sources. Writing of these years, Bramwell said, "We had to build the ship while we were at sea, and not only build the ship but master the laws of navigation."[26]

The growing number of corps and the widening scope and infiltration of these young pioneers saw the Army's annual budget exceed thirty thousand pounds in 1884. Clerical staff at Army headquarters in London frequently received and dispatched up to two thousand letters each day. This rapid growth stretched resources to the limit, and for Booth the problems of support and survival grew more and more intense.

In later years, Bramwell Booth remembered the struggle of these days:

> The money burden was never lifted. It remained a heavy cloud—perhaps divinely permitted to keep us of a practical turn of mind. Of well-to-do friends to whom we could look to for a five pound note, he had not about a dozen; and even when they did help him they generally wanted to fix their gift for some new effort, forgetting (what many people with kind intentions forget today!) that the ordinary work has still to be financed, and that the cost of the regular organization cannot be made to disappear by simply overlooking it![27]

More than ever before, volunteers had to be prepared for the hardship that accompanied the life of an officer. In 1882, when William sent word out to Salvationists of a team that was soon to leave for India, he described in detail the difficulties they would face.

> Remember that you are likely to be absolutely alone—it may be for months together. . . . In the villages the men must expect to have no furniture at all, except some mats, and must learn to sit on the ground like a tailor. . . . You will have to learn to cook just as Indians do and to wash your clothes at the stream with them. . . . You must make up your mind to leave entirely forever and behind you all your English ideas and habits.[28]

The difficulties arising from sparse resources were not confined to officers serving overseas. As early as 1878 William had been forced to issue a "General Order Against Starvation" to ensure the self-sacrificing attitudes of his officers did not lead to ill health or compromise the well-being of their families. In order to meet the expenses required to keep their corps going, officers lived and ate as simply as possible. At times they existed on stale bread crusts and spoiled fruit. Sometimes, for extended periods, they would not eat at all.

Despite these hardships, the Booths and their officers persevered with incredible commitment and stamina. No difficulty was allowed to bring the work of salvation to a halt. The state of souls was at stake! As the Army stretched out its arms to embrace the world, its members knew more than ever to prepare to pay the price. There was no denying it; the cost was great. Some had already lost their lives in this salvation war. Countless others had given up the right of a comfortable existence, choosing to go without luxuries in order to see others come into the kingdom of God. The results were worth it! Undaunted by poverty or persecution, these soldiers of Christ saw 250,000

One of the early Maori Salvation Army performing groups

souls saved between 1881 and 1885 alone.

Each new convert was challenged to follow the example of their leaders, some of whom had literally given their lives in the salvation war. Their general and his family had laid aside their own rights and dedicated their strength, their gifts, their time, and their material wealth to the purpose of the gospel of Jesus Christ. William encouraged his people to do likewise—to lay their own lives down for God, stating:

> True courage does not think about self; it rises above self—tramples it beneath its feet. It does not even measure and inquire the value and worth of its object. Enough for it that there is duty to be done, difficulties to be overcome, burdens to be borne and suffering to be relieved; regardless of self, and in a measure regardless of its ability to accomplish the task it sets itself upon, it goes straight at it; "to do or die"—nay, "to die and do," if the doing cannot be done without dying—may it be taken as its motto.[29]

The courage and selfless dedication of the Booths had permeated all levels of The Salvation Army. They led by example, laying down their lives to see souls saved. As a result, God worked powerfully in their midst. This was not an army advancing on the energy and influence of its leaders or soldiers alone. This was a holy army empowered by the Holy, Living God.

Although they had weathered persecution and had continued to fight a winning battle with financial needs, and although their early welfare work among the poor, ex-prisoners, and prostitutes was very successful, William and Catherine were yet to face their greatest challenges. The first arrived quite literally on their doorstep in the spring of 1885.

CHAPTER 9

On Trial for Righteousness

THE ARMSTRONG CASE (1885)

No statue was ever erected to the memory of a man or woman who thought it was best to "let well enough alone."

—*WATCHMAN EXAMINER*

Major William Fenny unlocked the front entrance of The Salvation Army headquarters on London's Queen Victoria Street to greet a beautiful spring day. As housekeeper and caretaker, it was his responsibility to ensure that the building was open by 7 A.M. sharp, ready for another busy day. He pushed open the heavy door, allowing the sunshine to stream into the foyer as he wondered what the day would hold. He was not kept wondering for long.

Crouched near the front gate was a disheveled young girl dressed in a scarlet dress made of fine silk. The girl clambered to her feet and faced the major. "I need to see the general," she demanded. At first sight the Salvationist had assumed the girl was one of London's poor wretches who had nowhere to lay her head. Now, as she stood before him, he recognized the Salvation Army songbook she gripped firmly in her hand. His heart melted as he looked into her tear-stained face. He immediately showed her inside.

A short time later, over a cup of hot tea, she nervously shared her story with Bramwell, the Army's chief of staff. Her name was Annie Swan. She was seventeen years of age. Until recently she had lived with her family in the village of Shoreham in Sussex. Annie had answered a newspaper advertisement and traveled to London to work in private domestic service.

On her arrival, however, she horrifically discovered that her new "home" was in fact a brothel and the private service expected of her was everything *but* the domestic duties she had imagined. She was locked in the house in Pimlico, South London, and escape seemed impossible. Annie barricaded herself in the cellar and flatly refused the suggestions of the "mistress." She would rather starve to death than work as a prostitute. Fortunately she was left alone rather than forced into compliance.

Annie had attended Salvation Army meetings in her village, and while in her state of anguish, she picked up her treasured songbook and discovered the address of The Salvation Army headquarters on the cover. A plan of escape began to form in her mind. At four o'clock one morning she crept out of the brothel via the side exit used by departing clients. Once free, she half walked, half ran the four miles to Army headquarters, clutching the precious songbook, her ticket to freedom.

As Bramwell listened to Annie, he recalled the horror stories recounted to him night after night by his wife when she first began working in the rescue home for women. Her heart had broken, over and over, while she cared for the girls, some only ten years old, and listened as they told of the abduction and abuse they had endured. At first Bramwell had questioned the validity of some of the young girls' stories—after all, they sounded so farfetched. Now, as he listened to Annie Swan, their claims were being confirmed. His eyes flooded with tears and his heart broke for the innocence stolen from so many of England's girls.

Annie was one of the fortunate ones. When the staff officer who was sent to the Pimlico brothel returned, her belongings in hand and her story confirmed, she was placed in the loving care of a Salvationist. She had escaped, largely unharmed, and was able to return to her family in Sussex.

For Annie, the ordeal had ended, but for the Booths it had only just begun. Bramwell immediately set out to investigate the matter further. Without a word to anyone, he went incognito to the neighborhoods renowned for prostitution. He wanted to see the facts for himself and get an understanding of the magnitude and nature of the problem. What he saw was even worse than he could have imagined.

When he conveyed the things he had learned from Annie and his own investigations to his parents, they were shocked. The stories of the brutality and appalling treatment endured by these young girls in the brothels were bad enough. Bramwell's evidence of the evil nature and the magnitude of the sex trade that brewed below the surface of respectable Victorian society compelled them to action. They encouraged their son to continue his investigations and do something—anything—to help the innocent young girls who were trapped in prostitution.

In 1885 English law offered virtually no protection for young girls against these brothel owners and white slave traders. Slavery as a whole had been abolished throughout the British Empire in 1833, but the consent laws seemed to offer a loophole to those who dealt in "auctioning off" these girls: Any form of consent, even that given in ignorance, would render a girl over thirteen years of age defenseless against a man of ill intentions, or even a man wishing to sell her off to another on the continent. Five years earlier, a committee of the House of Lords that had been established to investigate claims of an increase in juvenile prostitution had put forward a bill that would have raised the age of consent to sixteen. This proposal, however, had been rejected by the House of Commons. The legal age of consent in England remained set at thirteen.

While the police had the power to convict those guilty of acquiring young girls for the purpose of prostitution, they spent little time or effort in policing the brothels. As Bramwell continued his investigations, he followed with interest the progress of a court case against Mrs. Jeffries, a woman notorious for her ownership of twelve brothels. Her trial was a farce, a prearranged guilty plea resulting in a fine of just two hundred pounds. It was reputed that one of her wealthy clients alone paid her four times this amount each year to provide him with innocent young girls of his choice. The police officer arresting Mrs. Jeffries had refused to accept a bribe from her and was subsequently ridiculed by his superiors and driven to resignation when he stated in court that her houses were frequented by England's aristocracy.

Meanwhile, Bramwell met with Home Secretary Sir William Harcourt and laid before him the facts he had collated. This meeting prompted Harcourt to put forward once more the bill to raise the age of consent to sixteen. Once more it was blocked in the House of Commons, with one politician arguing that the age of consent should be lowered to ten. His reasoning—it was difficult for a man to face such a charge without being able to plead the consent of a child! This infuriated the Booths as they recalled the look of innocence in the eyes of their own children and wondered how any human being could justify such a statement.

With a sobering realization that Britain's lawmakers and law enforcers would not adequately address the prostitution industry, the Booths knew their only avenue was to go to the public. They enlisted the help of William T.

Stead, editor of the *Pall Mall Gazette*, and Mrs. Josephine Butler, a well-known campaigner against the trade of young girls.

At first Stead was hesitant to become involved. Many of Britain's most influential men had berated him for the thought of it. Although a keen supporter of The Salvation Army for some years, Stead was reluctant to risk his reputation by taking on what he believed was a lost cause. He finally consented to visit Army headquarters to hear the evidence Bramwell had gathered.

W. T. Stead, editor of the Pall Mall Gazette, *whose affiliation with The Salvation Army earned him a jail term*

A few days later Stead entered the Army's offices on Queen Victoria Street, ready to listen to the witnesses Bramwell had called together. His first meeting was with Mr. Benjamin Scott, recorder of the City of London, who explained the current legal situation concerning juvenile prostitution in England. When this meeting was complete, Stead met with three young girls, all less than sixteen years of age, and all rescued from prostitution by The Salvation Army.

One by one they spoke plainly of the abuse and shame they had experienced. Stead listened with amazement as one of the girls described how she had been drugged by a man introduced to her by a friend. When she awoke she found herself trapped in a brothel. She overheard the women in the house making plans to transport her with a group of young girls to Europe to serve as a prostitute there. Fearing a fate worse than death, she escaped by leaping from a window and found her way to safety through The Salvation Army.

After hearing the girls' testimonies, Bramwell brought in forty-five-year-old Rebecca Jarrett, a woman rescued by Salvationists from her life as an alcoholic brothel manager. Rebecca told how she herself had been raped as a fifteen-year-old and how she had gone on to work in the industry, procuring hundreds of girls for wealthy clientele. She described in detail the traps laid to lure young girls from parents who were so desperate they sold their children into prostitution for next to nothing. Stead was astounded as Rebecca exposed the elaborate system that organized the drugging and trafficking of children around England and into Europe for abuse by the professional, high society, and even royal clientele of the brothels. The accounts were unending and heartrending.

When Rebecca finally left the room, Bramwell sat quietly for a moment, then looked at Stead, who was obviously deeply affected by the testimonies he had heard. Unable to find the words to express his heartache for the girls, he raised his fist and pounded the writing table, uttering only one word as he did so: "Damn!"

"Yes!" declared Bramwell, "that is all very well, but it will not help us. The first thing to do is to get the facts in such a form that we can publish them."[1] Stead, his heart breaking for the thousands who were trapped in this evil system, agreed. They knelt together in prayer, vowing to expose the prostitution industry and seeking God's wisdom and help for the task.

Stead explored every possible avenue of assistance. He called on an old friend, Howard Vincent, former director of Scotland Yard's Criminal Investigation Department. Vincent confirmed the ugly truth revealed to Stead by the Salvationists and explained that the current laws provided little, if any, protection to girls over the age of thirteen. As far as the police were concerned, the brothel clientele and white slave traders were virtually untouchable.

Next on his list were his colleagues, the influential journalists of the day. But all he uncovered was a conspiracy of silence. While most were aware of the facts, they refused to do anything about them. Prostitution and white slave trading were subjects deemed taboo by the English press.

With his conscience awakened by the accounts he had heard, Stead knew he could not join the ranks of those who knew the truth but kept quiet about it. He organized a secret commission, a six-week examination of juvenile prostitution beginning on May 25, 1885. Under his guidance, workers from the *Pall Mall Gazette* began to gather the facts on the nature and extent of the organized system of white slave trading. To help with their investigations, a young Salvationist agreed to work her way into a brothel to collect information. To protect her, Stead posed as her exclusive client and visited her every night in the Wanstead house where she was held captive.

The information they gained was alarming. Thousands of girls, most under the age of sixteen, were regularly shipped out to the state-controlled brothels in Europe. It was a buyer's market, with many wealthy clients describing in detail the type of girls they wanted. Any girls who had proved difficult to handle were drugged and then shipped out of England in coffins nailed shut with air holes to keep them alive. Some who regained consciousness during the voyage actually died, overcome by fear while they tried desperately to escape the terrifying confines of the unyielding caskets.

After several days had gone, the undercover Salvationist heard a plan to ship her to Europe in charge of a party of young girls. Stead was alerted of this intention, and he immediately set in place a plan for her rescue, but he didn't have a chance to carry it out. After ten days of confinement in the brothel, the young girl made a serious mistake. The mistress of the brothel discovered her Salvation Army badge in a hidden fold sewn into her clothing and locked her in an upstairs room, away from the other girls. Fearing her fate, she leaped out of the window into the garden, determined to escape. But as she landed she twisted her ankle and crumpled into a heap on the ground, the pain so severe that she fainted.

However, through providence it appears, her fiancé had had enough of this ruse by now and missed her so greatly that he had organized a rescue mission. When he stormed the brothel with a group of Army officers, they found her lying unconscious in the garden not long after she had jumped. In the end, she was largely unharmed by the whole ordeal.

Stead's investigators continued their fact-finding mission, scouring the streets and making their way into houses renowned as brothels. The statistics they collated were horrifying. The prostitution industry was worth an estimated eight million pounds every year, an astonishing amount of money in 1885. Within London alone, as many as eighty thousand prostitutes worked the trade; one in every fifty Englishwomen was a streetwalker! Every night, girls no longer useful to the brothels were forced out onto the city streets, where they continued to sell their bodies but now for no more than ten shillings at a time.

Posing as a wealthy client, Stead worked his way into the confidence of the brothel madams and soon became privy to the grueling secrets of the evil trade. The best money came for young virgins, "fresh girls," as the industry labeled them. The most common way of luring them was through advertisements seeking country girls for domestic service in London homes. Irish girls were easy prey for women dressed as nuns. Other women scoured city parks looking for girls to befriend. As soon as their trust was gained they were taken to a secure place, drugged, and abducted. By the time they awoke, their belongings were gone and they were behind locked doors. Many were forcibly raped by clients or brothel workers, only to have the shame of their loss of innocence used against them, being told they were now worthy of nothing more than joining "the trade." Their only chance of survival, they were told, was to "work" for their food and board. Escape was virtually impossible.

To Stead's disgust, the brothel clientele included some of the most respectable of London's citizens. They ranged from Harley Street physicians to royalty and even clergymen. Men who were applauded publicly as upright and honorable members of society were in fact nothing more than perverted criminals. His findings rocked him to the core. "It is a sham, a horrible sham, the whole of our professed Christianity and civilization,"[2] he cried one night. As he knelt with Bramwell to pray for the girls, he broke down and wept uncontrollably. Nothing could ease the burden on his heart for the innocent.

Stead carefully compiled the facts they had gathered. They were comprehensive and would certainly alarm his readers, but they lacked the convincing touch of authenticity required to force a change in law. With all concern for his reputation now firmly pushed aside, Stead concocted an elaborate plan that when reported would lead to public outcry. He proposed to purchase a young girl from her mother for the purposes of prostitution and to arrange to have her delivered to him in a brothel. It was a risky plan, but they documented every aspect of the evil underworld system of the trafficking of young girls, knowing that when printed it would tell a story no one could deny. When he outlined his plan to the Booths, he received their full support.

While Stead and Bramwell set about putting this into action, William and Catherine began to address the issue publicly. Mass meetings were held as part of what became known as "The Purity Crusade." All over London, as well as in Manchester, Sheffield, Leeds, Portsmouth, and Newcastle, they spoke honestly of the terrible evils committed against young girls in secret every day.

At one meeting, Catherine declared,

> I question whether any face has burned with fiercer shame than mine. . . . Three years ago a committee of the House of Lords sat to consider these very things and they recommended improved legislation for the protection of young girls . . . and yet nothing has been done. I would like to ask those responsible for this state of things how many thousands of innocent victims have been sacrificed during those three years? . . . They have found time to legislate on the preservation of game, and the diseases of cattle! . . . time to legislate for British interests in far-off corners of the earth, surely they might have found time to legislate for the protection of the children of their own country! . . . The wretches who cater for the

child-destroying monsters perfectly well know the present state of the law. . . . Hence their anxiety to get children who are turned thirteen even if only by a day![3]

In addition to her lectures, Catherine wrote to Queen Victoria and Prime Minister Gladstone, urging them to use their power to bring the bill for raising the age of consent before Parliament again.

Meanwhile, Stead had discussed his plan with a solicitor, who assured him that without criminal intent there could be no crime. For his own protection, he outlined his intentions to three irreproachable witnesses: the archbishop of Canterbury, Cardinal Manning—head of the Roman Catholic Church in England—and the bishop of London.

Finally, at Bramwell's suggestion, he enlisted the assistance of Rebecca Jarrett. At first she had refused to return, even momentarily, to her former life. However, Stead proved convincing: "You've told me you've procured and ruined scores of innocent girls. If you're really penitent, make amends for your crime by procuring one, not for ruin but for rescue, whose purchase will save more girls being sold in future than all those you've ruined in the past."[4] Reluctantly, she agreed.

Stead's charade immediately swung into action. Rebecca contacted an old acquaintance, a woman she had once worked with in securing young girls for brothel clients. On June 2, 1885, she was introduced as the wife of a wealthy businessman who needed to hire a housemaid to thirteen-year-old Eliza Armstrong. Eliza was excited about the prospect of earning some money and leaving the cramped room she called home. Her alcoholic mother was happy with the money she received for her daughter and seemed not to care about her fate. Rebecca assured Stead that it was quite clear to Mrs. Armstrong that Eliza was headed for ruin. Her only oversight, one that later proved costly, was the assumption that Eliza's father knew of the deal.

The whole transaction was completed with ease for the sum of just five pounds—one pound for the girl's mother, two pounds to Rebecca's "friend" for setting up the deal, and two pounds for a midwife who performed the customary physical examination that was often requested by brothel clientele. The midwife, Madame Louise Mourez, had certified many virgins for brothels before and was more than happy to comply this time as well. Eliza, who was informed that a physical checkup was required before her work began, was unharmed but confided afterward to Rebecca that the midwife was "a dirty woman." The whole procedure was carried out as planned, without a hitch.

After visiting the midwife, Eliza, Rebecca, and Jacques, one of Stead's investigators, went to a house on Poland Street, Soho, where Stead was waiting. Together the party climbed the narrow stairs leading to the brothel rooms Stead had hired for the evening. After sharing a drink, Eliza was left alone to sleep. The charade was all but complete. Sometime later, Stead entered her room, expecting the young girl to be sleeping soundly. Eliza awoke when she sensed his presence, and screamed aloud, "There's a man in the room! Take me home; oh, take me home."[5] Without speaking, Stead left the room, and Rebecca came to reassure Eliza. The following day, plans were made for Rebecca and another Salvationist to escort Eliza to France where she would remain in the care of The Salvation Army. Within twenty-four hours she was out of England.

Stead was triumphant. They had attained undeniable evidence of the evil system that saw the ruin of thousands of young English girls every year. With the sweet taste of victory in his mouth, he began to write.

On Monday, July 6, 1885, the first of four articles entitled "The Maiden Tribute of Modern Babylon" appeared in the *Pall Mall Gazette*. These contained the findings of Stead's secret investigations, culminating in the account of the purchase of a young girl he called "Lily," for the purpose of prostitution. Stead held nothing back, clearly exposing both the sordid nature and immense magnitude of the abuse occurring daily against young girls in Britain. The articles were an instant sellout as the prostitution industry was blown open to public scrutiny.

London was thrown into turmoil. The public largely hailed Stead a hero, although some politicians branded him a pervert for publishing obscene material and demanded prosecution. Some news agents banned the sale of the *Gazette*, and a dozen newsboys were arrested for selling the papers. Slave traders recruited as many roughs as they could lay hands on and incited them to storm the building where Stead worked, desperately trying to meet each day's deadline for the series of articles. On Tuesday, July 7, when it appeared they might lose their building to the wild crowds, Stead sent word to William Booth, requesting his assistance. Without hesitation, William replied, "Tell Mr. Stead that we'll throw open this building for the sake of his paper. We'll do everything in our power to help him."[6]

Stead pressed on, the Army backing his every move. Army headquarters became a base from which the *Gazette* was sold, and cadets distributed it for sale on the streets. William and Catherine stepped up their public purity meetings, stirring the mass crowds to action. At a meeting in Exeter Hall,

London, Catherine brought home to many the awful reality of Stead's reports with a true account from their own files. A rich merchant had approached a brothel-keeper, paying cash in advance to secure a small girl for Sunday. The arrangements were made, and an innocent girl was easily enticed away from her Sunday school lesson. All went as planned—until the merchant entered the padded room and quickly withdrew in shock as he came face-to-face with his own daughter.[7]

Such stories added fuel to the fire, and letters began to pour in from the public, thanking Stead for his articles and calling for a change in the laws that failed to protect England's children.

The Booths' involvement in calling for reform did not in any way or at any time distract them from their primary purpose. As William explained,

> To prevent any misunderstanding here let it be known that we only know of one way of stripping the miseries of men—that is by stripping them of their sins. . . . If you want to bless mankind, go to the root! . . . Our work is to deliver people by turning them away from their iniquities. That is a fundamental principle. But we want help in that matter from the government. We want our lawmakers to make just laws. . . . I said to a friend who is mixed up with politics, "I think the time is come when you politicians ought to have another party—a party based on morality. . . . Whatever differences of opinion there may be with regard to the special forms of government there can be no difference of opinion with good men that a good government ought to be the father of its people and the protector of their children."[8]

The Booths took advantage of the rising tide of public opinion and prepared a petition calling for:

- Protection for children, boys and girls, to the end of their seventeenth year.
- The procuring of young persons for immoral purposes to be made a criminal act.
- Magistrates to be given the power to order entry into a house where believed that underaged girls may be detained against their will.
- Equality for men and women in the law—that it be made an offense for men to solicit women.

Protest meetings were held over a period of seventeen days, and the Army collected 393,000 signatures to their petition. On Thursday, July 30, 1885, the petition, which when stretched out measured over two and half miles, was carried by Salvation Army cadets and escorted by a group of mothers to the House of Commons. As a result of the petition and the public outcry over the evidence presented in Stead's articles, the Criminal Law Amendment Act was passed by the House of Commons on August 14. From that day on, the age of consent was set at sixteen. As the news spread, other nations, including Australia and some parts of the United States, began to follow suit.

William Booth, captured in a thoughtful moment.

Through an unwillingness to accept the evils of society and the courage to challenge the system, the Army had successfully initiated and supported a campaign that improved the laws of their nation. They set up a national service for helping young girls, including more homes for those rescued from prostitution. Within five years they had thirteen homes housing over three hundred girls in England and a further seventeen homes abroad. As always, however, their success did not come without a cost.

The Armstrongs had begun to worry about their daughter. Although her identity had not been disclosed in Stead's articles, they could not ignore the similarity between Eliza and "Lily." In mid-July, they stormed into their local police station and demanded their daughter's return. Those wanting to discredit the Booths and The Salvation Army wasted no time in seizing their opportunity. A series of articles appeared in a weekly newspaper, portraying the Armstrongs as innocent victims who had been robbed of their child. One member of Parliament who was well known for his opposition to changes in the law alerted the home secretary to these articles and called for the prosecution of all those involved in Eliza's alleged abduction.

An extradition warrant was issued to Mr. Armstrong, who traveled to Paris to collect his daughter. Eliza had been very happy in her service of The Salvation Army and begged to stay on, but by August 24 she was home in England, once more in the custody of her parents.

The police moved quickly, summonsing all those who had played some role in Stead's charade. Bramwell, Rebecca, Madame Mourez, Mrs. Combes, Stead, and Jacques all appeared before the Bow Street court to hear the charges laid against them. The preliminary hearing lasted almost three weeks amid stormy courthouse scenes. Angry slave traders and brothel workers gathered together mobs of roughs, inciting them to attack the defendants as they arrived and departed from the courthouse.

All were remanded to face trial on the abduction of Eliza Armstrong, a charge that hinged entirely upon the fact that Eliza's father had not given his consent to her removal from their home. In addition, Stead, Jacques, and Rebecca were charged with aiding and abetting an indecent assault. Madame Mourez was charged with indecent assault.

As the trial progressed, it became apparent to Stead and the others that the judge was clearly against them. The witness of the archbishop of Canterbury, in whom Stead had earlier confided, was not allowed into the court. When the jury attempted to show they saw a difference between offenses that were technical and those that were committed with criminal intent, the judge would not accept it. He refused to give any room for recommendations from the jury that would have favored Stead and Rebecca based on the motive behind their actions.

Rebecca's history as a procuress severely damaged her defense. When questioned about her past, she panicked and lied to protect former accomplices. Her lawyer tried to excuse her behavior, but the damage was already done.

Finally the jury's verdict was announced. Bramwell and Madame Combes were acquitted of all charges laid against them. Stead and Rebecca were found guilty of both the charges of abduction and aiding and abetting an indecent assault against Eliza Armstrong. Jacques was acquitted of the abduction charge but found guilty of aiding and abetting the assault, and Madame Mourez was found guilty of indecent assault. Stead was labeled a "disgrace to journalism" and was sentenced to three months of imprisonment. Rebecca was sentenced to six months without hard labor, Jacques to one month, and Madame Mourez to six months with hard labor.

Ironically, after Stead had served his time, he discovered that Eliza was in fact an illegitimate child. The judge's insistence that the jury base their decision entirely on the fact that the girl was taken from Mr. Armstrong without his consent was entirely unfounded. It would seem that any ill feeling between Mrs. Armstrong and the Salvationists quickly disappeared. Eliza's little sister was the first child placed in the Army's Marylebone crèche, and Eliza herself spent some of her teenage years in the care of The Salvation Army before getting married.

Rebecca endured her imprisonment, encouraged by the contact she had with the Salvationists. She remained with The Salvation Army until her death. For his part, Stead celebrated his imprisonment in the following years by donning his prison uniform on the anniversary of his conviction.

At first, skeptics and those who stood opposed to The Salvation Army predicted the Armstrong case would herald its downfall. But, as Railton later reported, it actually strengthened their position in England and overseas. He wrote,

> The Armstrong prosecution has done more to assist us in becoming the rescuers of those who have fallen, or are in danger of falling, than fifty years of desperate labor on our part could possibly have done. Not only are we fully recognized all over the world as being engaged with all our might in this rescue business, but are looked upon as the people who are never likely to be beaten because we are never likely to stop short at any difficulty or danger where a great object is to be attained. Consequently, we have not only the joy of harboring hundreds of these poor wanderers and striving to lead them to Christ and to a new life, but from the police, from parents, from friends and even from enemies, we have received inquiries as to those who were missing and whom we have already been privileged in a great many cases to restore to now happy homes.[9]

The Booths experienced once more the faithfulness of God. The very plans and purposes of the enemy to destroy their work in spreading the gospel were instead turned around and used for good. On November 14, 1885, William wrote in *The War Cry*,

> Let us fill the land with Hallelujahs! Not because the Chief of Staff is outside prison walls but because the Army is vindicated at the same time that its work has been more fully than ever proclaimed before the world. And now for personal re-consecration and increased devotion to the work not only for saving the girls, but the boys and the fathers and the mothers

from sin and perdition. . . . To the inquiry "What about Eliza Armstrong?" let us return the question "What about Jesus Christ and your never-dying soul and the salvation of the perishing millions around you?"[10]

The Salvation Army had survived its greatest challenge to date, and their welfare work was lifted into a sphere of greater public recognition. The stage was set for the unfolding of the Booths' masterpiece of social welfare, a strategy that would radically impact not only England but also the world.

CHAPTER 10

A Broken Heart

CATHERINE'S FINAL YEARS (1886–1890)

The great use of life is to spend it on something that will outlast it.

—CHARLES MAYES

Catherine looked out across the vast crowd of Salvationists gathered in London in June of 1886 for the Army's first international congress. She began:

> Twenty-one years ago, we stepped right out in the name of God, single-handed, with the one all-absorbing desire and determination that at all costs we would reach the people with the Gospel. . . . We have found the true idea, Jesus Christ's idea, of fraternity, the fraternity of all men, irrespective of difference of color, customs or speech. . . . "By this shall men know that ye are My disciples, if ye love one another." [See John 13:35] . . . Not only have we got this love, but we go on propagating it.[1]

The dedicated group of salvation soldiers seated before her was evidence of Catherine's claim. Officers from sixteen nations as far-flung as India, New Zealand, Canada, and South Africa had gathered to take part in the congress meetings. The Salvation Army had become an international force, with the great majority of its overseas officers being raised up from within their own nations.

While each division was responsible for its own funding, The Salvation Army International Headquarters in London managed a foreign fund to assist their work in other nations. Even with the Army ever expanding, the Booths still bore the brunt of the financial burden. William hated to ask for money, but at times he had no choice.

The Invercargill Salvation Army Band, 1886. Photo taken outside the town's law court building.

In 1886 one officer's unusual pledge caught William's attention. On the small yellow form used for pledging a donation to the Army's work, Major John Carleton had written, "By going without pudding every day for a year, I calculate I can save 50 shillings. This I will do, and will remit the amount named as quickly as possible."[2] Carleton's self-sacrificing attitude touched William's heart and inspired an idea for raising funds that became an annual event.

In autumn of 1866 The Salvation Army in the United Kingdom held their first Self-Denial Week. During these seven days, Salvationists were encouraged to deny themselves one thing and donate the money they saved to the Army. The first appeal was comprised of thousands of coins, mostly copper, amounting to £4,820! The Booths knew the pennies and half-pennies that poured in during Self-Denial Week represented some of the greatest sacrifices made by the Salvationists. To William and Catherine, they were more precious by far than checks written out by their wealthy supporters. Self-Denial Week was established as an annual event for the Army, not only in England but also in every nation where they had established their work. Each year the officers set out to smash the previous year's total, doing almost anything to raise a little extra money to fund the work.

With The Salvation Army spreading like wildfire, William began to travel extensively, directing the troops, encouraging them in their work, and preaching in nations around the world. It seemed as though the more ground the Army took, the more aware William was of the lives that remained untouched and unchanged. Even in England, where they had toiled for years, there was still so much to do.

In December of 1887 William and Catherine commenced a new campaign across England. The meetings were entitled *Two Days With God*. William and Catherine shared the preaching, compelling their listeners to consecrate their lives to God with a greater urgency than ever before. The response was incredible: In one place alone, over eight hundred people responded to the call to live a life of holiness in service to God.

Even though Catherine continued to preach as powerfully as ever, her health was declining noticeably by this time, and a new strategy was adopted to minimize her fatigue. When she preached, an accompanying officer was instructed to tug on her jacket after she had spoken for an hour. This was her cue to wind down to a close in order to save her strength. Even in spite of such measures, she had to be physically carried from many meetings due to sheer exhaustion.

In a letter written to Emma from Manchester in December of 1887, Catherine revealed her own fears for her health.

> I got on well I think this morning. I got a blessing yesterday. I *accepted* [this illness] if [it be] the Lord's will for me—the disease I have so dreaded in my life, against which I fear my heart has rebelled—and this has helped me as submission always helps us! This won't bring the disease if it is not to come, but it will make it much easier if it should come.[3]

Although not named, the disease Catherine feared was most likely cancer. She had nursed her own mother as she suffered and died from the dreaded sickness in 1869; now, as Catherine encouraged others to submit themselves wholeheartedly to God, she, too, laid down her life afresh. Come what may, she continued to obey, trusting her Lord with her life.

As they toured their nation, preaching in cities and towns, the Booths were filled anew with compassion for the poor. Remarkably, their senses never became dull to the suffering endured by so many. One cold December evening in 1887, William returned home by cab from a meeting in Whitstable, Kent. As the carriage rattled over London Bridge around midnight, his eyes took in a scene that cut to his heart. In every nook and hollow provided by the bridge, men huddled under scraps of cardboard and newspaper, seeking shelter from the bitter cold. They seemed oblivious of his stares as the cab passed them by, but William could not erase the pitiful sight from his mind. The acknowledgment of so many fellow human beings without food and shelter in the harsh English winter plagued him. How could he turn away?

The next day William spoke with Bramwell, describing in detail the scene he had witnessed during the night. "Did you know that men slept out all night on the bridge?" he questioned his chief of staff. When Bramwell admitted he was aware of the fact, William reprimanded him for not having done something about it before and demanded that he immediately find a way of providing shelter for the poor wretches. Bramwell wasted no time in obeying his general's orders.

In January of 1888 a building in Limehouse was hired for the purpose of providing refuge and food for the homeless living on London's streets. A donation of six hundred pounds covered the initial cost of setting up The Salvation Army's first food and shelter depot. By the end of the first week, more than two thousand people were being fed each

Bramwell Booth, son of William and Catherine, and The Salvation Army's second general

day, over seven hundred of them children. William and Catherine had learned many valuable lessons from their earlier attempts at welfare work and now insisted that a small fee be paid for meals and lodging. They were adamant that charity would not interfere with genuine conversions. Those who had no money and were fit for work were provided with tasks to do to earn their keep. Two more depots were opened by the end of February.

While Bramwell organized the establishment of the food and shelter depots, William began a thorough evaluation of the effectiveness of their work among the poor. When he had first begun to evangelize the East London masses, his one aim was to rescue them from eternal hell; relief from the temporal hell they endured on earth had seemed much less important. After years of working with the poor, of seeing the effects of drunkenness, hunger, disease, and all manner of evil desires, William's heart had changed. He had come to realize that for many, their desperate circumstances prevented them from responding to the gospel of Christ. Surely, by providing relief of their temporal miseries, The Salvation Army could make it easier for men and women to find their way to Jesus.

William was tired of seeing the indifference of the wealthy toward the poor. He was tired of hearing those who worked to provide welfare services conclude that there was no answer to society's evils, no way to change the state of the poor. As he reviewed the direction and purpose of The Salvation Army, he decided once more to take matters into his own hands. A strategy was needed—a plan that would provide for the welfare of the masses throughout England.

Utilizing his network of Army officers, who were in touch with the heart and soul of the nation, William began a thorough investigation of the magnitude and nature of the problems that assailed the poor in England. Day after day, reports and statistics poured into Salvation Army headquarters, telling story after story of the plight of the unemployed and the homeless.

The picture that was pieced together before them was horrifying. The predicament of those living in the slummy tenements was terrible, but even more alarming were the great hordes of men and women who had no place to call home. They would sleep upright six to a bench or stretch out on the icy bare ground with only their threadbare clothes to protect them from the cold. Their stories were diverse.

Said one man discovered sleeping on a bench,

> I'm a tailor, [and I] have slept here four nights running. Can't get work. Been out of a job three weeks. If I can muster cash, I sleep at a lodging-house in Vere Street, Clare Market. It was very wet last night. I left these seats and went to Covent Garden Market and slept under cover. There were about thirty of us. The police moved us on, but we went back as soon as they had gone. I've had a pen'orth of bread and pen'orth of soup during the last two days—often goes without altogether. There are women who sleep out here. They are decent people, mostly charwomen and such like who can't find work.

Replied another,

> I've slept here two nights. I'm a confectioner by trade; I come from Dartford. I got turned off because I'm getting elderly. They can get young

215

men cheaper, and I have the rheumatism so bad. I've earned nothing these two days; I thought I could get a job at Woolwich, so I walked there, but could get nothing. I found a bit of bread in the road wrapped up in a bit of newspaper. That did me for yesterday. I had a bit of bread and butter today. I'm fifty-four years old.[4]

For hundreds of men and women like these, unemployment had driven them to the streets. On the days they could find work, they had food to eat and a place to stay. When there was no work, they had to return to the streets, scrounging for food from garbage bins. Some were driven to suicide by their desperation. One such man was a fifty-year-old chemist. When he lost his job, he and his wife and child slowly spiraled into poverty. After twelve months the couple decided to end it all, taking their young child with them. When their attempt failed, they were both charged with the murder of their son. A letter addressed to the man's brother portrays the hardships that had driven them to these desperate measures:

> Twelve months have I now passed of a most miserable and struggling existence, and I really cannot stand it any more. I am completely worn out, and relations who could assist me won't do any more, for such was my uncle's last intimation. Never mind; he can't take his money and comfort with him, and in all probability will find himself in the same boat as myself. He never enquires whether I am starving or not. . . . I can face poverty and degradation no longer, and would sooner die than go to the workhouse, whatever may be the awful consequences of the steps we have taken. . . . My poor wife has done her best at needle-work, washing, house-minding, and in fact, anything and everything that would bring in a shilling; but it would only keep us in semi-starvation. I have now done six weeks' travel-ing from morning to night, and not received one farthing for it. If that is not enough to drive you mad—wickedly mad—I don't know what is. No bright prospects anywhere; no ray of hope. . . . If you could get three pound for our bed it will pay our rent, and our scanty furniture may fetch enough to bury us in a cheap way. Don't grieve over us or follow us, for we shall not be worthy of such respect. Our clergyman has never called on us or given us the least consolation, though I called on him a month ago. He is paid to preach, and there he considers his responsibility ends, the rich excepted.[5]

While the Booths collated story after story of the tragic circumstances of the poor, their own lives were struck a terrible blow. On February 21, 1888, William completed last-minute preparations for his tour of Holland. He was due to depart within the hour, but foremost on his mind was Catherine. He looked anxiously out of the window, searching for the first glimpse of her return. Finally he caught sight of her cab and rushed out to meet her.

One look into her eyes confirmed his worst fears. She tried bravely to smile through her tears, but nothing could hide the truth she had discovered. Sir James Paget, the renowned London surgeon, had diagnosed the small painful lump in her breast as a malignant cancer. The surgeon recommended immediate surgery. Without it, she was given no more than two years to live. Kneeling beside her beloved husband, she wiped away her tears and looked deeply into his troubled face. "Do you know what was my first thought?" she asked tenderly. "That I should not be there to nurse you at your last hour."[6] Her selfless confession broke William's heart and they wept together, stunned into silence by the awful reality. Finally they prayed, as they had so often done before, asking God for courage and strength for relief from the sentence of death.

After what seemed an eternity, they were jolted back to the present. William's transport arrived to take him to the station. At first he refused to go, but at Catherine's insistence he left for Holland, leaving instructions with Bramwell to find out more from the doctors. William's tour lasted only two days. The separation from Catherine was impossible for him to bear. He arranged for others to conduct the meetings and returned to London.

The news he received on his arrival home was no more encouraging. The second and third medical opinions confirmed the first. Despite her poor prognosis, Catherine obstinately refused to undergo surgery. She was aware of the risks associated with such an operation, and with her heart trouble she was not sure she would survive the ordeal. Various homeopathic treatments were tried, but all to no avail. Catherine's physical condition deteriorated very quickly after her cancer was diagnosed. Kate and Ballington made arrangements to return home to visit their mother, and the date for Emma's wedding to Commissioner Tucker was brought forward to April 10, 1888.

While Catherine's failing health required her to all but give up her busy preaching schedule, she continued her active involvement in Army affairs. Although she was not able to travel or address her beloved soldiers, she encouraged them with her letters, talked and prayed with them in her home, and continued to take part, whenever possible, in the leadership of the Army. Even in her personal suffering she gave little thought to her own comfort and ease, her life ever an example of self-sacrificing love.

The Salvationists who gathered to celebrate Emma's wedding were moved to tears by the courage displayed by their beloved Army Mother. Speaking of her illness, she said, "I have, as you know, been wounded and worsted in the fight and I have felt it hard, sometimes, not to be able to answer the bugle's call and jump to the front, as has been my custom for the last twenty-six years, when there has been need for me."[7]

From the midst of her pain she spoke lovingly and powerfully, urging them on in the fight of faith.

> You should thus present yourselves, your children, your all; for you know we all have a world to give up. It does not signify how we are trained or what were the particular circumstances of our antecedent life, there comes a crisis, a moment when every human soul which enters the Kingdom of God has to make its choice of that Kingdom in preference to everything that it holds and owns as its world; to give up all that, and to embrace and choose God.[8]

Even as her own world seemed so uncertain and so hard, Catherine continued to lay her life down for her Savior.

After Emma's wedding, it seemed Catherine's strength began to improve. The entire Army of Salvationists held her before the throne of grace in prayer, pleading for her healing and restoration. For a time it seemed their petitions were being answered. In May she took part in the *Two Days With God* meetings in Glasgow and London, sharing the preaching once more with William. Hopes for her recovery were, however, short-lived, and by the middle of June it was clear that the cancer was spreading in her body. On June 21, 1888, she stood before the people gathered in the City Temple and preached what was to be her final public message.[9]

Her words, as always, portrayed the depth of her devotion to God and to His Word. She encouraged the Salvationists to push on in the war for souls:

> Are not we who love the Lord Jesus Christ bound to do something for *His* sake? . . . He wants His prodigal children brought home. He won't ask you where you worshipped, or what creed you professed; but He *will* ask for His prodigals—those whom you have won for Him. Will you not set to work to do something for His sake? . . .
>
> Listen to what Jesus Christ commissioned His disciples to do. Not to ensconce themselves in comfortable buildings and invite the people to come, and then, if they would not come, leave them alone to be damned. No! No! He said, "Go ye," which means "go after them." . . .
>
> When we come to face eternity, and look back on the past, what will

be our regret? That we have done so much? Oh no! That we have done so little.[10]

With her own life's journey winding to conclusion, she left her people with no doubt of her desire for them to continue to follow hard after God.

Catherine's love of the ocean drew her to spend time at The Salvation Army officers' rest home overlooking the sea in Clacton, Essex. She spent a few weeks there before returning in October to their new home in London's Hadley Wood. Although physically weak and in pain, Catherine still continued her active involvement in Army affairs. Her home had always been a center of activity; now, as her health failed, her rest bed became a place of discussion, with meetings held and decisions made with her ever-valued input.

As William wrestled to come to terms with Catherine's deteriorating health, he sifted through the reports on the poor that continued to stream in from around England, bringing a welcome distraction from his own pain. The situation in the city of London was far worse than William had suspected. His officers' research indicated that an estimated three million people, ten percent of England's population, were experiencing life without the very basic standards of food, shelter, and work. The government, with little enthusiasm, had put in place a few schemes to help. Yet the only poor these schemes seemed to assist were those who were sober, industrious, and thoughtful enough to take advantage of the help they offered. Whenever help was offered, it seemed to be made as undesirable and unpleasant as possible in order to prevent people taking advantage of the state.

William discussed these findings with Catherine, and as he did so a Holy Spirit-inspired welfare strategy began to form in his mind. The strategy aimed to address the three basic needs of the poor—housing, food, and employment. His desire was to formulate a plan that would rescue them from their circumstances, lift them from the depths to which they had fallen, and provide them with the means by which they could improve their life. He again enlisted the help of W. T. Stead and began to set his agenda out in writing. Catherine's sickroom became a makeshift office for William's work on the book. He discussed every aspect of his writing with her, incorporating her ideas with his own as together they created an answer to England's social ills. Capitalizing on Stanley's bestselling work about his journey through Africa, *Through the Dark Continent*, William aptly entitled his book *In Darkest England and the Way Out*.

The book began by outlining what was termed "the cab horse ideal of existence." William likened the treatment of cab horses working in the streets of London to the basic standard of life that should be experienced by every person. Every cab horse had three things: shelter at night, food to eat, and work to do by which to earn its food. Whenever a cab horse tripped or fell in the middle of traffic in London, people responded immediately to get the animal on its legs again. Immediately the horse was helped up, the harness taken off, and everything done to restore the animal to full strength. There was never any delay as people argued or debated regarding why or how it fell. While the horse lived it had food, shelter, and work. This was the very basic standard that should be experienced by every person living in England.

After setting out the standard of living that his strategy would aim to bring to all people, William unveiled the magnitude of poverty currently experienced by three million of England's population. The statistics and stories of those living in "Darkest England" painted a grim picture. He described in detail the plight of the unemployed, the homeless, the alcoholics, those driven into prostitution and crime, and the most innocent of victims, the children. Heartrending stories of the brokenness caused by poverty filled the pages. The assistance provided to the poor by the government was described by William as being "well meaning, but more or less abortive attempts to cope with this great and appalling evil."[11]

Having described the problems, he began to outline his strategy to provide assistance for the lost, the homeless, and the helpless. He believed his plan, if carried out, would bring light into the heart of "Darkest England."

Every aspect of the Darkest England Scheme was based on seven foundational principles, which William described as "essentials to success."

The first essential of any successful plan for helping the poor was that it must deal with the heart of the man, especially where his failure in life has resulted from his character and conduct. As William well knew, "You may clothe the drunkard, fill his purse with gold, establish him in a well-furnished home, and in three, or six, or twelve months he will once more be on the Embankment, haunted by delirium tremens, dirty, squalid, and ragged."[12]

Second, the scheme must change the circumstances of an individual, especially when beyond his control. Although favorable circumstances would not change a man's heart, William believed they might make it easier for him to take the necessary steps to freedom.

The third essential for success was a strategy that was on a big enough scale to address the problem of poverty. "It is no use trying to bail out the ocean with a pint pot," William declared. His scheme was huge, and it would require a great amount of funding in order to succeed.

Fourth, the strategy must be permanent; it must be established into the framework of the nation in order to successfully alleviate the suffering of the poor in generations to come.

The fifth essential for success was a plan that was immediately feasible. A strategy that was not viable was not worth pursuing.

Sixth, the strategy to rescue the poor must not bring further damage to the people it sought to restore. William wrote, "Mere charity . . . while relieving the pinch of hunger, demoralizes the recipient; and whatever the remedy is that we employ, it must be of such a nature as to do good without doing evil at the same time."[13]

Finally, to be successful, the scheme must not endanger any others in society. There would be no point in saving one group of people by sacrificing another. Having laid the foundation by which he desired his strategy to be assessed, William presented his solution to the social problems encountered by the poor.

The Darkest England Scheme was divided into three parts; together, William believed they would work to transform the living hell of the homeless into communities of self-helping, self-sustaining families, based on the principles and disciplines of The Salvation Army. The three-phase strategy began in London and stretched out to the farthest corners of the British Empire.

Phase One: The City Colony

The first phase involved the establishment of institutions to rescue the poor, supply their immediate necessities, provide them with temporary employment, and begin to instruct them in godly principles that would assist in life. Some would be reestablished in the broader community through this colony, finding work or being reinstated with family who were able to support and help them. Others would be passed on to the next phase of the strategy.

Phase Two: The Farm Colony

Those who were unable to find permanent employment in the city would be moved out to a settlement in the country. The reformation of the character of the individuals would continue with education, vocational training, and instruction in godly principles and disciplines. Once again, many who were restored in this way would find employment or be reunited with supportive family in other parts of the country. Some would be trained and sent on to the third phase of the strategy.

Phase Three: The Colony Across the Sea

At this time in the history of the world, the doors of opportunity were flung wide open for settlement and development of industry in the British colonies of South Africa, East Africa, Canada, and Australia. Booth's strategy included the establishment of a settlement in the colonies that would become the home for some of England's destitute millions, giving them a new start and hope for a new life in the colonies of the British Empire.

William described in detail the multitude of schemes that would be instituted in each of the phases of his strategy. He proposed food and shelter depots, work factories, a labor exchange, waste recycling, rescue homes for women and prisoners, and a variety of other programs all designed to help set the poor on their feet again.

The Darkest England strategy was designed to reach those who could not help themselves. The essential ingredient of any scheme to be developed as part of the strategy was a focus on changing the man, not just his circumstances. William was fully convinced the only way to do this was by the power of God.

> To get a man soundly saved it is not enough to put on him a pair of new breeches, to give him regular work, or even to give him a university education. These things are all outside a man, and if the inside remains unchanged you have wasted your labor. You must in some way or other graft upon the man's nature a new nature, which has in it the element of the Divine. All that I propose . . . is governed by that principle.[14]

In spite of this belief, William's strategy would not force religion on anyone. Those who chose not to accept the salvation offered by God would receive the same practical help as those whose lives were transformed by Jesus Christ.

The book was concluded with a call for public support of the Darkest England Scheme. The Salvation Army was comprised of ten thousand full-time officers at the time of writing the book, yet William called for new recruits to help implement his strategy. He wrote,

> I want Recruits, but I cannot soften the conditions in order to attract

men to the Colors. I want no comrades on these terms, but those who know our rules and are prepared to submit to our discipline: who are one with us on the great principles which determine our action, and whose hearts are in this great work for the amelioration of the hard lot of the lapsed and lost. These I will welcome into the service.

It may be that you cannot deliver an open-air address, or conduct an indoor meeting. Public labor for souls has hitherto been outside your practice. In the Lord's vineyard, however, are many laborers, and all are not needed to do the same thing. If you have a practical acquaintance with any of the varied operations of which I have spoken in this book; if you are familiar with agriculture, understand the building trade, or have a practical knowledge of almost any form of manufacture, there is a place for you.

We cannot offer you great pay, social position, or any glitter and tinsel of man's glory; in fact, we can promise little more than rations, plenty of hard work, and probably no little of worldly scorn; but if on the whole you believe you can in no other way help your Lord so well and bless humanity so much, you will brave the opposition of friends, abandon earthly prospects, trample pride under foot, and come out and follow Him *in this new crusade*.[15]

In addition to this call, William asked for the public to commit financially to the scheme. In order to put his strategy into action, £100,000 was required. William concluded,

To you who believe in the remedy here proposed and the soundness of these plans, and have the ability to assist me, I now confidently appeal for practical evidence of the faith that is in you. The responsibility is no longer mine alone. It is yours as much as mine. . . . I am only one man among my fellows, and the same as you. The obligation to care for these lost and perishing multitudes does not rest on me any more than it does on you. To me has been given the idea, but to you the means by which it may be realized. The Plan has now been published to the world; it is for you to say whether it is to remain barren, or whether it is to bear fruit in unnumbered blessings to all the children of men.[16]

While the manuscript for *In Darkest England and the Way Out* was slowly pieced together, William arranged to move to Clacton so that he could spend as much time as possible with Catherine. The seaside location had proved to be more beneficial to her health than their home in London. A generous gift enabled them to rent the home from The Salvation Army, and they set the house up as their makeshift headquarters.

Catherine's condition worsened rapidly after her cancer was diagnosed. Stoically, she refused narcotic pain relief for many months, preferring to suffer than lose a moment's consciousness. By October of 1889, she was almost completely confined to bed, and it appeared the end was drawing near. Night after night her beloved family kept watch by her bedside, not expecting her to see the New Year. As January of 1890 dawned, however, Catherine's strength increased a little and her condition stabilized.

Despite the poor health and physical weakness that had troubled Catherine throughout her life, she had always been determined that nothing would hinder her service of God. The greatest struggle she faced as she lay stricken with cancer was her inability to continue in the war for souls. For the 1889 Self-Denial Appeal she wrote,

> If the Lord were to ask me to deny myself of almost all I possess how easy it would be in comparison with what He requires from me just now, for I am realizing more fully than ever how much harder it is to suffer than to serve: nevertheless my soul bows in submission to my Heavenly Father.[17]

Night after night William wrestled with God in prayer as he watched the woman he loved so deeply suffer great pain and grow weaker by the day. It crushed his heart to see the terrible effects of the cancer as it ate away her flesh and brought such painful agony. He cried out to God every day, trying desperately to come to terms with her suffering. His only consolation was the realization that such trials, though hard, were invaluable as they drove people to the Lord, the greatest source of comfort and peace. He saw this fact most clearly displayed in the eyes of his beloved.

Catherine had long ago realized that her greatest need was to have faith in God, regardless of her circumstances. Now, in the face of a cruel and painful death, her faith continued to hold strong. "Ought I not be willing," she said, "if it be God's will, even to go down into the dark valley without any realization, simply knowing that I am His and that He is mine?"[18]

In spite of her ever-increasing suffering, Catherine still continued to have input into the life of the Army. There were no new advancements, no fresh initiatives implemented, that were not first run past the Army Mother. When more than fifty thousand Salvationists gathered at the Crystal Palace for the Army's twenty-fifth anniversary celebration, she sent her greeting.

My dear children and friends,
My place is empty, but my heart is with you. You are my joy and my

crown. Your battles, sufferings, and victories have been the chief interest of my life these past twenty-five years. They are so still. Go forward. Live holy lives. Be true to the Army. God is your strength. Love and seek the lost; bring them to the Blood. Make the people good; inspire them with the Spirit of Jesus Christ. Love one another; help your comrades in dark hours. I am dying under the Army flag; it is yours to live and fight under. God is my Salvation and refuge in the storm. I send you my love and blessing.[19]

Long before the Salvation Army was birthed, God had whispered a promise to His devoted servant. "I will make thee a mother of nations,"[20] He had said. As often seems to be the case, the Word of the Lord had come at a time of great hardship. It was a promise given early in married life when, together with William, she faced leaving and losing all they had in order to follow God. It was a promise that seemed too good to be true—a virtual impossibility. Catherine had tucked it away in her heart. Now, as she lay on her deathbed, picturing the thousands of men and women from nineteen nations around the world that marched under the Army's flag, her heart rejoiced in the faithfulness of her God. As she had lived her life in obedience to her Lord, He had fulfilled His promise. Catherine Booth had become a mother of nations.

Catherine's days on earth were numbered, but her influence on the lives of many men and women was destined to live on. William's Darkest England Scheme was clearly shaped with her input and ideas. Many meetings and discussions were held around her bedside as she and William read and re-read the manuscript prepared by Stead. When, on a Sunday morning in September of 1890, the epic was finally complete, Stead declared prophetically to those gathered around her, "That work will echo around the world. Its influence for good, its effects upon others far beyond the ranks of the Army, will be quite incalculable. I rejoice with an exceeding great joy." Summoning all her strength, Catherine replied in a whisper, "And I most of all. Thank God. Thank God. Yes, thank God, we may rejoice that something on an adequate scale is to be done at last; through all these years I have labored and prayed that this matter might be done; but, thank God! Thank God!"[21]

By Thursday, October 2, 1890, Catherine's strength had all but failed, and death drew near. William sat alone by her side during the evening hours, enjoying the precious time that remained for them to share. Their journey through life together had been a beautiful experience of the deepest love and devotion. Together they had triumphed over tremendous opposition to see thousands upon thousands of souls added to the kingdom of God. The movement they pioneered had stretched out to reach the very ends of the earth, bringing great joy to their hearts. As they reflected together on their memories and moments, Catherine allowed her wedding ring to slip from her thin finger into William's hand. "By this token we were united for time," she whispered, "and by it now we are united for eternity."[22]

Although her body was failing, she survived the night and another day. On Saturday her beloved family and friends gathered once more around her bedside. William, Bramwell and his wife, Florence, Eva, Marian, Lucy, Catherine's nurses, and other staff members joined in song and prayer. Seeing her life ebb slowly away, they each kissed her and said their good-byes. With her hand in his, William waited for the final moment, praying for the grace to endure. Sensing somehow that the time had come, he bent to kiss his beloved wife and took her in his arms. She breathed his name one last time as her life slipped away.

In death as in life, Catherine continued to draw people to Jesus. The public

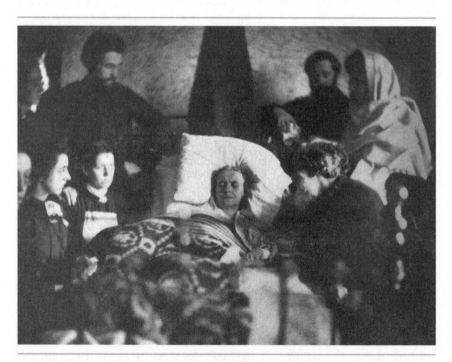

Beloved wife and mother; the family gather around Catherine's bedside during her "final battle" with cancer. She went to glory shortly after on October 4, 1890.

viewing saw over fifty thousand people file by to pay their last respects. Many had been saved as a result of her ministry; she had left her mark on them all. Bramwell's children knelt by the coffin as their mother spoke to them of heaven. Five-year-old Mary began to cry and, with her mother's arm around her, gave her heart to Jesus. In that very precious moment, her grandmother's death marked the beginning of her own spiritual life.

On Monday, October 13, thirty-six thousand people attended Catherine's funeral. At the close of the service, hundreds stood to their feet, surrendering their lives to God. The following day, four thousand Salvationists marched in the funeral procession as it moved through the city to Abney Park Cemetery. William stood to his feet and spoke passionately of his love for Catherine, of her friendship, her counsel, her mothering, and her wonderful devotion as a wife:

> My beloved Comrades and Friends:
>
> You will readily understand that I find it a difficulty to talk to you this afternoon. To begin with, I could not be willing to talk without an attempt to make you hear, and sorrow doesn't feel like shouting.
>
> Yet I have come riding through these, I suppose, hundreds of thousands of people this afternoon, who have bared their heads and who have blessed me in the name of the Lord at almost every revolution of the carriage wheels. My mind has been full of two feelings, which alternate—one is uppermost one moment, and the other the next—and yet which blend and amalgamate with each other; and these are the feeling of sorrow and the feeling of gratitude.
>
> Those who know me—and I don't think I am very difficult to understand—and those who knew my darling, my beloved, will, I am sure, understand how it is that my heart should be rent with sorrow.
>
> If you had had a tree that had grown up in your garden, under your window, which for forty years had been your shadow from the burning sun, whose flowers had been the adornment and beauty of your life, whose fruit had been almost the stay of your existence, and the gardener had come along and swung his glittering axe and cut it down before your eyes, I think you would feel as though you had a blank—it might not be a big one—but a little blank in your life!
>
> If you had had a servant, who for all this long time had served you without fee or reward, who had ministered, for very love, to your health and comfort, and who had suddenly passed away, you would miss that servant!
>
> If you had had a counselor who, in hours—continually occurring—of

perplexity and amazement, had ever advised you, and seldom advised wrong; whose advice you had followed and seldom had reason to regret it; and the counselor, while you are still in the same intricate mazes of your existence, had passed away, you would miss that counselor!

If you had had a friend who had understood your very nature, the rise and fall of your feelings, the bent of your thoughts and the purpose of your existence; a friend whose communion had ever been pleasant—the most pleasant of all other friends—to whom you had ever turned with satisfaction, and your friend had been taken away, you would feel some sorrow at the loss!

If you had had a mother for your children, who had cradled and nursed and trained them for the service of the living God, in which you most delighted—a mother, indeed, who had never ceased to bear their sorrows on her heart, and who had been ever willing to pour forth that heart's blood in order to nourish them—and that darling mother had been taken from your side, you would feel it a sorrow!

If you had had a wife, a sweet love of a wife, who for forty years had never given you real cause for grief; a wife who had stood with you side by side in the battle's front, who had been a comrade to you, ever willing to interpose herself between you and the enemy, and ever the strongest when the battle was fiercest, and your beloved one had fallen before your eyes, I am sure there would have been some excuse for sorrow!

Well, my comrades, you can roll all these qualities into one personality, and what would be lost in each I have lost in all. There has been taken away from me the delight of my eyes, the inspiration of my soul, and we are about to lay all that remains of her in the grave. I have been looking right at the bottom of it here, and calculating how soon they may bring and lay me alongside of her, and my cry to God has been that every remaining hour of my life may make me readier to come and join her in death, to go and embrace her in life in the Eternal City!

And yet, my comrades, my heart is full of gratitude too that swells and makes me forget my sorrow, that the long valley of the shadow of death has been trodden, and that out of the dark tunnel she has emerged into the light of day. Death came to her with all its terrors, brandishing his heart before her for two long years and nine months. Again and again she went down to the river's edge to receive her last thrust, as she thought, but ever coming back to life again. Thank God, she will see him no more—she is more than conqueror over the last enemy!

Death came to take her away from her loved employment. She loved the fight! Her great sorrow to the last moment was: "I cannot be with you when the clouds lower, when friends turn and leave you, and sorrows come sweeping over you; I shall no longer be there to put my arms round you and cheer you on!"

But she went away to help us! She promised me many a time that what she could do for us in the Eternal City should be done! The valley to her was a dark one in having to tear her heart away from so many whom she loved so well. Again and again she said, "The roots of my affections are very deep." But they had to be torn up. One after another she gave us up; she made the surrender with many loving words of counsel, and left us to her Lord.

This afternoon my heart has been full of gratitude because her soul is now with Jesus. She had a great capacity for suffering and a great capacity for you, and her heart is full of joy this afternoon.

My heart has also been full of gratitude because God lent me for so long a season such a treasure. I have been thinking, if I had to point out her three qualities to you here, they would be: First, she was good. She was washed in the Blood of the Lamb. To the last moment her cry was, "A sinner saved by grace." She was a thorough hater of shams, hypocrisies and make-believes.

Second, she was love. Her whole soul was full of tender, deep compassion. I was thinking this morning that she suffered more in her lifetime through her compassion for poor dumb animals than some suffer for the wide, wide world of sinning, sorrowing mortals! Oh, how she loved, how she compassioned, how she pitied the suffering poor! How she longed to put her arms round the sorrowful and help them!

Lastly, she was a warrior. She liked the fight. She was not one who said to others, "Go!" but "Here, let *me* go!" And when there was the necessity she cried, "I *will* go." I never knew her flinch until her poor body compelled her to lie aside.[23]

Grief overwhelmed William as the loss of his best friend and dearest companion sank into his soul. The thought of continuing without her was almost inconceivable. In spite of this, however, his mission remained unchanged. Standing by her graveside he concluded his address.

"My comrades," he declared,

I am going to meet her again. I have never turned from her these forty years for any journeyings on my mission of mercy but I have longed to get back, and have counted the weeks, days, and hours, which should take me again to her side. When she has gone away from me it has been just the same. And now she has gone away for the last time. What then is there left for me to do? Not to count the weeks, the days, and the hours which shall bring me again into her sweet company, seeing that I know not what will be on the morrow, nor what an hour may bring forth. My work plainly is to fill up the weeks, the days and the hours and cheer my poor heart as I go along with the thought that when I have served Christ and my generation according to the will of God—which I vow this afternoon I will, to the last drop of my blood—then I trust that she will bid me welcome to the skies, as He bade her. God bless you all.[24]

Tears flowed freely as Catherine's body was lowered into the ground. Commissioner Railton performed the Army's burial service, and Bramwell concluded by leading those present in a prayer of covenant. As William and his children finally turned away from Catherine's grave, the Army band struck up the familiar tune of a battle song. The Army Mother's war was over, but through the words of her son's song, she continued to urge them on.

To the front! The cry is ringing;
To the front! Your place is there;
In the conflict men are wanted,
Men of hope and faith and prayer.
Selfish ends shall claim no right.
From the battle's post to take us;
Fear shall vanish in the fight,
For triumphant God will make us.

Chorus:
No retreating, hell defeating,
Shoulder to shoulder we stand;
God look down, with glory crown
Our conquering band.
Victory for me
Through the Blood of Christ, my Savior;
Victory for me
Through the precious blood.

To the front! No more delaying,
Wounded spirits need they care;
To the front! The Lord obeying,
Stoop to help the dying there.
Broken hearts and blighted hopes,
Slaves of sin and degradation,
Wait for thee, in love to bring
Holy peace and liberation.[25]

CHAPTER 11

Finishing the Race

WILLIAM'S FINAL YEARS (1890–1912)

A leader is great, not because of his or her power, but because of his or her ability to empower others. Success without a successor is a failure.

—JOHN MAXWELL

In the days following Catherine's death, William completed the preface to his book, allowing the world a brief glimpse of his grief. *In Darkest England and the Way Out* was dedicated to the memory of his beloved wife: "To one who has been for nearly forty years indissolubly associated with me in every undertaking I owe much of the inspiration which has found expression in this book," he wrote.

> It is probably difficult for me to fully estimate the extent to which the splendid benevolence and unbounded sympathy of her character have pressed me forward in the life-long service of man, to which we have devoted both ourselves and our children. It will be an ever green and precious memory to me that amid the ceaseless suffering of a dreadful malady my dying wife found relief in considering and developing the suggestions for the moral and social and spiritual blessing of the people which are here set forth, and I do thank God she was taken from me only when the book was practically complete and the last chapters had been sent to the press.[1]

As general of The Salvation Army, William was given little chance to mourn. *In Darkest England and the Way Out* was released for sale a week after

231

William Booth, God's general

Catherine's funeral, and overnight the book became a bestseller, with ten thousand copies sold in one day! General William Booth became the most talked-about man in Britain. The timing was perfect; the nation was slowly awakening to the desperate cries of the underprivileged, and many reformers were joining the fight against poverty. Donations began to pour in to help the Army implement its welfare strategy.

Not everyone, however, was supportive of William's radical scheme. He immediately faced intense personal criticism from those who believed social welfare was related only to political and secular theories, not to God or religion. Throughout Britain, public debate raged over the issue of the state funding such a scheme.

In private, William mourned his beloved wife. He had waged war with her by his side for thirty-five years. Catherine had been his equal in every aspect of their work, and together they had shared the responsibilities and difficulties of leading what had become a monumental move of God. Her wisdom with people and the ways of God had been invaluable in growing The Salvation Army from its humble beginnings in East London to its expansion around the world. The loss and loneliness that engulfed William after her death was unimaginable; at the age of sixty-one, he faced the reality of living out the remainder of his days alone.

While grieving his loss in private, publicly William was once again the focus of slander and accusation. His critics labeled him "a sensual, dishonest, sanctimonious, and hypocritical scoundrel," a "brazen-faced charlatan," and a "masquerading hypocrite."[2] One of his greatest critics was Professor Thomas Huxley, a prominent and influential scientist who had won great support for Darwin's evolutionary theories. Through his scathing letters to the London *Times*, Huxley, an agnostic, attacked William's strategy, decrying his methods as "prostitution of the mind"[3] and arguing that religion should have nothing to do with political and social theory. Huxley's attitude is understandable for one who believed humankind was merely the product of natural selection. William, though, was accustomed to the spiritual degradation of the masses and knew that without the intervention of God, no amount of social theory could ever change hearts.

The cruel criticism was felt even more keenly by William in the absence of his fiercest defender, his most loyal supporter, his devoted companion. Even though he chose to ignore where possible the slander and criticism, William clearly felt the full brunt of the attack. Speaking of his many critics, he stated, "The day has gone when the priest and Levite are content to pass by the wounded man. They must . . . stop now, turn back, and punch the head of any Good Samaritan who dares to come to the rescue."[4]

Although their attitude angered him, he had learned long ago to leave them and vengeance with God. When Bramwell was irritated by the spiteful comments directed at his father, William wisely replied, "Bramwell, fifty years hence it will matter very little indeed how these people treated us. It will matter a great deal how we dealt with the work of God."[5] William resolutely chose to ignore his critics, focusing instead on the implementation of his strategy.

Workshops or labor yards were opened next to each Salvation Army shelter, providing work and a means of restoring self-respect for the unemployed seeking refuge. Employment was available for everyone to earn at least the four pence required for food and board in the Army's shelters. The work included basket- and brush-making, carpentry, tambourine-making, upholstery, sign writing, baking, and sandwich-board carrying. A household salvage brigade was set up to collect unwanted items from homes across London, restoring and recycling them where possible into saleable products.

The Army opened Britain's first labor exchange, a full twenty years before the government took up the idea of liaising between the unemployed and those requiring workers. The exchange was a huge success, placing over sixty-nine thousand people in employment in just seven years. A missing persons bureau was established to help families trace their loved ones who were among the nine thousand people who disappeared from London each year. Plans were made for a legal-aid service for the poor and a poor-man's bank with credit facilities for the establishment of new businesses by the unemployed. William was a visionary, and there seemed no limit to his innovative answers to the needs of the poor.

By the end of 1890 The Salvation Army social work entailed thirty-three rescue homes, thirty-three slum posts, ten prison-gate brigades, four food depots, five shelters for the destitute, a house for alcoholics, a factory, and two labor bureaus. In the face of critical opposition, the first phase of William's welfare strategy was successfully being implemented.

By January of 1891, £102,559 had been pledged to the Darkest England Scheme. The Darkest England Trust Deed was set up, appointing the general of The Salvation Army as the legal trustee, with the money and properties to be kept separate from the remainder of The Salvation Army funds. A temporary headquarters was established in London, and The Social Reform wing of the Army was appointed to run the scheme under the leadership of Commissioner Frank Smith and, on his resignation, Commissioner Elijah Cadman. As general of The Salvation Army and trustee of the Darkest England Scheme, William maintained oversight and guidance of his welfare strategy.

During the research for *In Darkest England and the Way Out*, Salvationists had unveiled the terrible exploitation of factory workers. None had appalled William more than the working conditions of the employees of England's match factories. Every day over four thousand workers, mostly women, as well as children as young as eight, went to work in the match factories. They toiled for sixteen hours a day, with no break for meals, and took home little more than one shilling for their labors. Even worse than the unreasonable hours and low pay, though, was the severe health risk to which they were exposed.

English companies, unlike other nations, still produced "strike anywhere" matches. These were made by dipping the match heads in yellow phosphorous, a substance that was lethal in minute amounts. Even the fumes of yellow phosphorous were highly toxic, and with the poor ventilation in the factories, the deadly vapor was inhaled day in and day out by the workers. As William's men investigated the industry, they discovered many of the women complained of severe toothaches. The cause of their pain, unknown to them, was "phossy jaw"—the rotting of the jawbone due to the toxic yellow phosphorous, which often resulted in gangrenous infection and death. The match manufacturers were aware of the medical risks they imposed upon their workers but refused to do anything about them. Their only concern was their profits.

In response to this deadly industry, the Army set up its own match factory in 1891. The factory was well ventilated and well lit. Its 120 workers were paid nearly double the rate paid by other factories, and they made sure each worker took breaks during the day. The "Lights in Darkest England" matchboxes contained only safety matches tipped with harmless red phosphorous. The good working conditions resulted in great productivity, and at its peak the factory turned out six million boxes of matches every year. News of the good environment at the factory spread quickly within the industry.

The safety matches were double the price of those made from yellow phosphorous, so a campaign was needed to alert people to the dangers of the cheaper product. Salvationists informed newsmen and politicians of the true cost of the matches made with yellow phosphorous. They took them to the homes of workers suffering from "phossy jaw" so they could see for themselves the terrible effects of the yellow phosphorous. In the cramped houses, the stench of rotting flesh was enough to convince any man of the damage. To push the point home, the gaslight was snuffed out, revealing a phosphorescent glow from the victim's jaw and hands. Tours were conducted around their own model factory, providing a great contrast to the pitiful state of the women affected by yellow phosphorous. To help their campaign, Salvationists across England were encouraged to demand safety matches from their grocers and to boycott the dangerous "strike-anywhere" variety.

The tide of public opinion was gradually turned toward the Army's safety matches. Pressure from the public and the government eventually forced match manufacturers in England to conform to the standard of safety set by this industry leader. By the turn of the century, all of England's large match manufacturers had ceased their use of yellow phosphorous. Ten years later, when the victory was won and match companies adopted the reforms necessary for the health and fair treatment of workers, the Army closed its factory and turned its attention to rectifying other social injustices.

The second phase of the Darkest England Scheme was put in motion with the purchase of eight hundred acres at Hadleigh on March 25, 1891; the farm colony was settled in May. Men were sent from London immediately to work on the land, and by the end of the year they had constructed temporary dormitories, kitchen and dining halls, bathrooms, offices, and a library. The farm could cater for up to three hundred men and officers who successfully developed the land in accordance with William's scheme. After just five years of operation, Hadleigh Farm boasted one of England's finest market gardens, a poultry farm, two brickfields, and a large number of sheep, cattle, dairy cows, and pigs. The farm colony successfully helped many men gain skills that enabled them to move on to lead a better life. Through the meetings held by the officers, a good number of the men also found new life in Christ.

There was hardly a need in the community that was not in some way catered for under the Darkest England Scheme. Although successful in many ways, however, the plan was fraught with difficulties. The public had pledged the initial £100,000 required to implement the program, but annual contributions were never large enough to cover the ongoing cost.

Opposition against the Darkest England Scheme continued, and in 1892, rumors were spread through the media accusing William of helping himself to the funds that had been provided. When the damning reports called for an audit of Salvation Army accounts, William agreed without hesitation. A thorough investigation by an independent committee of five auditors found no financial fault with the scheme. Their report stated that William had never drawn an income from either the Darkest England or Salvation Army funds. Despite being cleared of this charge, the damage had been done, and the scheme suffered from a continual funding shortfall. The overseas colony was never established due to a lack of finances and the inability to acquire land in the countries they approached.

Although the plan experienced setbacks, many aspects of this pioneering work were gradually adopted by England and other nations, including Australia, France, Germany, Holland, India, and the United States. The strategy fashioned by The Salvation Army became in part a blueprint for the welfare services implemented and supported by governments around the world.

Stead's prophecy had come true—William's scheme had impacted not only Britain but also the globe, its far-reaching influence continuing to this day. Although the strategy was never fully implemented, The Salvation Army pioneered the way for effectively combining social work with the gospel message. Salvationists around the world followed their general in bringing salvation, both temporal and eternal, to humankind. Their faith was made manifest as they fed the hungry, housed the homeless, and provided a "hand up" rather than a "hand out" for the poor. As one reporter, deeply moved by the selfless love of the officers, declared:

> They are men and women selected for their power of subordinating themselves to their cause, most assuredly a remarkable type of ecclesiastic: remarkable because there is no inequality between man and woman, because home life and married life are combined with a complete dedication of the individual to spiritual service. A beautiful spirit of love and personal service, of content and joy, permeates the service; there is a persistent note of courtesy to others and of open-mindedness to the world.[6]

The Army was saturated with the self-sacrificing spirit of love and obedient service epitomized in William and Catherine. All around the world, officers followed in the footsteps of their leaders, carrying on the great work they had begun. They were inspired by their general's faith in God and his passion for souls.

As Salvationists pioneered the Army's work on the continents of Africa, Asia, and South America, they learned firsthand the value and power of connecting with the heart of God through prayer. One story is told of two struggling officers who tried everything they could think of to establish a new work, but all to no avail. The opposition was fierce and relentless; they were ready to quit. Weary and discouraged, they wrote to their general, requesting the closure of their station. To William, defeat was not an option. He responded by telegram with just two words: "try tears." They did, and revival broke out![7]

All around the world, the Salvationists were seeing breakthrough as they launched their attack on the powers of darkness. William's handpicked team of five young officers sent to wage war in Zululand, South Africa, learned quickly what it meant to confront their spiritual enemy. Led by Scottish-born Captain Allister Smith, the team settled amongst the Zulu warriors on the shore of the Amatikulu River in October of 1891. The nature of their opposition was evident from the outset: The Zulu chief and his people revered the powerful witch doctors, whose occult practices struck great fear in their hearts. Smith and his team realized that while the witch doctors reigned over the lives of the Zulu, the progress of gospel would be minimal.

They went to "knee drill," crying out to God for the release of the Zulu to the gospel of Christ. The atmosphere was heavily charged with resistant forces, but these dedicated young warriors persisted in fervent prayer.

Their breakthrough opportunity came in August of 1892 as drought ravaged the Amatikulu district. When the Zulu's most powerful "rain doctor" failed to bring an end to the drought, the chief sent word to Captain Smith, saying, "Our hearts are dried up within us. Our courage is finished. The Great One has called the rain doctor, but he has failed to overcome the dry devil who beats us with his rod of hot air."[8]

The chief's request was presented to Smith: If the Army would hold a Sunday prayer meeting to Great-Great—the White Man's God—all the chief's people would be ordered to attend.

Boldly, Smith sent word back to the chief, informing him of their willingness to pray for rain in a public meeting on Sunday. What a challenge! Here was an opportunity for the power of God to be displayed. Answered prayer would almost certainly bring the breakthrough they were praying for, but what would happen if their prayers went unanswered?

In his book *The General Next to God*, Richard Collier relates the story of this "Mount Carmel" experience:

> No officer in Booth's Army ever prayed harder than Smith did now. Sunday saw hundreds of Zulus trudging across the parched valleys and plains, squatting on the forlorn brown grass outside the Catherine Booth settlement. To his secret joy, Smith saw that at least one Zulu, despite the crowd's scoffing, had brought a vast umbrella.
>
> "You could shelter your family under that tent, Jojo! Do you think it will rain?" As the banter died, the upright old man replied demurely: "Well, we are here today to pray for rain, and it might rain!" It was an answer, Smith thought, to shame many a Christian.
>
> Then, rising before his vast audience, he taught them a short simple prayer in the Zulu tongue: "Our Lord, send upon us the rain in Thy mercy. Help us with rain. Shower it upon us, O Great-Great."
>
> At once, Smith's handful of converts began fervently to pray. Uncertain at first, the Zulus followed. Voices rose and fell in exhortation, dying sometimes to a mumble as one man prayed alone, rising again in massed volume

to seek God's intervention. Three hours passed. The sun was white and pitiless in a blue, brassy sky, and Smith prayed on.

Suddenly, from far to the east, toward the Indian Ocean, came a heavy rumbling. Rapt with awe, the congregation saw, piling inland from the sea, massed thunderheads moving inexorably toward Amatikulu. The sun from the west blazed upon them, and they shone like high and snow-capped ridges.

As the thunder rolled louder, louder rose the prayers. A few feet away from Smith, a searing flash of forked lightning ripped the ground. Again thunder crashed, unbearably loud, drowning out all human sound. In solemn silence the congregation crouched.

Nkulu-nkulu, the Great-Great, was speaking with a warrior's majesty. Warm, wet drops of rain, as large as pennies, spattered on the Zulus' upturned faces. Hastily, with a last devout prayer, Smith brought the meeting to a close; soon the rivers and streams on the homeward journey would be raging white torrents.

He dared not, of course, look ahead to a moment, not far distant, when Chief Tshingwayo and all his kraal, even the witch doctors, would themselves embrace salvation. Nor could he envisage the first Army-sponsored Zulu school, where pupils from six to sixty came to learn not only to read and write, but brick-making and husbandry. Fat oxen, broken into the yoke, drew ploughs, which The Army helped the Zulus to purchase. The unfair burdens thrust on the women became properly those of men. . . . All this lay in the future.

On this August Sunday, Smith saw only the people rise and run in all directions, laughing and singing as the rain their prayers had brought beat on their naked bodies. Louder than any sang old Jojo, trudging homeward beneath the vast canopy of an umbrella justified by faith.[9]

Captain Smith and his team, like William, knew and experienced the power of prevailing prayer. The general's influence and his consistent orders to "pray, pray, pray" had penetrated the minds of his troops and forged a path to their knees.

From nations around the world, similar reports of revival were sent to the general, describing the battles won in the name of the Lord. By this time, in excess of five thousand letters and telegrams arrived weekly at the International Headquarters detailing the Army's movements throughout the world. In Java, Japan, Barbados, and Trinidad, new territories were claimed and hundreds of souls were snatched from darkness into light.

Since Catherine's death, William had a greater freedom to travel. He

In Tokyo, the Salvation Army marches on the red light district

covered many miles to visit his officers in England and around the world. His heart had a huge capacity to love people of every culture, and he looked upon them all as being part of one family—the family of God. Wherever he traveled he attracted huge crowds; people journeyed great distances to catch a glimpse of the general of The Salvation Army. Meeting halls were packed by those eager to hear him preach, and when he toured nations by rail, great crowds gathered on the station platforms, hoping to hear him speak before his train moved on.

By the turn of the century, the personal persecution and public opposition William had endured for so many years had all but disappeared. The Army had weathered the storm of criticism and doubt that so often assails a new work. Their success among the poor in England and around the world was obvious for all to see. National and international leaders sought to pay honor and respect to the general of The Salvation Army.

The cost of the call and the life he had chosen, however, remained a daily reality for the general. Perhaps the greatest troubles faced by William after Catherine's death were those within his own family. With the stabilizing influence of his beloved wife no longer tempering his incessant drive for success, serious rifts appeared in his relationship with some of his children.

The dissension was not directed entirely against William, though. Over the years, Bramwell had been granted greater control of the administrative affairs of the Army. He had been groomed for leadership since he was a teenager, and by the late 1800s he knew more about the day-to-day operations of the immense international organization than the general himself. Yet, due in part to his physical weaknesses, including deafness, he had never toiled in the field as had William's other children. As a result, his strong autocratic leadership style, modeled on his father's, was not always welcomed or respected by his siblings.[10]

Toward the end of 1895, while William was touring India, Bramwell proposed a reshuffle of the leadership positions held by his siblings in an effort to improve the efficiency of the Army. His plan included sending Herbert from Canada to Australia, Eva from London to Canada, Kate and her husband from France and Switzerland to Holland and Belgium, Lucy and her husband from India to France, Ballington and his wife from America to London, and Emma and her husband to America. His decision to transfer leadership was entirely consistent with Army guidelines, but it was neither wisely nor tactfully conveyed.

Although Ballington and his wife initially accepted the order to move from their position of leadership in America, it was clearly out of duty and discipline, not consent. A few days after announcing their transfer, they had a change of heart and chose instead to resist the move, arguing against the order. A mass rally was held in New York, during which Ballington's supporters urged Bramwell to change his mind. Eva and Herbert were sent to America to persuade their brother to return to London but were unable to do so. In 1896 Ballington and Maud Booth resigned from The Salvation Army and formed their own organization called Volunteers of America. It was founded along very similar lines to The Salvation Army, and they took with them many members of the American Corps.

Ballington's secession was the first fracture in the Booth family and by far the most public. Although the others obeyed their transfer orders, a growing sense of discontent permeated some of their lives. In a letter to his father, Herbert explained his belief that the Army, if it were to continue to grow and remain unified, required "a government in which its leading spirits throughout the world shall have a voice and a vote in some constituent assembly."[11] By 1902 both Kate and Herbert had also abandoned the Army, partly because of the authority structure they believed restricted their leadership as territorial commanders. Kate had been heartbroken when ordered to leave her beloved

In New York, Booth's soldiers march in opposition to alcohol, using a giant whiskey bottle for emphasis.

France, but her decision to resign from the Army was largely influenced by her husband's involvement in the movement started by healing evangelist John Alexander Dowie.

For William, the family troubles only highlighted his grief for Catherine. Had she still been alive, it is likely these misunderstandings would have been worked out to a more favorable conclusion. In the end, only Bramwell, Eva, and Emma remained William's devoted supporters and active workers in the Army. However, Emma was soon lost to him in another way.

On October 28, 1903, a train crash in the United States claimed many lives, among them forty-three-year-old Emma Booth-Tucker. She had worked tirelessly for the Army, serving alongside her husband in Britain, India, and America. Her death brought great sorrow to William, who described his pain as like "the loss of his left hand."

Yet William would let no amount of personal grief or heartache interfere with the advance of The Salvation Army. In June of 1904 the city of London hosted the Army's third International Congress. Thousands of Salvationists made the journey to receive inspiration and direction from their beloved general. During the course of the meetings, William encouraged his followers to remain true to their calling.

Now the real object for which The Salvation Army exists is known to us all. It is to save men. Not merely to civilize them. That will follow. Salvation is the shortest and surest cut to civilization. . . . Not merely to feed them; that is good, very good, so far as it goes. It is true that in our Social work we feed the starving and house the homeless, but it is only a step towards the purpose we wish to accomplish. The object is to save men from sin and hell. To bring them to God. To bring God to them. To build up the Kingdom of Heaven upon the earth. The end of The Salvation Army Officer is to convert men, to change their hearts and lives, and make them good Saints and Soldiers of Jesus Christ.[12]

He also encouraged them all to consecrate their lives once more to this great purpose, saying:

Many of you, I have no doubt, offered yourselves for a soul-saving life years ago. You knelt down, as I did, on the day you were converted— perhaps in the very act of being converted, and said, "Lord, help me to live for the salvation of those around me." But you have had much experience since then. You see what it means in the way of tears, of toils, of disappointments, of conflicts, to really follow the Lamb that was slain. What is asked from you by the Spirit from the Throne, is that with this increased knowledge and actual experience you should give yourself up to it again.[13]

Their battle-scarred general inspired them with faith and courage to lay their lives down afresh to fight for the souls of people everywhere.

On June 24, 1904, the eve of the Third International Congress, William was invited to Buckingham Palace to talk with King Edward VII. The king esteemed the Army's work, congratulating him on the overwhelming success of his ventures to assist the needy. His Majesty was aware of the criticism previously dealt out to the Army by the churches, and he inquired as to how they now viewed his work. "Sir," William replied, a cheeky twinkle in his eyes, "they imitate me."

While the journey had been both lonely and hard, the Army now enjoyed great favor earned by years of faithful perseverance. In towns and cities across England and even overseas, money was provided to Salvationists to carry out welfare work among the poor. While they discussed the impact of the Army's labors, the king was left with no doubt about the overriding passion in William's life. His inscription in the king's autograph book read:

Your Majesty,
Some men's ambition is art,
Some men's ambition is fame,
Some men's ambition is gold,
My ambition is the souls of men.[14]

William Booth on the steps of New Zealand Parliament with Prime Minister Seddon

The accolades continued to roll in. On October 26, 1905, seven hundred officers and four Army bands accompanied William as he marched through the streets of London to Guildhall. During the procession, Bramwell suddenly directed the officers marching alongside their leader to fall behind and allow him to walk alone. As the cheering crowds waved to the general, he removed his top hat in a humble sign of his respect and love for the people of London. When the parade arrived at the packed hall, the Lord Mayor awarded the seventy-six-year-old patriarch the honor of "The Freedom of the City of London."

Nottingham, the city that nurtured his compassion for the poor during childhood, soon followed suit. Even the University of Oxford esteemed him with an honorary doctorate of civil law for his "noble work . . . a work excelled in range and beneficence by no living man."[15] The honor and recognition came not only from his own nation: The kings of Norway and Sweden invited

William to visit, and he was also given the honor of opening the U.S. Senate with prayer.

Social and political leaders, who only ten years earlier had branded William Booth a heretic, a fool, and a fraud, now honored him as they saw with their own eyes the hard-won success achieved by the Army. The press, who for years had followed his movement, publishing scathing reports and criticisms, now praised his work. William humored them as always when they came to hear him preach, fixing his gaze on them as he prayed a blessing on those "who always arrive late, leave early, and never give anything to the collection."[16]

For most people the twilight years are a time to relax, a chance to reflect on their achievements and to enjoy the benefits of their life's work. William was different. It seemed that as the end of his life drew near, the state of those still living without Jesus haunted him with even greater intensity. In his younger days, the hundreds that flocked to the penitent-form brought great joy to his heart. Now it was those who turned away, refusing God's gift of salvation, that caught his attention. No amount or degree of honor from people could deter William from what remained his primary call—the work of salvation. His heart grieved passionately for those who did not know Jesus, and he was determined to continue to preach the gospel while he had breath.

In August of 1904, inspired by the introduction of the motorcar, the general set out on the first of a series of six motor campaigns. In just twenty-nine days his six-car procession rattled and bounced its way over 1,224 miles as he preached in 164 meetings across England. The going was tough for his younger companions, men like Railton and Elijah Cadman; it was even harder on the seventy-five-year-old saint. The thick dust from the unsealed, rut-ridden roads seemed to fill every pore of their skin. The ride was extremely rough and at times perilously dangerous: "Choose your rut carefully," William joked with his driver, "we may be in it for the next twenty miles."

The impact of this novel touring method was astounding. All over the country, packed crowds lined the highways to greet the old man who was fast becoming a national icon. The impact of his preaching was even greater; it was as though he knew his time was coming to a close, and the unfinished task of preaching the gospel to all creation seemed to grip him with unrelenting fervor more than ever. With great zeal for God and an ever-increasing passion for souls, William implored men, women, and children to surrender themselves to the living Christ. Thousands responded to his desperate pleas and found new life in Jesus.

Enthusiastic crowds across England lined the streets to catch a glimpse of the old General in the peaked cap.

General Booth arriving in a new city in his motorcade.

His days were clearly numbered, and William was insistent upon using every moment to its utmost. He loathed wasting time and maintained a pace of life that kept his secretary, half his age, run off his feet. The general never tolerated idleness among any of his workers, and some consequently found his leadership demanding and forceful at times. To William every moment was precious; he would easily convert a railway carriage or station platform into an office or meeting place when necessary to use his time to its fullest. "Every hour and every power for Christ and duty"[17] was his daily motto as he made the most of every opportunity, even those presented by delays.

For instance, while touring in the north of England, the motor convoy was unexpectedly brought to a standstill by a rope strung across the street. A group of practical jokers from the nearby factory had heard William was coming, and they lined the streets to enjoy their moment of fun. William had always enjoyed a joke, and he was not at all fazed by the disruption to his plans. He stood in the car and greeted the men, then began to speak to them, addressing their hearts. After a while he said, "Some of you men never pray—you gave up praying long ago. But I'm going to say to you, won't you pray for your children, that they may be different?"[18] The general's voice boomed out across the crowd who stood silently before him, transfixed by his words. Slowly, one by one, men began to kneel in the dusty street. Women and children looked on in amazement, tears filling their eyes, as the entire gathering of seven hundred men knelt in prayer.

The frantic months of touring England or traveling overseas to South Africa, Russia, Japan, Australia, New Zealand, or the Americas provided a stark contrast to quieter nights spent in his Hadley Wood home. William had never been a good sleeper, and in the quiet evening hours his mind was plagued by the terrible thought of men and women still living without the Savior. Bramwell lived nearby with his family and often called in during the evening to wish his father good-night. Late one evening, Bramwell found the general anxiously pacing the study floor. Concerned as always for his father's health, Bramwell suggested he go to bed. William refused, saying, "No, I am thinking." When his son inquired as to what was so urgent as to keep him awake at such a late hour, William replied solemnly, "Bramwell, I am thinking about the people's sins. What will they do with their sins?"[19] The God-given burden for souls still rested heavily on his heart.

As William faced the reality of his own limitations, his one consolation was the massive Army of warriors who had taken their place under his command in the war for souls. New territories established in the early 1900s included Panama, Costa Rica, Korea, Chile, Paraguay, and Peru. The Army's social-welfare work was also expanding; although William's plan for an overseas colony was never realized, The Salvation Army assisted thousands of English families in immigrating to the colonies. In April of 1905, the first Salvation Army ship, SS *Vancouver*, set sail from Liverpool with one thousand new citizens for Canada on board.

Homes were opened in England to care for the fatherless. Medical services were established by the Army in India, while in Java, Salvationists pioneered a leper colony. A Norwegian captain built the first Salvation Army Lifeboat and successfully rescued thousands of fishermen from the stormy waters along Norway's treacherous coastline, a precursor to the coast guards of today. In 1906, the American Salvationists pioneered the Army's first disaster relief work when San Francisco was rocked by a powerful earthquake that destroyed more than twenty-eight thousand homes. Within days a fund of fifteen thousand dollars had been set aside to provide food, clothing, and other relief assistance to the thousands left homeless by the tragedy. All around the world, Salvationists followed their leader in bringing both temporal and eternal salvation to the lost.

William Booth addresses a large wharfside crowd in Wellington, New Zealand, March 1899.

In July of 1909 William set out on his sixth motor tour of Britain. He planned to cover 1,460 miles in five weeks, an enormous undertaking for the eighty-year-old. The tour was abandoned when grit from the dusty roads wrecked havoc with his eyes. William had already had an operation during the previous year to remove a cataract from his right eye. The eye would not heal, and it had to be removed on August 21, 1909. Because his left eye was also affected by a cataract, after the loss of his right eye, he could barely see. William's sight was so dim that he had to use the communion rail to guide him along when he preached. Years of public speaking without the aid of a public-address system had also taken its toll on his voice. Physically his strength was failing, but spiritually and mentally William was as strong as ever.

In 1910 he preached in Switzerland, Holland, Denmark, Germany, and Italy before returning to conduct another grueling motor tour of Britain. Despite his physical frailty and his constant drive for success, William maintained his keen sense of humor. His messages were punctuated with humorous stories of people he had met, stories that caused his audiences to erupt with laughter. He knew how to capture people's attention, how to use emotion, humor, powerful illustrations, and penetrating truth to reach their hearts.

By far, the most powerful element of his preaching was the anointing of God—the measure of God's Spirit—that rested on his life. Through his years of preaching to the very worst of sinners, William continued to rely more and more upon the Holy Spirit. In a letter written to Bramwell, William had once declared, "The Holy Ghost convicting people of sin, making them saints and soldiers—sacrificing, weeping, toiling to save men from sin and hell—there is our power in a nutshell."[20]

As his physical body failed, William became a living testimony to the fact that God could use even the weakest vessels for His honor. In his eightieth-birthday letter to his followers, William wrote,

> O my comrades, do not seek to excuse yourselves on the ground of the humbleness of your position, or the apparent insignificance of your talents, your strength, or your past accomplishments. Do not forget that God has from the beginning chosen the "things which are not, to bring to nought things that are" [1 Corinthians 1:28]. . . . When that lad of fifteen walked out unsolicited and unnoticed to the Mercy Seat, and made a full conse-cration of his little all to the service of his King, who would have thought that God had such a wonderful future in store for him? That boy certainly at that time entertained no higher notions of his own powers and possibil-ities than to have the privilege of leading a cottage prayer meeting, or sing-ing "His blood can make the foulest clean" in the slums of his native town. And yet, see the honor that God has conferred upon him by making him the General of The Salvation Army![21]

In February of 1912 William toured Holland and Norway, and after cele-brating his eighty-third birthday on April 10, he traveled extensively in Brit-ain, preaching from Torquay to Glasgow. The general seemed unstoppable until his failing left eye demanded attention.

Despite his travels and need to withdraw for care, the tragedy that rocked the world just days after this birthday did not go unnoticed by William. When the *Titanic* struck an iceberg and sank on the evening of April 14, several Sal-vation Army officers and their families were on board, as well as longtime friend and fellow warrior against injustice W. T. Stead. It must have been a hard blow seeing his wife, a daughter, and this friend all pass before he did. The day the ship had set sail from Southampton for the U.S. had, in fact, been the general's birthday.

In a cable to U.S. President William Howard Taft, he shared his grief and shock at the enormity of the loss, but he also echoed that his own heartbeat for souls had never changed by stating that it should point out the need for salvation to others:

My heart is moved by the fearful calamity which has befallen the world in the loss of the *Titanic*—moved with sorrow for the dead, among whom are some of my long-tried friends; moved with sympathy for the living, whose loss can never be repaired, and moved in its deepest sources of feeling concerning that sudden and awful summons into the presence of God. I pray that it may speak to the multitudes of the reality and nearness of the world to come, and the urgency and overwhelming necessity of preparing for it. God bless and comfort you all![22]

When the *Carpathia*, the ship that had rescued the survivors of the disaster, landed in New York, Salvation Army soldiers were among those who met and aided them. Commander Evangeline Booth led the delegation.

On May 9, 1912, William stood before his beloved Army, gathered for the public celebration of his birthday at Royal Albert Hall, London. He told the crowd of seven thousand Salvationists that he was "going into dry dock for repairs." He then delivered what was to be his farewell speech to his faithful followers. William passionately summarized his life's work, calling on all present to continue to fight the good fight of faith.

I might have chosen as my life's work the housing of the poor. That, in early life, presented itself to me as a most important question. . . . I honor those who are devoting themselves to the solution of the problem. But has not The Salvation Army done something in this direction? If you look abroad, you will find hundreds and thousands up and down the world who tonight have comfortable homes through the influence of the Army; indeed, there are thousands of men, women and children who but for its assistance would have had no homes at all. For instance there are over 200,000 homeless men sleeping under our roofs each week.

I might have given myself up to the material benefit of the working classes. I might have drawn attention to the small rate of wages and striven to help them in that direction. But have we not done something for them? Are there not tens of thousands who, but for the Army, might have been almost starved? If we have not done much in the way of increasing income, have we not done a great deal in inculcating principles of economy and self-denial, which have taught the poor a better use of their wages? Their total abstinence from drink, tobacco, gambling and wasteful finery has made hundreds of thousands of people better off than they were before they came under our influence.

I might also have given myself up to promoting temperance reform. This is a most important business. Drunkenness seems to be the curse of every civilized nation under the sun; and I have all my life honored the

The General in latter years.

men and women who have devoted themselves to the solving of that problem. But has not The Salvation Army done something in that direction? Every Salvationist all the world over is a strict abstainer from intoxicating liquor, and the children are growing up to follow in their parent's footsteps. Tens of thousands of the most devilish and abandoned drunkards that the world has ever known have been reached and reclaimed, made into sober men and women, good fathers and mothers, good sons and daughters, and useful members of society.

I might have chosen as my life's object the physical improvement and health of the people by launching out on a medical career. As a matter of fact, I think the medical system is capable of improvement, and if I had been a doctor I should certainly have paid more attention to diet than to drugs. . . . We have done something in the way of medical aid, and possess at the present time twenty-four hospitals, while others are coming into existence, and there is no knowing to what extent the enterprise will reach in this direction. As it is, we deal with thousands of patients every year.

I might have chosen to devote my life to the interests of the criminal world. The hundreds of thousands of poor wretches who are pining in the prison cells while we are sitting here at ease, ought to have our sympathy and help. . . . Some 178 women prisoners have been admitted to our homes in this country during the year, and of these 130 have proved satisfactory. We have done something for the criminal, but it is only the commencement of a mighty work the Army is destined to do for the unhappy class.

I might have carried out my consecration for the improvement of the community by devoting myself to politics. . . . I saw something better than belonging to either party and, that by being the friend of every party, I was far more likely to secure the blessing of the multitude and the end I had in view.

And the object I chose all those years ago embraced every effort, contained in its heart the remedy for every form of misery and sin and wrong to be found upon the earth, and every method of reclamation needed by human nature.

In bringing the meeting to a close, Booth concluded with his famous final exhortation to his beloved soldiers:

The Army will not be allowed to suffer, either financially or spiritually, or in any other way by my absence; and in the long future I think it will be seen—I shall not be here to see, but you will—that the Army will answer every doubt and banish every fear and strangle every slander, and by its marvelous success show to the world that it is the work of God and that the General has been His servant. . . .

While women weep, as they do now, I'll fight; while little children go hungry, as they do now, I'll fight; while men go to prison, in and out, in and out, as they do now, I'll fight; while there is a drunkard left, while there is a poor lost girl upon the streets, while there remains one dark soul without the light of God, I'll fight—I'll fight to the very end![23]

May 23, 1912. Last known photograph of General Booth, as he anxiously awaited news of pending surgery that would cost him his sight. His dog, "faithful, Pat" sits at his feet.

Even as he spoke the words, he must have known his own fight was coming to a close. He looked with joy upon the dim sea of faces stretched out before him, men and women who had devoted their lives to war for souls. Though he could not see their faces, their colors were clear. With joy in his heart, he gave thanks to God that his beloved Army would continue their forward march.

Two weeks later a surgeon operated to remove the cataract from William's remaining eye. At first the reports were optimistic. The operation appeared successful, and William was recovering in his Hadley Wood home. Three days later, however, complications arose. The surgeon was worried and called for a colleague's assistance. Finally the truth was spoken: The operation had failed. William was now completely blind; he would never see again.

Bramwell was kneeling by the bedside when the news was broken to William. The general took his son's hand as he realized the magnitude of this outcome. "God must know best," he said, his faith unwavering as ever in the face of disaster. "I have done what I could for God and the people with my eyes. Now I shall see what I can do for God and the people without my eyes."[24]

Although his physical sight had been taken from him, William's spiritual vision never failed. His days of active warfare were concluding, but his leadership of the Army did not falter. In the twenty-two years since Catherine's death, William had leaned heavily upon his eldest son. Now, with greater urgency than ever before, he opened his heart to Bramwell, sharing his unfinished dreams and compelling him to continue the fight for the homeless and the lost. Writing on the tenth anniversary of his father's death, Bramwell stated: "The overwhelming thing which impresses me concerning him is the way in which the need of his fellow-men had seized him. Their sins and miseries scorched him like flame."[25] To the end, William's heart still beat with God's for souls to be saved. If he could not now carry it on for himself, at least he would continue to instill that passion in others. Around this time, Evangeline returned from America to spend some time with her father, and many other friends and family visited him as his days drew to a close. He implored them all to press ahead, to fulfill the destiny that had been entrusted to The Salvation Army. He knew his end was near.

On Sunday, August 18, William slipped into unconsciousness. For the next two days he drifted in and out of a semi-conscious state and seemed largely unaware of those who visited to say their final farewells. William's passionate love for souls was displayed to the very end of his life. On Tuesday, as she sat by his bedside, Lucy heard her father murmur, "Oh to save these people!"[26] His frail body lay motionless on the bed, but his restless fingers began to move in a definite and distinctive manner. Bramwell, Florence, Lucy, and the Salvationists gathered by his side knew immediately what their general was doing. He was counting; counting the penitents he saw in his mind as they flocked forward to receive Christ. He was as anxious as ever for the salvation of the lost. After a short time, the counting ended, and William's hand relaxed by his side. His shallow breathing quietly ceased, and the Army flag draped across his bed lay motionless, signaling the end of the great general's life.

A simple placard placed in the window of the international headquarters of The Salvation Army announced the news to the world: "The General has laid down his sword. God is with us."[27]

Over the next three days, the nation of England paid homage to the life of a man who had changed the course of history. More than 150,000 people filed past the casket that held the general's earthly remains. His funeral service on Tuesday, August 27, was attended by close to forty thousand people. Army officers from around the world stood shoulder-to-shoulder with the destitute and homeless as they rededicated their lives to God's service.

In life William had been a man of humility, a man who mixed as easily with prostitutes and drunkards as with royalty. His funeral drew both rich and poor as people from all walks of life united to honor the man who had touched and changed their world. Queen Mary made a last-minute decision to attend the funeral, and, as no seating had been reserved for her, she sat with Lord Shaftesbury in the rear of the huge hall among the people. On the aisle

Among the crush of the huge crowd, Queen Mary and Lord Shaftesbury found themselves sitting next to a prostitute. Rescued from a life of sin she was one of the hundreds of thousands whose overwhelming gratitude flowed forth unrestrained. As she shared her story with the Queen, she leaned over and whispered, "He cared for the likes of us."

seat next to the Queen sat a poor but neatly dressed woman who discreetly placed three faded red carnations on William's casket as it passed by. The woman had been a prostitute, rescued from the slavery by The Salvation Army. When asked why she was there, she quietly shared her story with the

Prior to Tuesday, August 27, the day of the funeral service, 150,000 filed past the casket that held the General's earthly remains. London came to a standstill as England mourned the passing of one of its most courageous sons.

Queen, declaring gratefully through her tears, "He cared for the likes of us."[28]

The following day the funeral procession of ten thousand Salvationists and forty Army bands slowly wound through the streets of London from international headquarters to Abney Park Cemetery. The acting Lord Mayor of London stood to salute the general as the procession passed by Mansion House. Flags representing the nations of the world were flown at half-mast in honor of the man whose vision and passion had extended to the very ends of the earth. Life in the great city of London came to a standstill as the entire nation mourned the loss of a great leader.

Bramwell Booth stood by the graveside. The day after William's death, he had been announced as the second general of The Salvation Army. According to the Army constitution, the departing general was responsible for the appointment of his successor. This was not a decision made by William alone; the nomination of his son was dated August 12, 1890, less than two months before Catherine's death. William and Catherine had chosen together the one who would lead their beloved Army into the future.

Now, as the casket carrying the earthly body of this stately warrior was lowered into the ground, the man groomed to lead the Army onward in its campaign for the salvation of all humankind tightened his grasp on the leadership baton. William Booth's race was over; his successor's had just begun.

The Challenge

On Thursday, June 21, 1888, Catherine Booth delivered what was to be her final public address to two thousand delegates gathered in London for a missionary convention. For more than an hour she challenged those present to consecrate themselves afresh to holiness and to the task of preaching the gospel and discipling the nations. The following excerpts, taken from this message, ring out to believers today with the same soul-stirring challenge.

I dare say that if I were to take a census of my audience this morning there would be many persons who would dispute as to the possibility of the world being converted. However this may be, I think there would be no division of opinion with respect to two or three facts relating to this subject.

In the first place, I believe that most of those who dissent from the possibility of the world being converted would admit that Jesus must have intended something more in that great commission, "Go ye into all the world, and preach the Gospel to every creature," than has yet been generally recognized. Even if the word translated "preach" were not capable of being rendered, "make disciples" of all nations, which you are aware it is, yet we must even then suppose that God intended more to be done than has generally been imagined. The same remark holds good with respect to the great commission of Paul, the Apostle of the Gentiles, who was sent "to open their eyes, and to turn them from darkness to light, and from the power of Satan unto God, that they may receive forgiveness of sins, and inheritance among them which are sanctified by faith which is in me." [Acts 26:18] There must have been more intended by this than a mere proclamation of the Gospel.

I have been appalled and amazed at the comparatively few whom I have met, of the thousands of people with whom I have conversed, who have understood that the realization of the forgiveness of sins is possible, and I have been appalled at the comparatively small number of professing Christians who enjoy this blessing. They do not appear to know that it is there for them, and that Jesus Christ is a positive, present Savior.

But supposing they do get pardoned from their past sins, they do not realize that Jesus has the power to deliver them from the sin reigning in their hearts; from their besetting sins; from that which constitutes their misery.

Perhaps on no point has The Salvation Army suffered persecution more than on this one point of its teaching: that it proclaims a Savior not only willing to pardon, but who does pardon absolutely, and who communicates a sense of that pardon by His Holy Spirit to the hearts of those who truly repent and sincerely believe; and that He not only washes their past sins away but has the power to keep them from their sins, and will, if they trust in Him, enable them to live in righteousness and holiness all their lives, walking in obedience to His commands, keeping that inner law of which we have just heard—the law of Christ—which is the most perfect law and fulfils all others—loving the Lord thy God with all the heart, mind, soul, and strength, and thy neighbor as thyself.

Oh, the hundreds of people I have seen open their eyes with astonishment at the mere propounding of such a doctrine! People who have sat under the Gospel for many years have never heard of such a thing, and do not understand it. They do not know it; much less does the poor world outside know it. Oh, as I have looked round our towns and cities, and observed the marks of misery depicted on thousands of faces I meet with, I feel, oh, for a trumpet voice! Oh, for some mighty herald that would get up on every curbstone, on every other available space, and proclaim to this poor world, full of hungry souls, that there is peace, pardon, purity for them, and power in a living Savior to keep them from sin, and to enable them to walk before Him and to enjoy His presence and smile!

Even in a Christian land this is not known, and consequently, we have professing Christians the most ready of all to persecute us when we announce such a doctrine. However, this teaching has spoken for itself, or, rather, God has spoken for it by the presence and power of His Holy Spirit, and there are today tens of thousands of people, the majority of them raised from the very lowest condition of the earth's population, standing forth and testifying; "We were once possessed of the devils of drink, debauchery and crime of every description, but now here we are—the devils are cast out, our past sins are purged away, and we are kept by the power of His grace from the sins which did so easily beset us, and we are walking in the light and fellowship of the Triune Jehovah." I say, Thank God that He has always testified of the truth of this teaching by the presence and power of His Holy Spirit whenever it has been put forth.

We have nothing to boast of short of Salvation. We have not a single disciple, baptized person, or professing Christian to be thankful for who has not experienced a change of heart, who has not been made out of falsehood into truth, out of dishonesty into honesty, out of uncleanness into purity; who is not transformed in the spirit of his mind, and renewed again after the likeness of God. Oh, that God may use me to be the means of imprinting this on your minds, and of helping you, in future, not to be satisfied with or glory over anything short of this in connection with all your religious work!

Jesus Christ came, I say, to rectify men's hearts, and He persistently taught that this would rectify all man's outward sorrows. That is, when you have got man right with God you will soon get him right with humanity, with himself, and in all his relationship with the world.

All who know anything of the Salvation of God must feel with me here: that if we cannot cover the earth with the knowledge of it then we should cover as much of it as we can. That we are bound, under obligation, to do this seems to be self-evident to those who believe Christianity to be for the benefit of the race. Putting aside the future life altogether, I think we are bound to do this for the peace, purity, goodwill, beneficence, truth, and justice which is always following the wake of true Christianity. "Ah," you say, "these things do not follow in the wake of all Christianity." But I am talking about the genuine thing, Christ's Christianity, and I say if these results do not follow, it is a bastard Christianity; its fruits prove it to be so.

Real Christianity is known by its fruits—peace, goodwill, purity, justice, and truth. It inculcates and implants the love that works no ill of any kind to his neighbor; the love that seeks the good even of its enemies, and heaps the coals of fire of benevolence on the heads of those who hate it. That is real Christianity, and wherever that goes peace and good-will are found. Therefore, for the happiness, deliverance, and emancipation of the slaves of the earth, for the rescue of the down-trodden women of the world, for the care and consideration it instills for the poor helpless children, for the ideas of justice which it brings wherever it goes—for these reasons we have found the spread of it to be a benefit to the whole race, both for this world and the next.

Again: are not we who love the Lord Jesus Christ bound to do something for *His* sake? What would satisfy Him, think you, as the end of His living, suffering, and dying? Will He be satisfied with a paltry percentage of the human race, as the result of the travail of His soul who tasted death for every man, and who wills that all men should be saved, and come to a knowledge of the truth? We cannot believe but that His great benevolent heart bounds with love for every son and daughter of Adam. Oh, my brother, my sister, you may be nearing eternity, and just on ahead of you may be the Judgment Seat of Christ, where you will have to render an account for the deeds done in the body, and receive according to that you have done, whether it be good or evil. That is not the Old Testament; that is not Salvation Army book. It is the New Testament; it is the Apostle Paul who is speaking to Christians. You will have to receive according to that you have done. We sing and talk about our mighty Savior, who shed His blood for us. We sing:

Were the whole realm of nature mine,
That were a present far too small. . . .

and then we grudge Him a little self-denial—a little money, or effort, cross carrying, or persecution, to secure that on which His heart is set. His heart is set on the Salvation of men. "What temple will ye build Me?" saith the Lord of Hosts. He does not want your grand temples, organs, music, ceremonials, or other paraphernalia. He wants *souls*. He wants His prodigal children brought home. He won't ask you where you worshipped, or what creed you professed; but He *will* ask for His prodigals—those whom you have won for Him. Will you not set to work to do something for His sake?

God has arranged to save men by *human* instrumentality, and if we have not succeeded in the past we are not to throw the blame on Him, as too many Christians do. A man who was sitting in his easy-chair, with his feet on an ottoman, said to me the other day: "But the Lord will come presently and put all things right." I replied: "I am afraid you are expecting the Lord to do what He has called us to do."

The Lord does not say *He* will go and preach the Gospel to every creature; He says *you* are to go and do it. He does not say *He* is going to convert the world; He says *you* are going to do it. He has shown you the lines on which to go, and given you the resources, just as much as, yes, more than, He has the agriculturist to cultivate and gather the fruits of the earth. If Christians were only half as diligent as husbandmen the world would have been saved long ago. Here are the lines—use your common sense.

There is no excuse for the ignorant and "all-thumb" kind of work that Christians are doing all over the world. We must not allow our blunders to be thrown back upon God. I say, we must have a more efficient force to do it. The force we have had has been imperfect and inadequate; therefore the work has not been done. If we are to better the future we must disturb the present, which some people very much dislike. They would rather be let alone, though they know they are wrong. What is wanted, I say, is a force of spiritually equipped and determined men and women to take the world for God—men and women trained to the business. What a poor job people make at trying to do a business if they don't understand it! You know better, in your temporal affairs, than to allow such people to do your work. If a man goes to work for you, and you find he does not understand your business, you soon give him notice. It is not so with the Lord Jesus; people do not think His worth a bit of trouble. They do not set before themselves the right models; they are not aiming at the right thing; therefore they are not likely to produce the right results.

Now we want a force of men and women given up to this work, sworn to bring the world to the foot stool of Jehovah, bound together spiritually to God and to each other, that will make it the business of their lives to subject the world to God.

Look at the world again for a minute. Here are the millions of men entrenched in their wickedness; entrenched behind all manner of refuges of lies, enamored of their sins—some gaiety, some drink, some impurity, some ambition, some money, some learning, some one thing, and some another. There they are, satisfied with their sin so far, because poor things, they will not allow themselves to think. They are not inclined to think. Oh, if a man would only shake himself up for an hour, and face God and eternity, he would not rest in his sins; but their great desire, and the great object of the Devil, is to keep these things from them; so he keeps them always preoccupied—always busy. How are you going to get them down from their tower of self-satisfaction, sin, and pleasure? Do you think they are coming down by your saying, "Here, come along; hear me; let me preach to you. Come and be converted"? Oh no! The Christian Church has been trying that game too long. The people are far too busy. They turn around and tell you so. They say, "I am doing a great work; I cannot come to you."

Listen to what Jesus Christ commissioned His disciples to do. Not to ensconce themselves in comfortable buildings and invite the people to come, and then, if they would not come, leave them alone to be damned. No, no! He said: "Go ye," which means, "Go after them." Where, Lord? "Into all the world." What to do? "Preach the Gospel to every creature."

Where, Lord? "Where the creatures are. Follow them!" If ever you are to get this work done it will be by pressing God's truth upon the attention of men, and making them hear, and think, and feel; and it must be done by men and women who have themselves experienced and are living in the practice of what they preach. It must be done by men and women who are renewed—saved, converted; men and women who have given up the paltry gewgaws of time for the greater and more lasting rewards of eternity; men and women who practice it; who show in their modes of speech, manner of life, dress, business, and everything about them, that they have renounced the world, with its fleshly lusts, and that they are given up to God, to subdue the world to Him; men and women in whom, as a consequence of this consecration, the Spirit of Christ dwells, and who are therefore equal to the work and who will never turn their back on any foe, nor scruple to suffer any difficulty or persecution.

These are the sort of people that are wanted. We need men and women who are trained for the fight. Not only people who have experienced a change of heart, but who are drilled in knowing how to use the weapons of the Spirit—knowing how to handle God's truth. You would think, if you heard some people's representation of the truth of God, that it was all honey and soap; you would not think there was any "cut" in it— any dividing asunder. A great deal of the truth preached nowadays would not cut the wings off a fly, much less pierce asunder the soul and spirit.

You must preach God's justice and vengeance against sin as well as His love for the sinner. You must preach Hell as well as Heaven. You must let your Gospel match the intuitions of humanity, or you may as well throw it into the sea, and thus save both trouble and money. A Gospel of love never matched anybody's souls. The great want in this day is truth that cuts; convicting truth; truth that convicts and convinces the sinner and pulls off the bandages from his eyes. The Lord knows the order in which His truth ought to be preached better than we do. Hence His commission to Paul, to go and "open the eyes" of sinners to their danger, and turn them round from the power of Satan unto God. This was to be done before they were converted. "Oh!" says someone, "do not talk to them about Hell, death, and judgment; show them the love of Christ." But we always get wrong when we reverse God's order. Tear the bandages off. Open their eyes, turn them round from the desire, the embrace and choice of evil to the embrace and choice of God. That they may receive forgiveness of sins.

Tell them the truth; tell a man the truth about himself. Drive in the red-hot, convicting truth of God on to his conscience, and make him realise that he is a sinner. Never mind how he howls, even if he groans as loud as the Psalmist did when the pains of Hell got hold of him. Until he has been made to feel himself a sinner he will never make anything of a saint. Then give him the Gospel. Say to him, "Have you had enough of the Devil? Will you give up your drink? Will you renounce that idol, or that unholy affection?"

Tell a man the truth about himself, then the truth about God, then the truth about his obligation to others, that is, if you believe the things I have been saying are true. If you do not, I would not go to chapel; I would not have the Bible. I would throw the whole thing overboard and live at peace; that is, as far as a man can, living a mere nominal existence. If it is not true, be done with it; if it is true, act upon it! Oh, may God help us!

And those of us who have acted upon it so much as to give up the greater portion of our lives to the service of God, when we come to face eternity, and look back on the past, what will be our regret? That we have done so much? Oh, no! That we have done so little; that we have not acted upon it to a greater extent; that we have not let God and eternity be the all-absorbing theme of our lives; that we have wasted any energy, time, or strength on less important things. Friends, take these few words home to your closet, and ask the Spirit of God if they are so; lay them on your hearts, and go and bring forth fruit according. May God bless and help you, and may we meet at the right hand of the Throne, for Jesus sake! Amen![1]

---

[1]"The Challenge" section (pages 252 to 258) can be photocopied and distributed without further permission for use in classroom, Bible studies, and discussion groups. Such copies must appear as in this book and contain this permission note: "From *William and Catherine: A New Biography*, © 2002 T. F. & J. B. Yaxley. Published by Bethany House Publishers, 2003. Reprinted with permission. All rights reserved."

Appendix A

English System of Currency in the Time of the Booths

The main measures were:

    12 pence = 1 shilling
    20 shillings = 1 pound (£)
    240 pence = 1 pound (£)

There were also the following coins at times:

    1 farthing = pence
    1 half-penny = ½ pence
    1 penny = 1 pence
    1 three-penny = 3 pence
    1 groat = 4 pence
    1 sixpence (or tanner) = 6 pence
    1 florin = 2 shillings (a slang term for shilling was "bob")
    1 half-crown (or half dollar) = 30 pence or 2 shillings, 6 pence
    1 double-florin = 4 shillings
    1 crown (or dollar) = 5 shillings or 60 pence
    1 half-sovereign = 10 shillings
    1 sovereign = 20 shillings or 1 pound (£)
    1 guinea = 21 shillings

APPENDIX B

A Timeline of
William and Catherine Booth
and The Salvation Army

Year	Age	Event	Elsewhere in the World
1829		January 17—Catherine Mumford's birth in Ashbourne, Derbyshire; April 10—William Booth's birth in Nottingham	Catholic Emancipation Act passed in Britain
1830	1		George IV dies and is succeeded by William IV
1831	2		
1832	3		First Reform Bill passed
1833	4	John Mumford (Catherine's younger brother) born	Slavery is abolished in the British Empire
1834	5	Mumford family moves to Boston, Lincolnshire	
1835	6		September 15—Charles Darwin gets his first sighting of the Galapagos Islands
1836	7		March 6—The Alamo falls to Mexican troops; George Muller (1805–1898) founds his first orphanages in England

(continued)

---

*Information for this timeline was taken from a number of different sources but primarily from W. T. Stead, Mrs.
Booth (London: James Nisbet & Co., 1900), 233–42, and George S. Railton,* The Authoritative Life of General
William Booth: Founder of The Salvation Army *(New York: George H. Doran Company, 1912), 326–31.*

Year	Age	Event	Elsewhere in the World
1837	8		William IV dies and is succeeded by his niece Victoria
1838	9		Regular Atlantic steamship service begins
1839	10		Abner Doubleday organizes the alleged first baseball game in Cooperstown, New York
1840	11		First New Zealand governor is William Hobson; The penny postage stamp is introduced in Great Britain; Samuel Morse invents the telegraph
1841	12	Catherine appointed secretary of Juvenile Temperance Society; Catherine attends private school in Boston	
1842	13	Summer—William is pulled out of school and starts as an apprentice to a pawnbroker (Samuel Booth's debts called in, forcing this move); Fall—Catherine attends second year of private school in Boston	Chartist Riots in England
1843	14	Catherine's last year at private school in Boston; Catherine's spinal complaint compels her to leave school; September 23—William's father (Samuel Booth) dies	The Great Migration begins on the Oregon Trail
1844	15	William's conversion; Mumford family moves to London	*The Christmas Carol* published by Charles Dickens
1845	16	Catherine joins Wesleyan Church in Brixton	England's Corn Laws repealed; February 29—Texas becomes the twenty-eighth state in the United States
1846	17	June 15—Catherine "knows" she is saved; Catherine contracts consumption	Potato failure in Europe
1847	18	Catherine goes to Brighton, delicate and ailing	
1848	19		Revolutions in Europe
1849	20	William moves to London	Gold discovered in Australia

(continued)

Year	Age	Event	Elsewhere in the World
1850	21	Catherine refuses to condemn the Methodist reformers and is expelled from the Wesleyan body; Catherine joins the reformers from 1850 to 1852 and takes a Sunday school class of girls at Binfield Hall, Clapham	September 9—California becomes the thirty-first state in the United States
1851	22	William is expelled from the Wesleyan Church for sympathizing with the reformers; June—William joins the reformers; William and Catherine meet for the first time in the house of Mr. Rabbits; William is appointed Minister of Binfield Hall	The Great Exhibition in London's Crystal Palace
1852	23	Edward Rabbits offers to sponsor William for three months so that he can dedicate himself to evangelism; April 9–10—William and Catherine share a cab to Catherine's house after a meeting on Cowper Street; William realizes he has fallen in love with Catherine; Also the first day of William's three-month sponsorship by Mr. Rabbits; May 15—William and Catherine are engaged; Catherine attends Congregational Chapel of Rev. D. Thomas; July—Mr. Rabbits' sponsorship ends and William refuses to renew it, feeling his ministry in London had come to little; November—William is appointed to the Spalding Circuit	Last convict ship dispatched to Eastern Australia
1853	24	Catherine writes her long letter to Rev. D. Thomas asserting women's right to preach	1853–1856 Crimean War; Dr. David Livingstone crosses Africa
1854	25	William leaves the reformers in Spalding and joins the New Connexion; William returns to London to study under Dr. Cooke for six months; Catherine's first article in *New Connexion Magazine* appears: "How to Retain New Converts"; William is appointed to the London Circuit but is permitted to travel to other areas to preach; William travels to Caistor, Guernsey, Longton, and Hanley	

(continued)

Year	Age	Event	Elsewhere in the World
1855	26	June 16—William and Catherine are married by Rev. Dr. D. Thomas at Stockwell New Chapel; July—Revival services in Guernsey and Jersey; August—Revival services in York and Hull; September–October—Revival services in Sheffield; November—Revival services in Dewsbury; Catherine's inflammation of the lungs is cured by homeopathy; December—Revival services in Leeds	Livingstone discovers Victoria Falls
1856	27	February—Revival services in Halifax; March 8—William Bramwell is born (#1); Revival services in Macclesfield; William is appointed evangelist for a year in Chester Conference; September—After a revival at Yarmouth, William returns to Sheffield; November 26—William is presented with his portrait in Sheffield; December—Mission at Birmingham	
1857	28	January—Revival services in Nottingham and Chester; Revival services in Bristol, Truro, and St. Agnes; June 6—Conference in Nottingham recalls William from revivalism and appoints him minister in Brighouse in Yorkshire by a vote of 44 to 40. July 28—Ballington is born (#2); Catherine holds her first class and begins to lecture on temperance	
1858	29	January—Catherine is laid aside for six weeks with a spinal complaint; February—William meets Mr. Caughey, the American revivalist in Sheffield; May—Conference in Hull appoints William to Gateshead for twelve months with the promise that he will be able to return to evangelism at the end of that time; September 18—Catherine (Kate, later known as *La Maréchale*) is born (#3)	May 11—Minnesota becomes the thirty-second state in the United States

(*continued*)

Year	Age	Event	Elsewhere in the World
1859	30	September—William starts his work among drunkards; Conference in Manchester reappoints William to Gateshead; Catherine writes her first pamphlet, "Female Ministry"	February 14—Oregon becomes the thirty-third state in the United States November 22—*On the Origin of Species* first published by Charles Darwin
1860	31	January 8—Emma Moss is born (#4); Catherine delivers her first public address; July—William's health breaks down, Catherine fills his place for nine weeks	
1861	32	Easter—Catherine visits Hartlepool—an extraordinary revival breaks out; Conference in Liverpool: William's appeal to be reinstated as an evangelist is rejected; Booths resign from the Methodist New Connexion; Booths return to London; William and Catherine go to Hayle and from there to St. Ives	March 4—Abraham Lincoln is inaugurated as president of the U.S.; April 12—Fort Sumter attacked, marking the beginning of the American Civil War
1862	33	Catherine holds her first women-only meeting in St. Just; June—The New Connexion accepts William's resignation; Wesleyan Conference forbids the use of their chapels by the Booths; Traditional Methodist groups ban the Booths; August 26—Herbert is born (#5)	
1863	34	February—William and Catherine leave Cornwall for Cardiff; Revival meetings in Walsall; William meets with an accident, and Catherine carries on the meetings in his stead	November 19—Lincoln gives "Gettysburg Address"; Red Cross established
1864	35	May 4—Marian is born (#6); William and Catherine conduct revival services in Padley, Pudsey, and Woodhouse Carr; July 5—East London Christian Mission founded	
1865	36	February 26—Catherine goes to London; William attends Midnight Meeting Movement; Catherine conducts first West End services; July 2—William starts East End work; William meets Samuel Morley; July 5—First headquarters opened on Whitechapel Road; December 25—Evangeline is born (#7)	April 9—Treaty of Appomattox signed: End of the American Civil War; April 14—Lincoln assassinated; Christian Revival Association established

(continued)

Year	Age	Event	Elsewhere in the World
1866	37	February–April—Catherine holds meetings at Peckham; Catherine is incapacitated by illness, goes to Tunbridge Wells for change	
1867	38	Services at Margate; April 28—Lucy Milward is born (#8)	England's Second Reform Bill
1868	39	First official headquarters of the East London Christian Mission established; Christian Mission commenced work in Scotland; Publication of magazine called *East London Evangelist*; Catherine opposes the teachings of Plymouth Brethren; Catherine goes to Norwood	Last convict ship dispatched to Western Australia
1869	40	Catherine holds meetings at Brighton; July/August—The East London Christian Mission expands to Croyden and Edinborough and takes the name The Christian Mission; December 16—Catherine's mother dies	Suez Canal is opened
1870	41	Publication of "How to Reach the Masses"; People's Market in Whitechapel purchased; Catherine conducts "All Nights of Prayer" and services at Stoke Newington and Hastings; April 10—The People's Mission Hall is opened; First experiment of establishing depots for the sale of cheap food to the poor; Second anniversary trip to Dunorlan; William ill for three months, Catherine runs mission	
1871	42	First book published: *How to Reach the Masses With the Gospel*	
1872	43	Branch of Mission started in America. Not successful, and the work ceases for a time.	
1873	44	Henry John Andrews (Georgie Booth?) (#9) is adopted by the Booth family and raised as their own by Emma; Catherine goes to Plymouth; October—Catherine commences campaign in Chatham. At the third meeting she is seized with severe heart attack and has to give up for a fortnight; November—Takes children to Hastings because of the whooping cough. Holds meetings in Royal Circus	

(continued)

Year	Age	Event	Elsewhere in the World
1874	45	June—Annual Conference of Mission Workers; Catherine starts special agency for the rescue of drunkards; June 10—Catherine gives temperance addresses in Whitechapel, Hull, William Neal Dow present; Catherine starts drunkards rescue bands; August—Two months' campaign at Ryde	
1875	46	Publication of the first volume of music; June—Catherine prostrated with another heart attack, ill for several weeks. Tries hydropath and gets great relief; William puts his knee out of joint falling out of pony carriage. He and Catherine absent from mission work for five months	
1876	47	January—Catherine revisits Portsmouth; Bramwell Booth ill; William has gastric fever. Catherine nurses him and breaks down	Thomas Edison invents the phonograph
1877	48	December—The Christian Mission becomes The Salvation Army	
1878	49	Special uniform adopted; Booths' children commence public work; First Corps flag presented by Catherine; August—Last of Christian Mission Conferences held; "Practical Christianity" published by Catherine; December 25—William assumes title of "General"	
1879	50	May 17—Catherine presents flags in the Newcastle Circus to nine of the newly formed corps; William meets Mr. Denny; July—Catherine meets W. T. Stead; October 5—The first "unofficial" meeting in the U.S./By the Shirleys: Eliza Shirley and her parents; December 29—Formation of first Salvation Army band at Consett; First publication of The War Cry	Zulu War in South Africa

(continued)

Year	Age	Event	Elsewhere in the World
1880	51	William addresses Wesleyan Conference; March 10—Salvation Army officially starts in the U.S. and Australia/Under the direction of G.S. Railton, Shirleys are key workers at this point; First foreign mission Headquarters removed to Queen Victoria Street; Opening of first training college; Publication of first "Orders and Regulations"; "Godliness" published by Catherine; Catherine takes seriously ill at Glasgow. Manages to address meeting; May—First training home for women opened—Principal, Miss Emma Booth; Celebration of William and Catherine's silver wedding anniversary at Whitechapel; Fall—Training Home opened for male cadets under Ballington Booth; Bishop of Carlisle preaches against Salvation Army. Catherine answers him; Ballington sent to prison for preaching in the streets of Manchester; Captain Louisa Loch imprisoned at Loche; 20,000 people protest	Riot at Whitechapel
1881	52	Work extended to France; Corps formed in Australia; Kate starts work in Paris; Headquarters transferred to Queen Victoria Street; "Eagle" Public House and Grecian Theater bought for £16,000; Inauguration of meetings in Exeter Hall; First number of the "Little Soldier" issued	
1882	53	Opening of the Congress Hall and International Training College at Clapton; Marriage of W. Bramwell Booth and Captain Florence Soper; Work extended to Switzerland, Canada, Sweden, and India; Publication of "Life and Death" by Catherine; September—Miss Booth imprisoned at Neuchatel; tried at Boudry and acquitted; First Prison-Gate Home opened in London	Married Women's Property Act allows women to buy, own, and sell property and to keep their earnings; Sheffield Riot (taken up by Mr. Bright); during twelve months 669 Salvationists assaulted

(*continued*)

Year	Age	Event	Elsewhere in the World
1883	54	Work extended to South Africa and New Zealand; Spring—Catherine delivers lectures at Cannon Street Hotel on "Relations of The Salvation Army to Church and State"	
1884	55	"The Training of Children" by William Booth published; Over 900 corps members, 260 overseas—America, Canada, Australia; Catherine delivers addresses on "Popular Christianity"; First rescue home started under Mrs. Bramwell Booth; First "Band Journal" issued	Great Britain's Third Reform Act
1885	56	Bramwell assists Mr. Stead in gathering information for "Maiden Tribute of Modern Babylon"; June—The vision of "Who Cares?" published; July—"Maiden Tribute" published in the *Gazette*; Catherine writes to the Queen, receives sympathetic reply; First Calvary Fort started, publicly dedicated by Catherine; "All The World" first published; October–November—The Armstrong Trial; Catherine unable to take part in public meetings for several months	Petition submitted requesting new age of consent to be eighteen, with 343,000 signatures/These signatures were obtained in just seventeen days; Criminal Law Amendment Act passed
1886	57	Catherine visits Cambridge, Derby, Learnington, Portsmouth, Castleford, Norwich, and Tunbridge Wells; Death of the Army's first French martyr; William's first visit to France, the U.S., and Canada; Fall—First International Congress held in London; September 17—Commander Ballington Booth marries; Work extended to Germany; "Musical Salvationist" published; Self-Denial Week established; First "Orders and Regulations for Field Officers" published; first "Orders and Regulations for Staff Officers" published	

(*continued*)

Year	Age	Event	Elsewhere in the World
1887	58	Thousand British Corps established; February 8—Kate marries; First slum settlement established; Work extended to Holland, Denmark, and Zululand; First Crystal Palace Anniversary Demonstration; Auxiliary League founded; "Popular Christianity" published by Catherine	Queen Victoria's Golden Jubilee
1888	59	April 10—Emma Booth marries; Commandant Herbert Booth marries; First food depot opened at Limehouse; Work extended to Norway, Argentine, Finland, and Belgium; Catherine stricken with cancer; refuses operation; tries Mattei medicines; June 21—Catherine gives her last public address; Fall—Catherine goes to Clacton-on-Sea. Returns in October to London. Tries electricity; unsuccessful. Resorts again to Mattei medicines	
1889	60	August—Catherine returns to Clacton; November 29—Deputation of officers visit Catherine; The petition for the Sunday closing of public-houses, with 456,500 signatures, presented to the House of Commons by William; Publication of "The Deliverer"	
1890	61	Twenty-fifth anniversary of the Army celebrated at the Crystal Palace; January 30—Deputation from Army brass band visit Catherine; October 4—Catherine dies at three-thirty in the afternoon; October 6—Remains brought to Clapton Hall; 50,000 people pass through the hall in two days; October 13—Funeral service at Olympia—36,000 present; October 14—Funeral at Abney Park; Publication of *In Darkest England and the Way Out*	

(*continued*)

Year	Age	Event	Elsewhere in the World
1891	62	Work extended to Italy and Uruguay; Opening of Industrial and Land Colony at Hadleigh, Essex; William visits South Africa, Australia, New Zealand, and India; William signs the "Darkest England" Trust Deed; Publication of *Social Gazette*	
1892	63	Publication of *Life of Catherine Booth*; William visits Denmark, Germany, and Switzerland; Work extended to West Indies	
1893	64	William visits Denmark, Sweden, Belgium, Holland, and Norway	
1894	65	International Congress in connection with the General's Jubilee held in London; Work extended to Java	
1895	66	Work extended to Japan and British Guiana; Naval and Military League established	
1896	67	First Salvation Army Exhibition—Agricultural Hall, London; Work extended to Malta	
1897	68	William inspects work in European countries	
1898	69	William visits U.S., Canada, and European countries; "Orders and Regulations for Social Officers" published	The Spanish-American War
1899	70	William visits Australia, New Zealand, Ceylon, and various European countries; Officers sent to the front to work among both sides in the South African War	1899–1902—Boer War
1900	71	William visits European countries	
1901	72	Opening of first inebriates' home at Hadleigh	Queen Victoria dies and is succeeded by King Edward VII; The six Australian colonies form the Commonwealth of Australia; First Prime Minister of Australia elected, Sir Edmund Barton

(continued)

Year	Age	Event	Elsewhere in the World
1902	73	William publishes "Religion For Everyday"	Women are granted the right to vote and be elected to Parliament in Australia
1903	74	William visits the U.S., Canada, and various European countries; William received by President Roosevelt in America	
1904	75	June 24—William received by His Majesty, King Edward VII, at Buckingham Palace; June 25—International Congress opened by William in London; July 23—William received by Her Majesty, Queen Alexandra, at Buckingham Palace; August—William commences his Motor Campaign; Work extended to Panama	1904–1905—Russo-Japanese War
1905	76	First emigration ship sails from Liverpool for Canada with 1,000 emigrants; William visits Palestine, Australia, and various European countries; William receives Freedom Cities of London and Nottingham	Russian Revolution
1906	77	Establishment of Anti-Suicide Bureau	
1907	78	William visits Japan, the U.S., and Canada, among other nations; Pentecostal revival breaks out in a mission on Azusa Street in Los Angeles; William received by kings of Denmark and Norway, queen of Sweden, and emperor of Japan	
1908	79	Work extended to Korea; William visits South Africa	
1909	80	Eightieth birthday celebration at Albert Hall, London; William received by kings of Norway and Sweden; William received by prince and princess of Wales, now king and queen of England; William visits Russia, Finland, and other European countries; William received by Queen Alexandra and the dowager empress of Russia; Meets with accident resulting the loss of sight in one eye	Peary reaches the North Pole

(continued)

Year	Age	Event	Elsewhere in the World
1910	81	William visits various European countries	King George V takes the British throne
1911	82	William conducts International Social Council of London, attended by officers from all over the world; William visits Italy and other European countries	Amundsen reaches the South Pole
1912	83	William visits North European Staff Council in Norway; May 23—Operation on William's remaining eye, followed by complete loss of sight; August 20—William's death	April 14—*Titanic* strikes an iceberg on her maiden voyage and sinks; W. T. Stead, a close friend of the Booths, is among the casualties; 1912–13—War in the Balkans

The Booth Family Tree

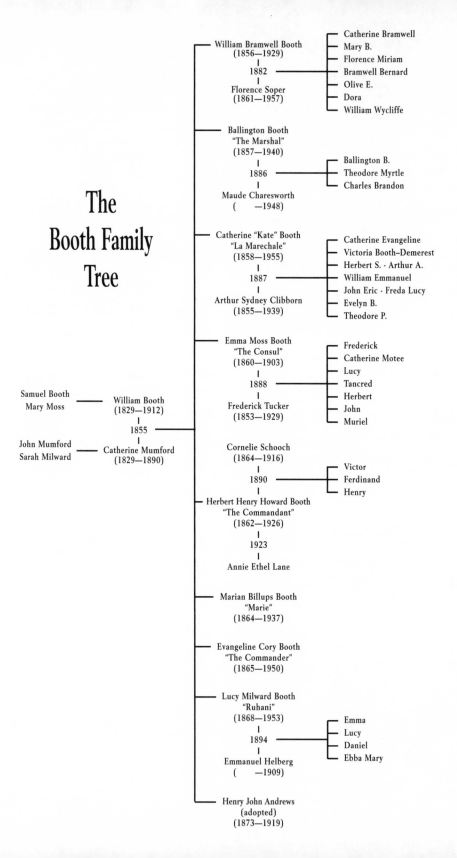

Samuel Booth
Mary Moss
— William Booth
(1829—1912)
|
1855
|
John Mumford
Sarah Milward
— Catherine Mumford
(1829—1890)

William Bramwell Booth
(1856—1929)
|
1882
|
Florence Soper
(1861—1957)

- Catherine Bramwell
- Mary B.
- Florence Miriam
- Bramwell Bernard
- Olive E.
- Dora
- William Wycliffe

Ballington Booth
"The Marshal"
(1857—1940)
|
1886
|
Maude Charesworth
(—1948)

- Ballington B.
- Theodore Myrtle
- Charles Brandon

Catherine "Kate" Booth
"La Marechale"
(1858—1955)
|
1887
|
Arthur Sydney Clibborn
(1855—1939)

- Catherine Evangeline
- Victoria Booth–Demerest
- Herbert S. - Arthur A.
- William Emmanuel
- John Eric - Freda Lucy
- Evelyn B.
- Theodore P.

Emma Moss Booth
"The Consul"
(1860—1903)
|
1888
|
Frederick Tucker
(1853—1929)

- Frederick
- Catherine Motee
- Lucy
- Tancred
- Herbert
- John
- Muriel

Cornelie Schooch
(1864—1916)
|
1890
|
Herbert Henry Howard Booth
"The Commandant"
(1862—1926)
|
1923
|
Annie Ethel Lane

- Victor
- Ferdinand
- Henry

Marian Billups Booth
"Marie"
(1864—1937)

Evangeline Cory Booth
"The Commander"
(1865—1950)

Lucy Milward Booth
"Ruhani"
(1868—1953)
|
1894
|
Emmanuel Helberg
(—1909)

- Emma
- Lucy
- Daniel
- Ebba Mary

Henry John Andrews
(adopted)
(1873—1919)

ENDNOTES

Foreword

1. Richard Collier, *The General Next to God* (London: Collins, 1965), 47.
2. *The Day Drawing Near*, Vol. 2, 4, quoted in Gary E. Gilley, "Turning to God, Part One," *Think on These Things*, Vol. 6, Issue 11, online at *www.svchapel.org/ThinkOnTheseThingsMinistries/publications/html/turning1.html*

Preface

1. William Booth, *The Seven Spirits* (Atlanta: The Salvation Army, 1985), 21–22.
2. Catherine Booth, Letter to Ballington Booth, date unknown, quoted in Catherine Bramwell-Booth, *Catherine Booth* (London: Hodder and Stoughton, 1970), 216.
3. Catherine Booth, "Aggressive Christianity," quoted in *Catherine Booth*, 216.
4. William Booth, *The Seven Spirits*, 40.
5. Ibid., 38.
6. Ibid., 23.

Chapter 1

1. Fredrick de Lautour Booth-Tucker, *The Life of Catherine Booth: The Mother of The Salvation Army*, Vol. 1 (London: Salvationist Publishing and Supplies, Ltd., 1924 [3rd printing]), 18–19.
2. Catherine Booth, "Reminiscences," quoted in Catherine Bramwell-Booth, *Catherine Booth* (London: Hodder and Stoughton, 1970), 17.
3. Booth-Tucker, *The Life of Catherine Booth*, Vol. 1, 13.
4. Bramwell-Booth, *Catherine Booth*, 32.
5. Catherine Booth, "Reminiscences," quoted in Bramwell-Booth, *Catherine Booth*, 23.
6. Ibid., 23.
7. W. T. Stead, *Mrs. Booth* (London: James Nisbet & Co., 1900), 25.
8. Catherine Mumford, Letter to William, British Library Microfilm 64799, 16 January 1853.
9. Booth-Tucker, *The Life of Catherine Booth*, Vol.1, 29–31.
10. Stead, *Mrs. Booth*, 27–28.
11. Ibid., 33.
12. Ibid., 35.
13. Bramwell-Booth, *Catherine Booth*, 33.
14. Ibid., 33.
15. Ibid., 33.

16. Booth-Tucker, *The Life of Catherine Booth*, Vol. 1, 36–37.
17. Charles Wesley, in *The Methodist Hymn Book* (London: Novello & Co., 1933), Hymn 406.
18. Stead, *Mrs. Booth*, 38.
19. Ibid., 39.
20. Bramwell-Booth, *Catherine Booth*, 37.
21. Catherine Booth, "Aggressive Christianity" (London: The Salvation Army, 1880, reprinted in Atlanta, 1986), 76.
22. Stead, *Mrs. Booth*, 42.
23. Booth-Tucker, *The Life of Catherine Booth*, Vol. 1, 39–40.
24. Stead, *Mrs. Booth*, 41.
25. C. M. to W. B., January 1854, quoted in Bramwell-Booth, *Catherine Booth*, 48–49.
26. Stead, *Mrs. Booth*, 57–59.
27. Ibid., 59–60.

Chapter 2

1. Author unknown, *Isaac Mardsen of Doncaster*, quoted in Harold Begbie, *The Life of General William Booth: The Founder of The Salvation Army*, Vol. 1 (London: MacMillan, 1920), 44.
2. Jenty Fairbank, *William and Catherine Booth: God's Soldiers* (London: Hodder and Stoughton, 1974), 24.
3. Harold Begbie, *Life of William Booth: The Founder of The Salvation Army*, 43.
4. Ibid., 52–53.
5. Ibid., 53.
6. Ibid., 53–54.
7. William Booth, *The Salvationist*, Jan 1879, quoted in *The Founder Speaks Again* (London: Salvationist Publishing and Supplies, 1960), 47.
8. Fairbank, *William and Catherine Booth*, 24.
9. Richard Collier, *The General Next to God* (London: Collins, 1965), 189.
10. Fairbank, *William and Catherine Booth*, 29.
11. Collier, *The General Next to God*, 23–24.
12. Fairbank, *William and Catherine Booth*, 29–30.
13. Stead, *Mrs. Booth*, 61.
14. William Booth, Letter to a friend, date unknown, quoted in General Frederick Coutts, *No Discharge in This War* (London: Hodder and Stoughton, 1974), 12.
15. Stead, *Mrs. Booth*, 61.
16. Edward Bishop, *Blood and Fire* (London: Longmans, 1964), 19.
17. Robert Sandall, *The History of The Salvation Army*, Vol. 1 (London: Thomas Nelson, 1947), 6.
18. Collier, *The General Next to God*, 27.
19. William Booth, *The Salvationist*, Jan. 1879 in *The Founder Speaks Again* (London: Salvationist Publishing and Supplies, 1960), 59–60.

Chapter 3

1. *The Life of General William Booth*.
2. Booth-Tucker, *The Life of Catherine Booth*, Vol. 1, 58–59.
3. Ibid., 60–62.
4. Catherine Booth, "Reminiscences," quoted in Bramwell-Booth, *Catherine Booth*, 58–60.
5. William Booth, Letter to Catherine, British Library Microfilm 64799, date uncertain: compiler's note was "April/May 1852."

6. Catherine Mumford, Letter to William, British Library Microfilm 64799, 11 May 1852.

7. William Booth, Letter to Catherine, undated, quoted in Bramwell-Booth, *Catherine Booth*, 64.

8. Catherine Mumford, Letter to William, British Library Microfilm 64799, 13 May 1852.

9. Begbie, *Life of General William Booth*, Vol. 1, 130–1.

10. Catherine Mumford, Letter to William, May 1852, quoted in Bramwell-Booth, *Catherine Booth*, 66–67.

11. Collier, *The General Next to God*, 29.

12. Catherine Mumford, diary entry, British Library Microfilm 64806, Sunday 30 May 1852.

13. Catherine Booth, "Reminiscences," quoted in Begbie, *Life of William Booth*, Vol. 1, 139.

14. Ibid.

15. Roy Hattersley, *Blood and Fire: William and Catherine Booth and Their Salvation Army* (New York: Doubleday, 1999), 51.

16. William Booth, Letter to Catherine, British Library Microfilm 64799, 9 June 1852.

17. See Appendix A for a chart of the relationships between pounds, shillings, and pence.

18. Catherine Mumford, Letter to William, British Library Microfilm 64799, date uncertain: compiler's note was "after 13 June 1852."

19. Catherine Mumford, Letter to William, British Library Microfilm 64799, date uncertain: compiler's note was "19–24 December 1852."

20. Catherine Mumford, Letter to William, undated, quoted in Bramwell-Booth, *Catherine Booth*, 85.

21. Catherine Mumford, Letter to William, British Library Microfilm 64799, 16 January 1853.

22. Catherine Mumford, Letter to William, British Library Microfilm 64800, 20 March 1853.

23. Catherine Mumford, Letter to William, British Library Microfilm 64800, 3 April 1853.

24. Catherine Mumford, Letter to William, undated, quoted in Bramwell-Booth, *Catherine Booth*, 92–93.

25. Catherine Mumford, Letter to Rev. Dr. D. Thomas, British Library Microfilm 64806, 1855.

26. Catherine Mumford, Letter to William, British Library Microfilm 64802, 9 April 1855.

27. Ibid.

28. William Booth, Letter to Catherine, 12 April 1855, quoted in Bramwell-Booth, *Catherine Booth*, 121–22.

29. Catherine Mumford, Letter to William, 4 September 1854, quoted in Bramwell-Booth, *Catherine Booth*, 111–13.

30. William Booth, Letter to Catherine, 5 January 1855, quoted in Bramwell-Booth, *Catherine Booth*, 114.

31. William Booth, Letter to Catherine, 29 January 1855, quoted in Bramwell-Booth, *Catherine Booth*, 115.

32. Booth-Tucker, *The Life of Catherine Booth*, Vol. 1, 85.

Chapter 4

1. William Booth, Letter to Catherine, 4 August 1855, quoted in Bramwell-Booth, *Catherine Booth*, 124.

2. William Booth, Letter to Catherine, 8 August 1855, quoted in Bramwell-Booth, *Catherine Booth: The Story of Her Loves* (London: Hodder and Stoughton Limited, 1970, Third Impression 1971), 147.

3. Catherine Booth, Letter to her parents, 5 November 1855, quoted in Bramwell-Booth, *Catherine Booth* (Third Impression 1971), 157.

4. Catherine Booth, Letter to her parents, British Library Microfilm 64803, 5 November 1855.

5. Catherine Booth, "Reminiscences," quoted in Bramwell-Booth, *Catherine Booth*, 129.

6. Catherine Booth, Letter to her parents, British Library Microfilm 64803, 13 December 1855.

7. Catherine Booth, Letter to her parents, British Library Microfilm 64803, date not specified: compiler's note was "22 October 1855."

8. William and Catherine Booth, Letter to Catherine's parents, British Library Microfilm 64803, 5 February 1856.

9. Catherine Booth, Letter to her mother, British Library Microfilm 64803, 10 December 1856.

10. Bramwell-Booth, *Catherine Booth*, 136.

11. Collier, *The General Next to God*, 33.

12. Sandall, *The History of The Salvation Army*, Vol. 1, 7.

13. Catherine Booth, Letter to her mother, undated, quoted in Bramwell-Booth, *Catherine Booth*, 138.

14. Catherine Booth, Letter to her mother, British Library Microfilm 64804, 21 June 1857.

15. Catherine Booth, Letter to her mother, undated 1858, quoted in Bramwell-Booth, *Catherine Booth*, 150.

16. Bramwell-Booth, *Catherine Booth*, 150.

17. Collier, *The General Next to God*, 33.

18. Stead, *Mrs. Booth*, 152–55.

19. Cyril Barnes, ed., *Words of Catherine Booth* (London: Salvationist Publishing, 1981), 26.

20. Catherine Booth, Letter to her mother, undated, quoted in Bramwell-Booth, *Catherine Booth*, 156.

21. Catherine Booth, Letter to her mother, undated, quoted in Bramwell-Booth, *Catherine Booth*, 154.

22. Catherine Booth, "Aggressive Christianity," quoted in Bramwell-Booth, *Catherine Booth*, 157.

23. Stead, *Mrs. Booth* (London: James Nisbet & Co., 1900), 157.

24. Ibid., 158–59.

25. Bramwell-Booth, *Catherine Booth*, 158.

26. Ibid., 159.

27. Catherine Booth, "Aggressive Christianity," quoted in Bramwell-Booth, *Catherine Booth*, 160.

28. Catherine Booth, Letter to her mother, British Library Microfilm 64805, 23 July 1860.

29. Chick Yuill, "Restoring the Image," quoted in Clifford W. Kew, ed., *Catherine Booth—Her Continuing Relevance* (St. Albans: The Campfield Press, 1990), 53.

30. William Booth, *The Seven Spirits* (Atlanta: The Salvation Army, 1985), 28.

31. Ibid., 30.

32. Catherine Booth, Letter to her mother, 4 February 1861, quoted in Bramwell-Booth, *Catherine Booth*, 173.

33. Yuill, "Restoring the Image" in Kew, ed., *Catherine Booth—Her Continuing Relevance*, 67.

34. Ibid., 83.

35. Ibid., 83–84.

Chapter 5

1. William Booth, Letter to New Connexion Conference, 5 March 1861, quoted in Bramwell-Booth, *Catherine Booth*, 176.

2. Catherine Booth, Letter to her parents, British Library Microfilm 64805, April 1861.

3. Catherine Booth, Letter to her parents, British Library Microfilm 64805, June 1861.

4. Catherine Booth, Letter to her parents, British Library Microfilm 64805, 24 June 1861.

5. Collier, *The General Next to God*, 36.

6. Catherine Booth, Letter to her parents, undated, quoted in Bramwell-Booth, *Catherine Booth*, 185.
7. Catherine Booth, Letter to her parents, undated, quoted in Bramwell-Booth, *Catherine Booth*, 186.
8. Booth-Tucker, *The Life of Catherine Booth*, Vol.1, 336.
9. Collier, *The General Next to God*, 36.
10. Catherine Booth, Letter to her mother, British Library Microfilm 64806, 23 February 1863.
11. Catherine Booth, Letter to her mother, British Library Microfilm 64806, February 1863.
12. Sandall, *The History of The Salvation Army*, Vol. 1, 45.
13. A colorless, flammable liquid obtained from crude petroleum.
14. Ibid., 45.
15. Begbie, *The Life of General William Booth*, Vol. 1, 366.
16. Ibid., 367–68.
17. Collier, *The General Next to God*, 19.
18. Begbie, *The Life of General William Booth*, Vol. 1, 370–71.
19. Ibid., 371.
20. Bramwell Booth, *Our First Captain* (London: Salvationist Publishing), 6.
21. Sandall, *The History of The Salvation Army*, Vol. 1, 42.
22. William Booth, *The War Cry*, 20 January 1881, quoted in Cyril Barnes, ed., *The Founder Speaks Again* (London: Salvationist Publishing and Supplies, 1960), 100.
23. Ibid., 100–01.
24. Ibid., 100.
25. William Booth, "A New Years Eve Greeting," 1906, quoted in Barnes, ed., *The Founder Speaks Again*, 162.
26. Spoken by Leonard Ravenhill on a visit to his house by the authors six months prior to his death.
27. E. M. Bounds, *The Complete Works of E. M. Bounds on Prayer* (Grand Rapids: Baker Books, 1990), 104.
28. Collier, *The General Next to God*, 189.
29. Ibid.

Chapter 6

1. Sandall, *The History of The Salvation Army*, Vol. 1, 53.
2. Collier, *The General Next to God*, 38.
3. Ibid., 195.
4. Ibid., 44.
5. Booth-Tucker, *The Life of Catherine Booth*, Vol.1, 404.
6. Sandall, *The History of The Salvation Army*, Vol. 1, 52.
7. William Booth, Letter to Catherine, 12 April 1855, quoted in Bramwell-Booth, *Catherine Booth*, 122.
8. Bramwell Booth, *Our First Captain*, 10.
9. Sandall, *The History of The Salvation Army*, Vol. 1, 65.
10. William Booth, *Christian Mission Magazine*, May 1876, 238, quoted in Bramwell-Booth, *Catherine Booth*, 219.
11. Collier, *The General Next to God*, 67.
12. Catherine Booth, "Reminiscences," quoted in Bramwell-Booth, *Catherine Booth*, 153.
13. Stead, *Mrs. Booth*, 198.

14. Collier, *The General Next to God*, 49.
15. Sandall, *The History of The Salvation Army*, Vol. 1, 294.
16. Booth-Tucker, *The Life of Catherine Booth*, Vol. 1, 410.
17. Collier, *The General Next to God*, 43.
18. Sandall, *The History of The Salvation Army*, Vol. 1, 93.
19. Ibid., 98.
20. Ibid., 98.
21. William Booth, *Faith-Healing* (London: Salvationist Publishing and Supplies, 1902), 7.
22. William Booth, *The Christian Mission Magazine*, Jan. 1870 in Barnes, ed., *The Founder Speaks Again*, 76.
23. Sandall, *The History of The Salvation Army*, Vol. 1, 60.
24. Ibid., 101.
25. Ibid., 108.
26. From *The East London Evangelist*, Vol. 1, No. 1, quoted in Sandall, *The History of The Salvation Army*, Vol. 1, 112.
27. Sandall, *The History of The Salvation Army*, Vol. 1, 128.
28. Ibid., 127.
29. Collier, *The General Next to God*, 50.
30. Coutts, *No Discharge in This War*, 25.
31. Robert Sandall, *The History of The Salvation Army*, Vol. 3 (London: Thomas Nelson, 1947), xiv.
32. Ibid., xiii.
33. Stead, *Mrs. Booth*, 167.
34. Bramwell Booth, "Echoes and Memories," quoted in "Adopted Children of the Booths," The Salvation Army Heritage Site, 2000, online at *www.salvationarmy.org/heritage.nsf/36c-107e27b0ba7a98025692e0032abaa/360acc736dd7876280256950003af170*
35. Sandall, *The History of The Salvation Army*, Vol. 1, 146.
36. William Booth, Letter to Bramwell, July 1872, quoted in Bramwell-Booth, *Catherine Booth*, 220.
37. Sandall, *The History of The Salvation Army*, Vol. 1, 154.
38. Coutts, *No Discharge in This War*, 31–32.
39. Sandall, *The History of The Salvation Army*, Vol. 1, 190.
40. Collier, *The General Next to God*, 55.
41. Ibid., 55.
42. Severe sudden and intense spasms of pain in the chest induced by physical or emotional exertion and associated with an insufficient supply of blood to the heart.
43. Sandall, *The History of The Salvation Army*, Vol. 1, 207.
44. Ibid.
45. William Booth, *Christian Mission Magazine*, 236, 240, quoted in Bramwell-Booth, *Catherine Booth*, 232.
46. Collier, *The General Next to God*, 56.
47. Ibid.
48. Sandall, *The History of The Salvation Army*, Vol. 1, 237.
49. William Booth, *The Salvationist*, Jan. 1879, quoted in Barnes, ed., *The Founder Speaks Again*, 45, 48.

Chapter 7

1. Collier, *The General Next to God*, 47.

2. Sandall, *The History of The Salvation Army*, 5.
3. Fairbank, *William and Catherine Booth*, 82.
4. Ibid., 85.
5. Collier, *The General Next to God*, 54.
6. Another name for a pub or a place that sold alcoholic beverages; a dram is a small measure in which alcohol was often sold.
7. Sandall, *The History of The Salvation Army*, Vol. 2, 11.
8. Catherine Booth, *Christian Mission Magazine*, June 1879, 143, quoted in Bramwell-Booth, *Catherine Booth*, 233.
9. Collier, *The General Next to God*, 57.
10. Sandall, *The History of The Salvation Army*, Vol. 2, 38.
11. Catherine Booth, *Christian Mission Magazine*, June 1879, 145, quoted in Bramwell-Booth, *Catherine Booth*, 240.
12. Edward Bishop, *Blood and Fire* (London: Longmans, 1964), 44.
13. Collier, *The General Next to God*, 60.
14. Inscription on a photograph signed by William Booth that hangs in the Salvation Army office in Kalgoorlie-Boulder, Australia.
15. Catherine Booth, *The War Cry*, 16 October 1880, quoted in Bramwell-Booth, *Catherine Booth*, 247–48.
16. William Booth, *The War Cry*, 21 February 1885, quoted in Cyril Barnes, ed., *The Founder Speaks Again*, 233.
17. William Booth, "Eightieth Birthday Letter," quoted in Barnes, ed., *The Founder Speaks Again*, 168.
18. William Booth, "A New Years Greeting, 1906," quoted in Barnes, ed., *The Founder Speaks Again*, 163.
19. Collier, *The General Next to God*, 48.
20. Catherine Booth, "Practical Religion," 4, quoted by Jean James, "Training Christians from Babyhood" in Kew, ed., *Catherine Booth—Her Continuing Relevance*, 98.
21. Catherine Booth, "Practical Religion," 8, quoted by Jean James, "Training Christians from Babyhood" in Kew, ed., *Catherine Booth—Her Continuing Relevance*, 101.
22. Catherine Booth, "Practical Religion," 9, quoted by Jean James, "Training Christians from Babyhood" in Kew, ed., *Catherine Booth—Her Continuing Relevance*, 103.
23. Collier, *The General Next to God*, 49.
24. Booth-Tucker, *The Life of Catherine Booth*, Vol. 1, 179.
25. Stead, *Mrs. Booth*, 131.
26. Catherine Booth, "Practical Religion," 7, quoted in Bramwell-Booth, *Catherine Booth*, 262.
27. Catherine Booth, "Practical Religion," 15, quoted in Bramwell-Booth, *Catherine Booth*, 262.
28. Stead, *Mrs. Booth*, 127–28.
29. Evangeline Booth, "The Officers' Review," 1940, 330, quoted by Jean James, "Training Christians from Babyhood" in Kew, ed., *Catherine Booth—Her Continuing Relevance*, 104.
30. Catherine Booth, "Practical Religion," 13, quoted by Jean James, "Training Christians from Babyhood" in Kew, ed., *Catherine Booth—Her Continuing Relevance*, 107.
31. Catherine Booth, "Practical Religion," 26, quoted in Bramwell-Booth, *Catherine Booth*, 267.
32. Catherine Mumford, Letter to William, British Library Microfilm 64800, 13 June 1853.
33. Cyril Barnes, ed., *Words of Catherine Booth* (London: The Camperfield Press, 1981), 29.
34. Ibid., 30–31.
35. From "Adopted Children of the Booths," The Salvation Army Heritage Site, 2000, online at

www.salvationarmy.org/heritage.nsf/36c107e27b0ba7a98025692e0032   abaa/ 360acc736dd7876280256950003af170.

36. Sandall, *The History of The Salvation Army*, Vol. 1, 145.
37. Catherine Booth, *The War Cry*, 5 December 1855, quoted in Bramwell-Booth, *Catherine Booth*, 306.
38. Stead, *Mrs. Booth*, 174.
39. Catherine Booth, "Aggressive Christianity," quoted in Bramwell-Booth, *Catherine Booth*, 307–08.
40. Catherine Booth, "Church and State," quoted in Bramwell-Booth, *Catherine Booth*, 308.
41. Ibid.
42. Catherine Booth, "Practical Religion," quoted in Bramwell-Booth, *Catherine Booth*, 308.
43. From *The East London Evangelist*, Vol. 1, No. 1, quoted in Sandall, *The History of The Salvation Army*, Vol. 1, 112.
44. Booth-Tucker, *The Life of Catherine Booth*, Vol. 2, 225–26.
45. Collier, *The General Next to God*, 78.
46. Ibid., 160.
47. Catherine Booth, "Popular Christianity," quoted in Bramwell-Booth, *Catherine Booth*, 310.

Chapter 8

1. Collier, *The General Next to God*, 130.
2. Inscription on a photograph of William Booth, reviewed by the author.
3. A Special Correspondent, "The Salvation Army: An All Night Meeting," *Newcastle Daily Chronicle*, 21 May 1879, quoted in "Stories and Teachings from the Revival Archives," online at *http://members.truepath.com/hf/boothg2.htm.*
4. "A Notice to the Inhabitants of the City of Salisbury," 1881, quoted in Coutts, *No Discharge in This War*, 92.
5. Collier, *The General Next to God*, 93.
6. Ibid., 92.
7. Ibid., 93.
8. Catherine Booth, *The War Cry*, 17 February 1881, quoted in Bramwell-Booth, *Catherine Booth*, 303–04.
9. Fairbank, *William and Catherine Booth*, 101.
10. Katie Booth, telegraph to her parents, quoted in Bramwell-Booth, *Catherine Booth*, 323.
11. Catherine Booth, Letter to Katie, 19 September 1883, quoted in Bramwell-Booth, *Catherine Booth*, 323–4.
12. Sandall, *The History of The Salvation Army*, Vol. 2, 131.
13. Collier, *The General Next to God*, 96.
14. William Booth, *The Seven Spirits*, 91–92.
15. From a *Saturday Review* article reprinted in *Christian Mission Magazine*, May 1879, 199, 201, quoted in Bramwell-Booth, *Catherine Booth*, 245.
16. Catherine Booth, Letter to Mrs. Billups, date unknown, quoted in Bramwell-Booth, *Catherine Booth*, 246.
17. Ibid., 13.
18. Collier, *The General Next to God*, 134.
19. Sandall, *The History of The Salvation Army*, Vol. 3, 4.
20. Ibid., 7.
21. Sandall, *The History of The Salvation Army*, Vol. 2, 98.

22. A daycare or nursery, often for foundling children.
23. Collier, *The General Next to God*, 156.
24. Stead, *Mrs. Booth*, 190.
25. Ibid., 191.
26. Ibid., 130.
27. Bramwell Booth, *Our First Captain*, 16.
28. Collier, *The General Next to God*, 78.
29. William Booth, *The War Cry*, May 23, 1885, quoted in Cyril Barnes, ed., *The Founder Speaks Again*, 175.

Chapter 9

1. Sandall, *The History of The Salvation Army*, Vol. 3, 29.
2. Collier, *The General Next to God*, 113.
3. Catherine Booth, *The War Cry*, 1 August 1885, quoted in Bramwell-Booth, *Catherine Booth*, 330.
4. Collier, *The General Next to God*, 115.
5. Ibid., 120.
6. Ibid., 122.
7. Ibid., 123.
8. Sandall, *The History of The Salvation Army*, Vol. 3, 35.
9. Ibid., 39.
10. Ibid., Vol 3, 47.

Chapter 10

1. Catherine Booth, *The War Cry*, 28 August 1886, quoted in Bramwell-Booth, *Catherine Booth*, 338.
2. Collier, *The General Next to God*, 131.
3. Catherine Booth, Letter to Emma, 30 January 1888, quoted in Bramwell-Booth, *Catherine Booth*, 342–43.
4. William Booth, *In Darkest England and the Way Out* (London: The Salvation Army, 1890), 27.
5. Ibid., 41–42.
6. Collier, *The General Next to God*, 159.
7. Catherine Booth, "Address at the Anglo-Indian Wedding," 10, quoted in Roger J. Green, *Catherine Booth* (Crowborough: Monarch, 1997), 281.
8. Catherine Booth, *The War Cry*, 21 April 1888, quoted in Bramwell-Booth, *Catherine Booth*, 350.
9. See the epilogue for more text from this address.
10. Booth-Tucker, *The Life of Catherine Booth*, Vol. 2, 424–27.
11. William Booth, *In Darkest England and the Way Out*, 67.
12. Ibid., 85.
13. Ibid., 87.
14. Ibid., 45.
15. Ibid., 284.
16. Ibid., 285.
17. Catherine Booth, *The War Cry*, 28 September 1889, quoted in Bramwell-Booth, *Catherine Booth*, 357.

18. Catherine Booth, *The War Cry*, 4 January 1890, quoted in Bramwell-Booth, *Catherine Booth*, 357.
19. Stead, *Mrs. Booth*, 210.
20. Ibid., 172.
21. Ibid., 213.
22. William Booth, diary entry, quoted in Begbie, *The Life of General William Booth*, Vol. 2, 100.
23. Green, *Catherine Booth*, 294–96.
24. Ibid., 296–97.
25. Song Book No. 692, 1953 edition, quoted in Bramwell-Booth, *Catherine Booth*, 377–78.

Chapter 11

1. William Booth, *In Darkest England and the Way Out*, preface.
2. Collier, *The General Next to God*, 173.
3. Huxley, quoted in Collier, *The General Next to God*, 173.
4. Begbie, *The Life of General William Booth*, Vol. 1, 375.
5. Collier, *The General Next to God*, 173.
6. Coutts, *No Discharge in This War*, 124.
7. Leonard Ravenhill, *Why Revival Tarries* (Minneapolis: Bethany House Publishers, 1959), 51.
8. Collier, *The General Next to God*, 199–200.
9. Ibid., 200–01.
10. Roy Hattersley, *Blood and Fire* (New York: Doubleday, 1999), 406.
11. Ibid., 421.
12. William Booth, *The Seven Spirits*, 49.
13. Ibid., 50.
14. Collier, *The General Next to God*, 193.
15. Coutts, *No Discharge in This War*, 139.
16. J. Evan Smith, *Booth The Beloved: Personal Recollections of William Booth, Founder of The Salvation Army* (London: Oxford University Press, 1949), 38.
17. Ibid., 20.
18. Collier, *The General Next to God*, 214.
19. Ibid., 214.
20. Harold Begbie, *The Life of General William Booth*, Vol. 2, 180.
21. William Booth, "Eightieth Birthday Letter," in Barnes, ed., *The Founder Speaks Again*, 33–34.
22. From "The Sinking of the Titanic," The Salvation Army Heritage site, 2000, *www.salvationarmy.org/heritage.nsf/36c107e27b0ba7a98025692e0032abaa/f51002b455947dba8025692e004d363d*
23. William Booth, "The Last Public Address," quoted in Barnes, ed., *The Founder Speaks Again*, 169–71.
24. Collier, *The General Next to God*, 221.
25. Bramwell Booth, *Our First Captain*, 5.
26. Fairbank, *William and Catherine Booth*, 125.
27. J. Evan Smith, *Booth The Beloved*, 131.
28. Collier, *The General Next to God*, 223.

BIBLIOGRAPHY

Barnes, Cyril, ed. *The Founder Speaks Again*. London: Salvationist Publishing and Supplies, 1960.

———. *Words of Catherine Booth*. London: Salvationist Publishing, 1981.

———. *The Words of William Booth*. London: Salvation Army Publishing and Supplies, 1975.

Begbie, Harold. *The Life of General William Booth: The Founder of The Salvation Army*. Vol. I & II. New York: Macmillan, 1920.

Bishop, Edward. *Blood and Fire: The Story of General William Booth and The Salvation Army*. Chicago: Moody Press, 1964.

Booth, Bramwell. *Our First Captain*. London: The Salvation Army, (no date).

Booth, Catherine. *Agressive Christianity*. London: The Salvation Army, 1880, reprinted in Atlanta, 1986.

Booth, William. *Booth Papers; May, 1852–January, 1855*. London: The British Library. Microfilm.

———. *Booth Papers; January 22, 1855–March, 1859*. London: The British Library. Microfilm.

———. *Booth Papers; March, 1859–*. London: The British Library. Microfilm.

———. *The Training of Children*. London: The Salvation Army, 1884.

———. *In Darkest England and the Way Out*. London: International Headquarters of the Salvation Army, 1890.

———. *Faith Healing*. London: Salvationist Publishing and Supplies, 1902.

———. *Religion for Every Day*. London: The Salvation Army, 1902.

———. *Religion for Every Day Volume II: Love, Marriage, and Home*. London: The Salvation Army.

———. *The Seven Spirits*. Atlanta: The Salvation Army, 1985.

Booth-Tucker, Fredrick de Lautour. *The Life of Catherine Booth: The Mother of The Salvation Army*, Vol. 1. London: Salvationist Publishing and Supplies, Ltd., 1924 (3rd printing).

Bradwell, Cyril R. *Fight The Good Fight—The Story of The Salvation Army in New Zealand*. Wellington, New Zealand: Reed Ltd., 1982.

Bramwell-Booth, Catherine. *Catherine Booth*. London: Hodder and Stoughton, 1970.

Collier, Richard. *The General Next to God*. London: Collins, 1965.

Coutts, General Frederick. *No Discharge in This War*. London: Hodder and Stoughton, 1974.

Ervine, St. John. *God's Soldier: General William Booth*. Vol. I & II. New York: The Macmillan Company, 1935.

Fairbank, Jenty. *William and Catherine Booth: God's Soldiers*. London: Hodder and Stoughton, 1974.

Green, Roger J. *Catherine Booth*. Grand Rapids, Baker Books, 1996.

Hattersley, Roy. *Blood and Fire: William and Catherine Booth and Their Salvation Army*. New York: Doubleday, 1999.

Kew, Clifford W., ed. *Catherine Booth—Her Continuing Relevance*. St. Albans: The Campfield Press, 1990.

Larsson, Flora. *My Best Men Are Women*. London: Hodder and Stoughton, 1974.

McKinley, Edward H. *Marching to Glory: The History of The Salvation Army in the United States, 1880–1992*. Grand Rapids: William B. Eerdmans Publishing Company, 1995.

Murdock, Norman H. *Origins of The Salvation Army*. Knoxville, Tennessee: The University of Tennessee Press, 1994.

Railton, George Scott. *The Authoritative Life of General William Booth: Founder of The Salvation Army*. New York: George H. Doran Company, 1912.

Reinsborg, Neil C. *Sallies of The South—Centennial History of The Salvation Army in Southland*. Invercargil, New Zealand: Craigs Printers and Publishers, 1984.

Sandall, Robert. *The History of The Salvation Army*. Vol. 1–3. New York: The Salvation Army, 1950.

Search, Pamela. *Happy Warriors: The Story of the Social Work of The Salvation Army*. London: Arco Ltd., 1956.

Smith, J. Evan. *Booth the Beloved: Personal Recollections of William Booth, Founder of The Salvation Army*. London: Oxford University Press, 1949.

Stead, W. T. *Mrs. Booth*. London: James Nisbet & Co., 1900.

Steele, Harold C. *I Was a Stranger: The Faith of William Booth, Founder of The Salvation Army*. New York: Exposition Press, 1954.

Troutt, Margaret. *The General Was a Lady: The Story of Evangeline Booth*. Nashville: A. J. Holman Co., 1980.

Waite, John C. *Dear Mr. Booth*. St. Albans: The Campfield Press.

Watson, Bernard. *A Hundred Years' War: The Salvation Army: 1865–1965*. London: Hodder and Stoughton, 1964.

Wilson, P. W. *General Evangeline Booth of The Salvation Army*. New York: Charles Scribner's Sons, 1948.

INDEX

Alcoholism   31, 58, 139, 155, 185, 200, 204, 220, 234, 242, 287

Allen, John   138, 139

America   20, 55, 66, 101, 153, 173, 237, 241, 242, 248, 255, 270, 271, 272, 275, 277, 278, 301

Armstrong, Eliza   204–210

Articles of War   155

Australia   61, 173, 189, 191, 207, 222, 236, 241, 248, 268, 269, 272, 274, 275, 277, 278, 287

Bands   156, 157, 158, 179, 180, 183, 212, 213, 230, 244, 258, 273, 276

Barbados   239

Barker, James   189–190

Basingstoke riots   178

Besom, Jack   57–58

Binfield Road Chapel   45, 62, 65

Booth, Ballington   96, 104, 167, 170, 217, 241, 270, 274, 275, 280, 281

Booth, Bramwell   94, 103, 123, 126, 140, 142–144, 148, 155, 158, 163, 166, 167, 188, 189, 193, 194, 197–201, 203, 204, 208, 214, 217, 227, 230, 233, 241, 242, 244, 248, 250, 255, 258, 270, 273–275, 280–291

Booth, Catherine
   Bible study   43, 45, 83, 162
   Birth   28–29
   Parents   31
   Home schooling   163
   Temperance   28, 30, 31, 32, 42, 66, 268c, 270, 273
   Spinal complaint   35
   Conversion   38–41
   Holiness, views on   18, 106, 169, 259, 260

Begins to preach   103–104

Meets William   65

Courtship and marriage   65–87

Illness   93, 134, 213, 218, 272

Cancer   213, 217, 218, 224, 226, 276

Death   225, 226

Funeral   227

Booth, Catherine Bramwell (Bramwell's daughter)   280, 281

Booth, Emma   102, 167, 170, 191, 213, 217, 218, 241, 242, 271, 272, 274, 276, 280, 289

Booth, Evangeline   132, 162, 164, 167, 159, 251, 255, 271, 280, 287, 292

Booth, Florence (Bramwell's wife)   189, 255, 274, 280

Booth, Herbert   114, 167, 241, 271, 276, 280

Booth, Kate   100, 104, 167, 180–182, 217, 241, 270, 274, 276, 280

Booth, Lucy   134, 146, 167, 226, 241, 255, 272, 280

Booth, Marian   115, 167, 226, 280

Booth, Mary (Bramwell's daughter)   227, 280

Booth, Mary Moss (William's mother)   48, 280

Booth, Samuel (William's father)   48, 51, 268, 280

Booth, William

   Birth   48, 267, 280

   Parents   48–49, 267, 280

   Apprenticeship   49–52, 268

   Chartist movement   52, 268

   Conversion   48, 55, 62, 106, 268

   Passion for souls   56, 59, 62–64, 70, 78, 87, 97, 100, 158, 172, 237, 244, 245

   Moves to London   60, 112, 268

   Lay preacher   57

   Meets Catherine   65

   Courtship and marriage   65–87

   Traveling evangelist   70, 72, 84

   New Connexion minister   81, 82, 84, 109, 112, 269, 271

   Circuit work   60, 79, 81, 82, 96, 97, 100, 109

   Resignation   109–112

   Finds his destiny   116, 119, 120

   Illness   105, 142

   Overseas travel   213, 240, 248, 279

   Failing eyesight   249, 250, 254, 255, 278, 279

   Final public address   251–254

   Death   255

Funeral   256–258
Booth, William Bramwell (see Booth, Bramwell)
Brick making   239
Brighouse   95, 96, 270
Brixton Methodist Church   42, 44
Brothels   178, 188, 198–206, 208
Butler, Josephine   200

Cadman, Elijah   150, 151, 234, 245
Canada   173, 211, 222, 241, 248, 274, 275, 277, 278
Cardiff   114, 166, 271
Caughey, Rev. James   55–57, 80, 160, 270
Chile   248
Christian Mission   134, 141, 148, 271–273
Christian Mission Magazine, The   143
Christian Revival Association   121, 271
Clacton   219, 223, 276
Clapton Common   170
Combe, Elizabeth   208
Compassion   16, 17, 28, 30–33, 35, 45, 51, 52, 56, 57, 71, 89, 96, 97, 102, 115–
   117, 130, 139, 140, 167, 168, 193, 213, 229, 244
Congregationalists   75–77
Consecration   18, 90, 107, 108, 121–123, 127, 172, 182, 209, 250, 253, 264
Conversion experiences   29, 38, 41–44, 48, 55, 62, 80, 89, 102, 106, 115, 119,
   127, 128, 138, 160, 167, 170, 176–178
Cooke, Rev. Dr. William   81, 82, 96, 110, 269
Cornwall Revival   94, 113, 114
Costa Rica   248
Cottrill, Elizabeth   187–189
Courage   28, 43, 84, 98, 154, 185, 195, 207, 217, 218, 238, 243
Crèches   192
Criminal Amendment Act of 1885   207
Critics   95, 101, 121, 137, 155, 181, 184–186, 233, 234, 243, 245

Darkest England Scheme   219–223, 225, 231, 234, 236, 276, 277
Disaster work   248, 251
Discipleship   169

Eames, Francis   49, 50, 52, 55, 57, 58, 60
East London Christian Mission   134, 140, 271, 272
East London Evangelist, The   138, 169, 272
Edward VII, King   243

Faith   12, 19, 30, 33–37, 39, 41, 42, 45, 53, 73, 74, 78, 95, 106, 107, 111, 112, 121, 123–125, 127, 129–131, 133, 135, 137, 144, 151, 160, 161, 169, 173, 181, 182, 185, 193, 218, 223, 224, 230, 237, 239, 243, 251, 255, 260
Family life   106
Farm Colony, Hadleigh   236, 277
Financial strain   42, 49, 60, 70, 126, 133, 139, 143, 161, 170, 171, 196, 212
Financial support   134, 135, 161, 174
Flag   29, 153, 154, 181, 225, 255, 273
Food and Shelter depots   214, 222
Food-for-the-Million shops   140
France   167, 180, 181, 205, 236, 241, 242, 274, 275
"Free and Easy" meetings   137
Freedom of The City of London   244
Fry family, The   180

Gateshead   97, 100, 102–106, 110, 111, 120, 131, 270, 271
General Order Against Starvation   194
Germany   236, 249, 275, 277
Guernsey   88–89, 269, 270
Guildford riots   183

Hadleigh   236
Hadley Wood   219, 248, 254
Hallelujah Lasses   152, 175, 176
Hammersmith home   116, 118, 125
Harcourt, Sir William   186, 187, 199
Holiness meetings   19, 174
Holland   216, 217, 236, 241, 249, 250, 276, 277
Holy Spirit empowerment   105, 159, 185
Home visitation   99
Homeless   111, 214, 215, 220, 221, 237, 243, 248, 251, 255, 256
Honorary doctorate   244

Immigration   173
Imprisonment   35, 181, 182, 208, 209
In Darkest England and the Way Out   219, 223, 231, 234, 276
India   167, 194, 211, 236, 241, 242, 248, 274, 277
Innovative methods   137, 234
International Congress   172, 211, 242, 243, 275, 277, 278
International Headquarters   211, 239, 255, 258
Isle of Wight   88

Japan   239, 248, 277, 278

Jarrett, Rebecca   200, 204
Java   239, 248, 277

"Knee Drill"   238
Korea   248, 278

Labor exchange   222, 234
Labor yards   234
Leadership style   77, 145–146, 155, 241, 247,
Legal-aid schemes   234
Leper colonies   248
Lifeboat, Salvation Army   248
Lights in Darkest England matches   235

"Maiden Tribute to Modern Babylon, A"   205
Marriage, equality of husband and wife in   86–87
Marsden, Isaac   47–48, 53, 160
Mary, Queen   256–258
Match factories   235
Meeting venues   114, 115, 120
Methodist New Connexion   81–82, 84, 95, 97, 100, 109, 111–114, 130
Methodist reformers   44–45, 61–63, 65, 74, 78, 81
Mile End Waste   116–118, 138
Military structure   146, 148, 153–155
Missing Persons Bureau   234
Monk, Peter   119
Morley, Samuel   121
Motorcar campaigns   245, 247
Mourez, Mme. Louise   204, 208
Mumford, Sarah   28–31, 34, 37, 69
Music   124, 156–158, 181, 262

New Zealand   190, 211, 244, 248–249
Norway   244, 248, 250
Nottingham   18, 47–49, 52, 55, 57, 60, 94, 101, 117, 126, 130, 244

Obedience   54, 95, 102, 106, 108–109, 113, 120–122, 141, 144, 150, 164, 180, 225
Open-air meetings   57–61, 101, 116, 121, 125–126, 130, 136, 152, 157, 180, 182–183, 186
Overseas colony   61, 133, 222, 236, 248

Paget, Sir James   217
Pall Mall Gazette   200–201, 205

Panama   248
Paraguay   248
People's Mission Hall, The   141
Penitent-form   127, 138, 145, 168, 175, 193, 245
Persecution   18, 90, 171, 173, 178–179, 180–184, 187, 240
Peru   248
Prayer, power of   43, 100, 117, 119, 123, 136–137, 162, 178, 224, 237, 239
Prayer meetings   44, 80, 93, 99, 102, 114, 127, 137, 238, 250
Prison-Gate Brigade   190
Prostitution   49, 120, 188, 199–205
Purity crusades   203, 205

Queen Victoria Street Headquarters   155, 197, 200

Rabbits, Edward   61–62, 65–67, 74, 78, 81–82
Railton, Commissioner George   145–148, 209, 230, 245
Recycling household rubbish   222, 234
Rescue Homes for Women   189, 198, 222, 234
Revival meetings   79, 81–82, 88–93, 98, 101, 111–117
Riots   49, 181, 185, 261, 267
Russia   248

Sacraments   184–185
Salvation Army, formation of   124
Sansom, Will   47, 48, 52, 57, 130
Self-Denial Week   212, 224
Sexual equality   83–84, 87, 185, 206, 237
"Sheffield Blades"   179
Skeleton Armies   184, 186
Slum Corps   191, 234
Smith, Captain Ada   187
Smith, Captain Allister   237–239
Soper, Florence (see Booth, Florence)
South Africa   211, 222, 237, 248
Soup kitchens   132, 134, 140, 190
Spalding   78–81
Spiritual manifestations   79, 177
Stead, William T.   142, 199–209, 219, 225, 237, 250
Swan, Annie   197–198
Sweated labor   192
Sweden   244
Switzerland   167, 181, 241, 249

Testimony, power of personal   42
Training homes   172, 191
Training of children   160, 162–165, 167
Trinidad   239

Uniforms   11, 154, 180, 189
Unity within marriage   86–88, 143

Victoria, Queen   153, 204
Volunteers of America   241

Walsall   115, 166
Walworth Chapel   60–61
War Cry, The   21, 158, 169, 191, 209
War Congress   147, 155, 172, 211, 242
Welfare work   130, 132, 140, 192, 196, 210, 214, 219, 233, 237, 243
Wesley, John   35, 38, 56, 61, 106, 160
Whitby   151
White slave traders   199, 201
Whitechapel   116, 125, 128, 133, 139, 141, 183, 189
Women in ministry   83–84, 102, 104
Workshops   234
Worthing riots   186–187

Zulu, work among the   237–239

About the Authors

Born in Britain in 1946, **Trevor Yaxley** grew up in the South End of London before immigrating to New Zealand at the age of sixteen. Shortly after settling in New Zealand, he set up his first business as a painter and specialized coating contractor.

Both Mr. Yaxley and his wife, Jan, experienced a total life transformation through Christian conversion shortly before their marriage in 1965. They became involved in a local church in Auckland where they served for the next nineteen years.

Following this, Mr. Yaxley was instrumental in the foundation and development of a plastics company, which pioneered "bubble" packaging. As a result of the efforts and innovation of Mr. Yaxley, his business partner, and those they worked with, Conform Plastics Ltd. received the 1978 Export Award for their invention of bubble-plastic mailing bags and pool covers.

In late 1985 Trevor and Jan were released from business to pursue their heart's passion—evangelism. They began their mission to see people motivated and trained to impact and transform the nation of New Zealand with the gospel of Jesus Christ. Trevor and Jan endeavor to lead by example—serving God and people—as they motivate, educate, and equip others to bring positive change to families and communities across New Zealand.

Through the team they work with, they have seen the successful establishment of an evangelistic training center known as Lifeway College, a community home for the disabled, a family-safe television station (Family Television Network), a roller-hockey rink for the local children, and the creation of a cartoon series committed to teaching children timeless values. Thousands have come to a saving knowledge of Jesus Christ through these outreaches, and many others have been released into effective ministries through the training and development of Lifeway College and other aspects of their organizations.

While busy with their businesses and ministry, however, Trevor and Jan remain passionate about family. Their firstborn, Mark, who has suffered from Down's syndrome since birth, is a continual delight to all around him. Tragically, their second son, David, who was an up-and-coming evangelist, was killed in a tragic auto accident at the age of sixteen-and-a-half. In the last year of his life, though, he'd led eighty young people to Christ and was a constant example to all in his faith, integrity, and enthusiasm. Rebecca, their gentle-hearted daughter, also has an incredible love and compassion for all around her. She and her husband, David Price, have produced three beautiful granddaughters who truly bring a sparkle to Trevor and Jan's eyes.

Carolyn Vanderwal grew up in a small farming community in Western Australia. She committed her life to Jesus Christ at the age of eleven and reaffirmed that commitment during her late teens. Carolyn studied and worked as a pharmacist before meeting her husband, Peter, and attending Lifeway Bible College in New Zealand. She began writing for Trevor and Jan Yaxley while serving as their personal assistant at the completion of her studies. She and Peter now live in Kalgoorlie, Western Australia, where they are involved in leadership of a local church ministry. They are passionate about connecting people with Jesus Christ and seeing their lives radically changed by His transforming power.

THE FIRST WAVE ARMY

So I prophesied as he commanded me, and the breath came into them,
and they lived, and stood up upon their feet, an exceeding great army.
—Ezekiel 37:10

Give me one hundred preachers who hate nothing but sin and love
nothing but God—and I care not a straw whether they be clergy or lay-
men. Such alone will shake the gates of hell and set up the kingdom of
Heaven on earth. God does nothing but in answer to prayer.
—John Wesley

Not only learn to use your weapons, and your armor, and the rules of
war, but how to put them into practice. It is only by fighting that you will
make warriors.

—William Booth

In direct response to the challenge of the Great Commission, Lifeway
Trust developed a six-month, intensive training program called "The First
Wave Army," which began in March of 2000. This training was specially
designed to equip those called to the ministry with the essentials they need to
evangelize, plant, and establish strong foundations for new believers and
churches in the areas they are needed most. This course is now a regular part
of Lifeway's curriculum and is run twice yearly with sessions beginning every
February and July.

Since soon after the first group graduated, First Wave Army members have
worked alongside local churches from all four corners of New Zealand and
swept through every town and city, sharing their faith, praying for the sick,
and mobilizing the saints to action. They concentrate their efforts to bring
effective and lasting positive change wherever they go through their passion
for God and a fiery love for souls that is both contagious and transforming.

First Wave Army groups have also begun works in such places as

Singapore, Liverpool, Belgium, Germany, and Tanzania, with plans to continue expansion into Thailand, Mongolia, Siberia, China, and other countries. These new soldiers of God's army are ready to go wherever called to carry out His will on the earth.

Is being part of this Army God's destiny for your life?

If you are interested in finding out more about how to become part of The First Wave Army, please contact us for more information and a free prospectus at:

Trevor & Jan Yaxley
First Wave Army
Lifeway Trust, Inc.
P.O. Box 303
Warkworth, New Zealand
Phone: +64-9-425-4054
Fax: +64-9-425-4053
E-mail: *army@lifeway.ac.nz*

He is no fool who gives up what he cannot keep in order to gain what he cannot lose.

—JIM ELLIOT, MARTYRED MISSIONARY TO THE AUCA INDIANS

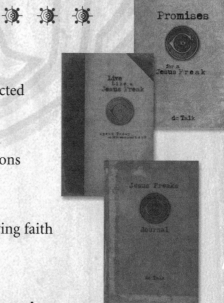